# CALVIN AND THE COMPANY OF PASTORS

Papers Presented at the 14th Colloquium of the Calvin Studies Society
May 22-24, 2003

The University of Notre Dame
Notre Dame, Indiana

Edited by David Foxgrover

Published for the Calvin Studies Society by
CRC Product Services
Grand Rapids, Michigan
2004

Cover: Calvin's letter to Edward VI, facsimile in *Letters of Calvin*, trans. Jules Bonnet (Philadelphia: Presbyterian Board of Publication, 1858), vol. 1, title page.

The image of Calvin is from Emile Doumergue, *Iconographie Calvinienne* (Lausanne: Georges Bridel & Cie Editeurs, 1909), plate V, 34.

# Contents

# Preface

The studies in this volume display a varied approach to the study of the "Company of Pastors" in Calvin's Geneva. Some of our contributors examined the topic from the perspective of Scripture and theology, while others emphasized historical studies. Some of the papers take a detailed look at the "Company" as it functioned in Geneva, and some offer comparisons with other cities and even other countries. The variety of approaches, the insights offered and the questions raised make it clear that the topic of the 14th CSS Colloquium was a good choice.

*Irena Backus* observes that although historians have devoted considerable attention to the role of Scripture in Calvin's ecclesiastical model, no one has examined the role of the history of the post-apostolic church in Calvin's views. Prof. Backus analyses ministerial and episcopal functions in the *Institutes* 4.4 – 4.5 as compared to Calvin's commentaries on Acts and his sermons on 1 Timothy.

*Erik de Boer's* thesis is seen in his title and in the question raised in his opening paragraph: "Is my translation of the term *congrégations* as 'Bible study meetings' accurate?" Based on a detailed study of *The Registers of the Company of Pastors,* Prof. de Boer concludes that the "method of working in the *congrégations*" is "training in exegesis." Prof. de Boer also asks if the emphasis on doctrine in the *congrégations* corresponds to the method of expounding the books of the Bible.

*Amy Nelson Burnett* examines pastoral ministry in Basel, Strasbourg and Geneva and finds "some surprising results" in the structure of ministry and the provision of pastoral care. Four areas in particular are examined: preaching and pastoral care before the Reformation, the significance of the parish after the Reform, the number of pastors and their turnover rate, and the overall composition of the pastoral corps.

*Laurel Carrington* finds a "significant degree of common ground" between Calvin and Erasmus on the spiritual formation of pastors, while noting their differences in scriptural exegesis and calling for more study of the interrelationships between theology, ecclesiology and exegetical method in Calvin's and Erasmus' writings and practice.

*Darlene K. Flaming* poses the question: "How does the practice of pastoral ministry as set up in Geneva correspond to Calvin's model of ministry as a true imitation of the apostles?" Her study leads her to conclude that, for Calvin, trying to replicate every detail of apostolic practice would be a "senseless 'aping' of the apostles."

*R. Ward Holder* asks the question: "If Calvin were teaching in the practical division of a modern seminary, what might he have to say?" The bulk of Prof. Holder's answer is based on Calvin's guidance given in his commentaries when he "breaks his train of thought" to speak about the actions or characteristics of the pastor—almost as if Calvin is pausing to offer the "breadth of his experience to other ministers."

*Glenn S. Sunshine* begins his paper by pointing out that "local political structure" was a significant factor in the creation of church institutions during the Reform movement. In studying France and Hungary where the civil governments opposed the Reform movement, Prof. Sunshine examines the role of pastors in shaping the reform in the two kingdoms.

The CSS is very pleased that the "Company of Pastors" of the Presbyterian Church (U.S.A.) is sending a copy of this volume to each of its 600 members for their study. The CSS is grateful for the continued support of the Office of Theology and Worship of the PCUSA and its Chair, Joseph D. Small, in helping to publish the Society's papers. Dr. Small has contributed a Foreword to the volume, along with Sheldon W. Sorge of the same Office who was an active supporter of and participant in the Colloquium. The Forewords by Dr. Small and Dr. Sorge emphasize the continuing significance of the "company of pastors."

The Calvin Studies Society wishes to express its profound gratitude to the Theology Department of Notre Dame and in particular to its Chair, John Cavidini. Members of the Department chaired several sessions and offered their appreciation of the quality of the papers presented, the responses and the ensuing discussions. The Department also helped support the Colloquium with a generous grant. We look forward to the possibility of returning to Notre Dame for a future Colloquium.

David Foxgrover, Editor

# Acknowledgements

The Calvin Studies Society gratefully acknowledges the support of the Office of Theology and Worship, Presbyterian Church U. S. A., in publishing the 2003 papers.

The Calvin Studies Society is also grateful for gifts to help publish this volume from the following members of the Society:

James A. De Jong
Betty Ann Donohue
David Foxgrover
I. John Hesselink
Merwyn S. Johnson
Earl William Kennedy
Hyun Tae Kim
Robert M. Kingdon
Elsie Anne McKee
John L. Thompson
Andrew J. Waskey
Roger D. Woods

# Foreword I
# A Company of Pastors

*Joseph D. Small*

## I. Introduction

The renewal of the church (perhaps even its reform) is necessary always and everywhere. Although the need is more apparent in some times and places than others, there is little doubt that all is not well within the contemporary North American church. Mainline Protestantism has played out the possibilities of cultural establishment. Catholicism offers an uncertain route between traditional ecclesial teaching and emerging American moral practice. Evangelicalism consorts uneasily with new paradigm churches. Pentecostalism finds itself on the threshold of religious respectability, uncertain if it wants to enter the club. Although there is widespread awareness of our difficulties, there is considerable doubt about the shape of renewal. Something new is required from all of us, but we are not sure what the something new is.

John Calvin was clear that reform of the church is based on the three pillars of "doctrine," "administering the sacraments," and "governing the church."[1] He was also clear that ministry—the pastoral office—is essential to the revival and maintenance of the church's faithful theology, worship, and order. "For neither the light and heat of the sun, nor food and drink, are so necessary to nourish and sustain the present life," Calvin asserted, "as the apostolic and pastoral office is necessary to preserve the church on earth."[2] Along with other great 16th century reformers, Calvin held the ministry in highest regard because he was convinced that the church's fidelity to the gospel depends on proclamation of the Word in preaching and sacraments, worship that glorifies God, and church order that honors the Spirit's leading.

Esteem for pastoral ministry was not a form of reflexive clericalism or an assertion of customary privilege. Rather, it depended on Calvin's insistence that "everyone who rules in the Church shall also teach" and that "none are to be

---

[1] John Calvin, "The Necessity of Reforming the Church," in *Calvin: Theological Treatises*, J.K.S. Reid, trans. and ed. (Philadelphia: Westminster Press, 1964), 184-216.

[2] *Institutes*, 4.3.2.

continued in the office but those who are diligent in performing its duties."[3] It was by virtue of its vocation to preach the Word and teach the faith that the ministerial office was "the chief sinew by which believers are held together in one body."[4] Until recently, my own Presbyterian Church incorporated this understanding in its *Book of Order* by calling ministers "teaching elders." Loss of this term is unfortunate, although the current designation, "Ministers of the Word and Sacrament," indicates the centrality of theological, liturgical, and ecclesial calling in the life and work of the church's pastors. The Reformed tradition has always understood that pastoral ministry is a God-given means for preserving the whole church in safety, unity, and fidelity.

## II. What is a minister, anyway?

Confusion about the nature of ministry is at the center of the church's uncertainty about the shape of its renewal. Contemporary pastors, like their predecessors, are beset by a bewildering range of congregational and denominational expectations. Demands on pastor's time and energy include regular visitation and successful stewardship programs, membership growth and an efficient committee structure, presbytery service and good sermons, community outreach and an attractive church school program. The list is endless.

The difficulty goes deeper, however. Beneath every demand on time and energy lies the reality that the vocational core of ministry is no longer discernible. The church does not have a cohesive understanding of ministry that can be shared by pastors in congregational settings (much less by other ministers in various forms of service). Ministers are presented with a bewildering and unstable bundle of images depicting the essence of ministry: preacher, teacher, community builder, programmer, marketer, therapist, change agent, care giver, manager . . . the list goes on! These images are more than another collection of tasks, however; they are comprehensive models of ministry that offer competing options without a compelling rationale for choice.

The absence of a coherent, cohesive ministerial identity is more than a mildly interesting sociological phenomenon. Its effects are apparent in the alarming escalation of conflict within congregations, the appalling incidence of clergy sexual misconduct, the high percentage of ministers "seeking a new call," the accelerating burn-out rate, and the number of mildly depressed pastors who have settled for playing out their days. Presbyteries and *classes*, "the pastors' pastors," seldom help because they are the product of the same fragmented identity.

Calvin was right. Encouraging and enhancing the *theological* vocation of pastors is one of the most urgent tasks before the church. Underscoring pastors'

---

[3] Calvin, "Necessity of Reforming," 206.

[4] Calvin, *Institutes*, 4.3.2.

theological calling is not intended to add one more image—theologian—to an already too long list. Rather, it recognizes that as ministers recover and deepen their vocation to "think the faith," they are better able to discern the shape of distinctly Christian pastoral and congregational life in the midst of disparate cultural claims. Pastoral discernment that encourages congregational discernment is the necessary starting point for the church's renewal in the gospel.

The theological vocation of pastors is not the solitary exercise of scholarly discipline, as if ministers were called to be little professors who transform congregations into mini-seminaries. Theology is a ministry of the whole people of God. All Christians are called to think prayerfully about the grace of the Lord Jesus Christ, the love of God, and the communion of the Holy Spirit. As they come together in congregations they are called into committed conversation about the shape of shared faith and common service. Congregations are called to widen the conversation denominationally, ecumenically, and globally so that all may benefit from diverse experiences and expressions of faith. It is through the committed conversation of the whole people of God that the church can recover the unity in faith that leads to unity in mission.

Pastors bear particular responsibility for nourishing congregational reflection on the faith. But who nourishes pastors' reflection on the faith?

## III. The Venerable Company of Pastors

Modern presbyteries and *classes* have developed from two ecclesial institutions in Calvin's Geneva: the Geneva Consistory and the Venerable Company of Pastors. The Consistory, composed of pastors and elders, was responsible for church order and discipline. The Company of Pastors was responsible for examination and ordination of ministers, continuing biblical and theological education, mutual theological and ethical encouragement, and missionary work in neighboring countries.[5]

Ordination and mission have joined order and discipline as major responsibilities of modern presbyteries/*classes,* but sustained theological work and mutual encouragement are no longer central to governing body life. Pastors continue to need deeply collegial relationships, however. Without the corporate engagement of pastors in biblical, theological, and ecclesiological inquiry, ecclesial order is easily bureaucratized while discipline is either ignored or factionalized. At this time in the life of Reformed churches, there is a conspicuous need for pastoral communities of spiritual, intellectual, and vocational discipline. Since governing bodies are unlikely locations for such community, a contemporary Company of Pastors, inspired by Calvin's Geneva Company, may provide new possibilities for Ministers of the Word and Sacrament.

---

[5] For a detailed discussion, see Robert M. Kingdon, "Calvin and 'Presbytery': The Geneva Company of Pastors," *Pacific Theological Review,* XVIII (2), 43-55.

Calvin set the basic shape of the Venerable Company of Pastors in the Draft Ecclesiastical Ordinances of 1541. Because he believed that faithful ministers were essential for the renewal of the church he recognized the necessity for continuous renewal of ministers themselves. A *company* of pastors provided the properly communal context for mutual education, encouragement, and supervision. No less than the 16th century pastors of Geneva, today's pastors deserve the fullest opportunity to pray the faith together, think the faith together, and live the faith together, so that the whole body of Christ may be built up and grow together into Christ.

A glance at Calvin's ecclesiastical ordinances suggests contemporary possibilities.

> *First it will be expedient that all the ministers, for preserving purity and concord among themselves, meet together one certain day each week, for discussion of the Scriptures.*[6]

Geneva's Venerable Company of Pastors embodied a commitment to collegial leadership. Meeting weekly, the Company engaged in biblical and theological study, enhancing one another's capacity to think the faith. Many of the meetings centered on interpreting the Scriptures, perhaps related to Calvin's lectures on books of the Bible. Pastors also presented theological papers for discussion.

Weekly meetings of pastors for prayer and study are almost unimaginable in the contemporary church. The reasons for this reality are worth pondering, but it is probably more useful to encourage workable possibilities for periodic gatherings that enable pastors to engage in study of the Scriptures, to discuss central theological issues that shape the church's faith and life, and to pray with and for one another.

> *If there appear differences of doctrine, let the ministers come together to discuss the matter. Afterwards, if need be, let them call the elders to assist in composing the contention.*[7]

Discussion of biblical and theological matters was not a polite academic exercise in Geneva. The search for truth sometimes required vigorous debate and mutual critique because the issues were not merely private matters of personal opinion. The Company's theological work mattered for the life of the whole church.

"Difference of doctrine" is not in short supply in the contemporary church, but "coming together to discuss the matter" is too often reduced to debating and voting in an essentially political context. Working together on difficult theological and ethical issues does not produce automatic agreement, but it can provide a more faithful way of struggling with questions that matter for the life of the whole church.

---

[6] John Calvin, "Draft Ecclesiastical Ordinances" (1541), in *Calvin: Theological Treatises*, 60.

[7] *Ibid.*

*To obviate all scandals of living, it will be proper that there be a form of correction to which all submit themselves. It will also be the means by which the ministry may retain respect, and the Word of God be neither dishonoured nor scorned.[8]*

The Venerable Company of Pastors was a disciplined community. Its meetings were more than conversation about abstractions, for their purpose was to encourage pastors to grow in love of God and thereby to grow in faith, hope, and love of neighbors. All of this was for the sake of the gospel—its proclamation, reception, and fulfillment throughout God's creation.

Recent unpleasant experience shows that the practice of mutual correction can become dangerous, but patterns of mutual encouragement and counsel are both possible and necessary. Ministerial support groups are important ways of dealing with pastors' isolation and loneliness. However, these groups are better able to deal with fundamental vocational issues and problems when they move beyond personal support to become groups of sustained study and prayer.

Geneva's Venerable Company of Pastors recorded its roster and the proceedings of its meetings in *The Register of the Company of Pastors*. These 16th century records reveal a gathering of pastors who placed Scripture and worship, theology and prayer, at the center of the church's life and the heart of pastoral vocation. In an age of ecclesial uncertainty and pastoral confusion, the pattern is suggestive.

## IV. Today's Company of Pastors

The Presbyterian Church (U.S.A.)'s Office of Theology and Worship has inaugurated a contemporary Company of Pastors. Spread across the country, it is a community of spiritual, intellectual, and vocational disciplines for ministers. The Company of Pastors encourages and enhances the theological vocation of the church's ministers by creating a community that is committed to daily disciplines of Scripture reading, prayer, and conversation with the tradition. The discipline of the Company of Pastors also entails common reading and reflection on significant theological works, the deepening of vocational awareness, regular meetings with other members of the Company, and opportunities to contribute to the Company's theological journal, *The Register of the Company of Pastors*.

The Company of Pastors is not restricted to ministers in the Presbyterian Church (U.S.A.), although ministers in the Reformed tradition are most likely to appreciate The Company's ethos, disciplines, and resources. The covenant of The Company of Pastors is simple, yet its ramifications are profound.

*Daily Disciplines:* Members of the Company of Pastors read the Scriptures according to the two-year cycle of the Daily Lectionary. Semi-continuous readings from the Old Testament, the Epistles, and the Gospels expose pastors daily

---

[8] *Ibid.*

to the grand sweep of God's way in the world. Faithful reading of the daily lections is very different from reading the Lord's Day lectionary to determine a text for preaching, or reading portions of Scripture in preparation for leading a Bible study. The daily lectionary opens pastors to the possibility of hearing God's Word for their own lives and ministries. In addition to reading and reflecting on biblical texts, members of the Company of Pastors pray the psalms for the day as well as prayers of thanksgiving and intercession for their congregations, their denomination, the church catholic, their colleagues in the Company, and the world. Use of the forms for Daily Prayer in the PCUSA *Book of Common Worship* is suggested, but certainly not required.

In addition to Scripture and prayer, members of the Company of Pastors read assigned portions of *The Book of Confessions* each day. Lord's Day readings alternate between the Nicene and Apostles' Creeds, while the other confessions are read in continuous sections, covering the entire confessional collection each year. For Presbyterian members of The Company, confessional readings go beyond exposure to classical documents of the Reformed tradition. In PCUSA ordination vows, ministers promise to "receive and adopt" the confessions' "essential tenets" and to be "led, guided, and instructed" by them. Thus, together with Scripture and prayer, the confessions help to locate the core of pastoral ministry.

*Reading in Common:* In addition to the daily disciplines, members of the Company of Pastors agree to engage in common reading of theological books and journals. Books are sent automatically four times each year, together with a brief reading guide. Beyond encouraging pastors to read significant theological works, there is value in reading books in common with others so that members of the Company can talk with one another about what they have read. Similarly, the Company's theological journal, *The Register of the Company of Pastors,* provides a common base of readings. *The Register* is a theological journal with a twist: no professors need apply! All articles and reviews are written by pastors for pastors, providing a publication opportunity for quality theological work that emerges from pastoral/congregational life.

*Regional Meetings:* Members of the Company of Pastors agree to meet regionally for prayer and study. Many members live close enough to colleagues that half-day gatherings are possible, while isolated members may meet via the Internet. All of the disciplines are aided by a Company of Pastors daybook that includes the Daily Lectionary and table of confessional readings, together with the Company's covenant, roster, and other resources.

## V. Pastors Matter

The Company of Pastors is not a panacea for what ails the church, or a prescription for the renewal of ministry. It is, however, a modest effort to encourage pastors to recover a shared sense of the ministry's grounding in the Faith and to enhance the ability of pastors to live out a ministry of the Word and

Sacrament. Several years ago, the Presbyterian Church (U.S.A.)'s General Assembly declared (as if making a discovery) that "theology matters." As an issue of both faith and faithfulness, theology does matter. *Pastors* matter, too. Pastors deserve more from the church than a market-oriented boutique of institutional roles and functions. Their distinctive theological vocation should be encouraged and enhanced—not as an additional option, but as the defining center of pastoral calling. A *company* of pastors also matters, for ministerial isolation makes possible the institutional tyranny that ensnares pastors in a web of customary expectations and organizational ambitions. The Company of Pastors is not the only community that pastors need, but it is one significant response to the church's desperate need for pastors whose primary responsibility is studying, teaching, and proclaiming the gospel.

*Information about the Company of Pastors is available by contacting the Office of Theology and Worship, at www.pcusa.org/theologyandworship/whatwedo/company/htm or 100 Witherspoon Street, Louisville, KY 40202.*

# Foreword II

# Company Trajectories:
# Emerging Patterns in The Presbyterian Church (U.S.A.)'s *Company of Pastors*

*Sheldon W. Sorge*

Joseph Small's Foreword to this volume, "A Company of Pastors," was originally composed for the launch of the "Company of Pastors" in the Presbyterian Church (U.S.A.) some six years ago. Small argues incisively both for the need of an ongoing vocational nurture nexus among pastors, and for the particular appropriateness in our place and time for such a nexus to be modeled significantly after John Calvin's "Venerable Company of Pastors." In developing its proposal for a present-day PCUSA Company of Pastors, the Office of Theology and Worship had the good sense to drop the "venerable" designation, and indeed the project has, at least so far, been marked at least as much by modesty as by venerability.

Since its inception, the Company of Pastors has enrolled some 1200 members, about 600 of whom continue to maintain active membership.[1] This means that, on average, each of the PCUSA's 173 presbyteries has enrolled 6 or 7 members, 3 or 4 of whom are currently active. Since most presbyteries represent fairly large geographic regions, the average presbytery does not have enough members in geographic proximity to one another to make regular local gatherings of the Company feasible. Of the three primary commitments of the Company covenant that Small adumbrates in his essay – daily prayer, disciplined study, and regular gathering with Company colleagues – the last has proven the most difficult to actuate.

---

[1] Active membership in the Company of Pastors involves annual renewal of the covenant, which includes a subscription fee to cover administrative expenses as well as costs for the annual calendar, new publications in the Office of Theology and Worship's "Church Issues" and "Occasional Papers" series, and subscription to the Company's journal, *The Register of the Company of Pastors*. We know anecdotally that some have let their active membership lapse due to the expense involved in the annual subscription. Others have left the Company because they did not want to continue to receive (and pay for) Company book selections. Still others have left because they hoped the Company membership would include regular face-to-face conversation and prayer with ministry colleagues that did not materialize. Some have left simply because they have felt guilty over their repeated failures to live up to the commitments entailed in the covenant.

The Office of Theology and Worship pinned hopes for convening local gatherings on the advocacy of participating pastors in each region. Several efforts to establish regular Company gatherings were mounted by Company members in a few presbyteries, but none proved sustainable. A new strategy is currently under development, in which the Office's staff will meet with regional groups of pastors to launch local companies, with the modest goal of motivating participants to continue meeting regularly for prayer and mutual encouragement in clusters of two to four (weekly to monthly), with the whole company meeting occasionally (annually or semiannually) for sustained study. Theology and Worship hopes that such a pattern will prove more accommodating to the realities of pastoral life, and therefore more sustainable, than earlier efforts to gather larger groups regularly.

Features of the Company that members most often report as helpful are the covenant of daily prayer and the pattern of daily reading from Scripture and confessions. Whether members of the Company or not, most pastors have every intention to cultivate regular disciplines that promote vocational growth; yet the press of ministry demands often precludes the daily exercise of those disciplines. Embracing a specific covenant in company with other pastors strengthens the resolve of many to keep practicing the spiritual disciplines that sustain lively pastoral vocation.

The Company's circulation of significant theological texts has met with mixed reception. Some members receive them eagerly, while others patently resent being told what to read and when to read it. Not surprisingly, books enjoy the warmest reception when they are read in critical conversation with fellow pastors. The Company of Pastors remains firmly resolved to distribute books to its members that encourage them to maintain a habit of sustained theological reflection and conversation.

While it is certainly encouraging that so many pastors have joined the Company, it still remains an unfortunately well-kept secret on the larger canvas of the entire PCUSA. When Office of Theology and Worship staff travel around the church, they discover in most settings that no more than one quarter of the pastors know of the Company. There remains much room in the PCUSA for the Company of Pastors to grow and a great need in the church for what it offers.

Maintaining disciplines that nourish faithful, fruitful, and fulfilling pastoral ministry is, in a word, hard. That is why pastors need to do so in company with others who share the need to nurture a common vocation. They need the encouragement; they need the accountability; they need the mutuality. Through all its early growing pains, the PCUSA's Company of Pastors still has afforded pastors a unique opportunity to engage a covenant that directly addresses these critical needs. For many members, the Company has been the catalyst that moves them from the realm of merely good intentions to actual engagement with regular disciplines of mind and heart that nourish and sustain good ministry.

John Calvin identified his own conversion with a divine turning of his heart toward teachability. If teachability is indeed a hallmark of genuine Christian discipleship, how could pastors possibly promote the Christian life effectively without themselves embodying it? Among other things, Calvin's Venerable Company of Pastors provided assurance that pastors would continue for a lifetime to teach and be taught by one another.

Understood in this way, the pastoral vocation is an inescapably collegial vocation. In PCUSA parlance, a pastor who serves a congregation as its only paid minister of word and sacrament is designated a "solo pastor." While the term is certainly not intended to encourage isolation from other pastors, it may have an unintended effect of perpetuating an understanding of pastoral vocation that is woefully inadequate. Pastoral ministry can no more be practiced well "solo" than can Beethoven's Ninth Symphony be played and sung well by a solo musician.

The Office of Theology and Worship is pleased to support this publication of the papers from the Calvin Studies Society's May 2003 consultation on "John Calvin and the Company of Pastors." Each current member of the PCUSA's Company of Pastors will receive a copy of this collection as part of the Company's regular circulation of books. We encourage all members of the Company to read this splendid volume in conversation with other pastors. These pages are richly filled with much of great value to pastors today, from lively accounts of the shape and practices of Calvin's own Company to suggestive proposals for how Calvin's experiment might still serve the church well as a lively model for vocational nurture that promotes faithfulness, fruitfulness, and fulfillment in pastoral ministry.

# Contributors

**Irena Backus**, Professor of Reformation History, Institute of Reformation History, University of Geneva, Switzerland

**Erik A. de Boer**, Minister of the Reformed Churches; Research Associate, Theological University in Kampen (Broederweg) and the University of Free State, South Africa.

**Amy Nelson Burnett**, Associate professor of History, University of Nebraska-Lincoln

**J. Laurel Carrington**, Associate Professor of History, St. Olaf College

**Thomas J. Davis**, Associate Professor of Religious Studies, Indiana University-Purdue University at Indianapolis; Managing Editor, *Religion and Culture*

**Darlene K. Flaming**, Assistant Professor of Christianity, Mercer University Macon, Georgia

**Gary Neal Hansen**, Assistant Professor of Church History, University of Dubuque Theological Seminary, Dubuque, Iowa

**R. Ward Holder**, Assistant Professor of Theology, Saint Anselm College, Manchester, New Hampshire

**Anthony N. S. Lane**, Professor of Historical Theology and Director of Research, London School of Theology, London

**G. Sujin Pak**, Instructor in the History of Christianity, Garrett-Evangelical Theological Seminary, Evanston, Illinois

**Joseph A. Small**, Chair, Office of Theology and Worship, Presbyterian Church (U.S.A.), Louisville, Kentucky

**Sheldon W. Sorge**, Associate for Theology and Worship, Presbyterian Church (U.S.A.), Louisville, Kentucky

**Glenn S. Sunshine**, Associate Professor, Department of History, Central Connecticut State University

**Tom M. Trinidad**, Ph.D. Candidate, University of Notre Dame, South Bend, Indiana

# Abbreviations

CO     *Ioannis Calvini Opera Omnia Quae Supersunt,* ed. G. Baum, E. Cunitz and E. Reuss. 59 vols. Brunsvigae: C. A. Schwetschke, 1863-1900.

CNTC     *Calvin's New Testament Commentaries.* 12 vols., ed. D. W. and T. F. Torrance. Grand Rapids: Eerdmans Publishing Company, 1959-1972.

CO     *Ioannis Calvini Opera Omnia Quae Supersunt,* ed. G. Baum, E. Cunitz and E. Reuss, 59 vols. Brunsvigae: C. A. Schwetschke, 1863-1900.

CR     *Corpus Reformatorum,* ed. C. G. Bretschneider. Halis, Saxoum: C.A. Schwetschke and Sons, 1842.

CSEL     *Corpus scriptorum ecclesiasticorum Latinorum* (Vienna: F. Tempsky, 1866- ).

LCC     *Calvin: Institutes of the Christian Religion,* ed. John T. McNeill, trans. Ford Lewis Battles. Library of Christian Classics, vols. 20-21. Philadelphia: The Westminster Press, 1960.

MPL     J.-P. Migne, ed. *Patrologiae cursus completes ...series Latina,* 221 vols. (Paris: J.-P. Migne, 1844-1864).

OE     *Opera Exegetica,* Series II of Ioannis Calvini Opera Omnia Denuo Recognita . . . Geneva: Librairie Droz, 1992-.

OS     *Ioannis Calvini Opera Selecta,* ed. P. Barth, W. Niesel and D. Scheuner. 5 vols. Monachii in Adeibus: Chr. Kaiser Verlag, 1926-1952.

RCP     *Registres de la Compagnie des Pasteurs de Genève au temps de Calvin,* vol. I (1546-1553), ed. Jean-Francois Bergier (Genève: Librairie Droz, 1964); vol. II (1553-1564), ed. Jean-Francois Bergier and Robert M. Kingdon (1962); vol. III (1565-1574), ed. Olivier Fatio and O. Labarthe (1969); vol. IX (1604-1606), ed. G. Cahier, M. Campagnolo and M. Louis-Courvoisier (1989); vol. X (1607-1609), ed. G. Cahier, M. Campagnolo and M. Louis-Courvoisier (1991).

# These holy men: Calvin's Patristic Models for Establishing the Company of Pastors

*Irena Backus*

## I. Introduction

In an article published in 1987, this is how Robert Kingdon described the episcopal functions of the Company of Pastors:

> In Calvin's Geneva the powers traditionally exercised by a bishop were now exercised by two new institutions: the Company of Pastors and the Consistory. The Company of Pastors exercised collectively the sacramental powers of a bishop, above all, the power to ordain new clergy; it also exercised some of the jurisdictional powers of a bishop, notably the power to supervise teaching. The Consistory exercised other jurisdictional powers of a bishop, notably the power to maintain discipline, especially in resolving family and marital disputes of all types and it enforced its decisions in this arena by frequent use of the power of excommunication. The Company of Pastors was made up of all the preaching clergy in the city of Geneva and the rural villages dependent upon it, plus the teachers in the local Academy. The Consistory was made up of lay elders elected by the city government plus the preaching clergy ex officio. The presiding officer of the Company of Pastors was a clergyman called the Moderator. The presiding officer of the Consistory was a layman, one of the four syndics...[1]

Kingdon then goes on to argue that in Calvin's time the office of the Moderator was ambivalent in that it retained some episcopal function, if only by virtue of the same person, i. e., Calvin, exercising it for over twenty years. He also argues that after Calvin's death government control over the Company of Pastors increased and that therefore, after 1564, the Genevan church comes to correspond more and more to the other Protestant and Lutheran churches, which transferred episcopal function from the church to the state.[2] Indepen-

---

[1] Robert Kingdon, "The Episcopal function in Protestant churches in the sixteenth and seventeenth centuries." In *Miscellanea Historiae ecclesiasticae VIII. Colloque de Strasbourg, septembre 1983 sur L'Institution et les pouvoirs dans les églises, de l'Antiquité à nos jours*, ed. Bernard Vogler (Bibliothèque de la Revue d'histoire ecclésiastique, fascicule 72), Brussels: Ed. Nauwelaerts, 1987, 207-220.

[2] Ibid., 216-220.

dently of the question of secularisation of the Genevan church after Calvin's death (which I do not propose to go into here), most historians, including Kingdon, take it for granted that Calvin's model of the church and of the episcopate in particular was entirely founded on a new reading of the Scripture and that the reformer and his early followers believed that they were recreating the apostolic church in its pristine purity, seeing subsequent development of the church as nothing other than gradual decline.

In recent years, Elsie McKee has devoted two books, one on the office of deacon and the other on the office of elder, to showing that Calvins's view of those two offices within the church was an affirmation of the sole authority of Scripture.[3] Indeed, if we concentrate on Calvin's Scriptural commentaries and on his Sermons, and if we bear in mind *Institutes* 4. 3 which is based almost entirely on biblical quotations, there are good grounds for believing that his view of the ministry was founded on Scripture alone and that Scripture was his sole basis for seeing the ministry as a collegiate function evenly distributed between laypeople and clerics. [4]

However, if we are to accept the view that Calvin saw the apostolic model of the church as the only viable one, several questions arise. Firstly, what is one to make of the abolition of the imposition of hands in the ordination of ministers? The draft of the Geneva Church Ordinances of 1541 acknowledged this to be something of an embarrassment, given that the custom was apostolic.[5] The authorised text of the same Ordinances, on the other hand, did not advert to the fact that the abolition of imposition of hands contravened apostolic practice and stated categorically: "As for how ministers should be introduced, seeing as past ceremonies have given rise to much superstition because of the corruption of the times, it is enough that one of the ministers declares that the

---

[3] Elsie McKee, *John Calvin on the Diaconate and Liturgical Almsgiving* (Geneva: Droz, 1984), 267: "The Reformed in the Strasbourg-Genevan tradition read Acts (6, 1-6) and First Timothy (3, 8-13) together: the diaconate chosen to care for temporal need in Acts 6 and ordained by the laying on of hands, is a permanent and necessary ecclesiastical office in any church order because Luke's history is made normative by Paul's general rule." Elsie McKee, *Elders and the Plural Ministry. The Role of Exegetical History in Illuminating John Calvin's Theology* (Geneva: Droz, 1988), 220: "Strange as it may seem, Calvin's interpretation of the biblical texts for his teaching on the ministry can be seen as an affirmation of the sole authority of Scripture and an application of the dictum that Scripture must be interpreted by Scripture."

[4] Kingdon, "The Episcopal Function," 219.

[5] RCP I, 3, note 1: "Quant à la maniere de l'introduire, il seroyt bon de user de l'imposition des mains, laquelle ceremonye a esté gardee des apostres et puys en l'esglise ancienne, moyennant que cela se face sans superstition et sans offence. Mais, pource qu'il y a eu beaucoup de superstition au temps passé, et qu'il s'en pourroit ensuivre du scandalle, on s'en abstient pour l'infirmité du temps." See also OS II, 330.

ordination is taking place, and that prayers are held that the Lord grants the new minister his grace."[6]

The abolition of the imposition of hands is a very clear instance of a discrepancy between the Genevan and the apostolic practice. Other instances of such discrepancies abound, the most obvious one being Calvin's lifelong occupation of the post of Moderator and his disinclination to discredit completely the episcopal nomenclature and the office of bishop.[7] Whereas historians have devoted some considerable attention to examining the role of Scripture and its interpretation in Calvin's ecclesiastical model, no one has so far examined the possible role that the history of the post-apostolic church might have played in it. There are some arguments for considering this question irrelevant: Calvin's apparent attachment to the Scriptural model of the apostolic church, his emphasis on it in his Sermons and biblical commentaries. However, if we read the *Institutes* 4. 4. 1 – 4. 5. 4 which deal with the ministry, not in the apostolic times (which is the theme of *Institutes* 4. 3), but in the post-apostolic period, we find it to be nothing other than a careful, historical enquiry into the legal aspect of practices of the post-apostolic and post-Nicene early church, going right up to the time of Gregory I. This paper therefore proposes to examine the apparent discrepancy between the importance of the apostolic model in *Institutes* 4. 3 and in Calvin's Commentaries and Sermons and the importance of the history of the early church in the *Institutes* 4. 4. 1 - 4, and 4. 5. 4. Do the two conflict or can they be said to complement each other in determining Calvin's doctrine of the ministry, including his notion of the episcopal function?

I propose to analyse *Institutes* 4. 4. 1 – 4. 5. 4 and compare its doctrine of ministerial and episcopal function to that developed in Calvin's Commentary on Acts and Sermons on I Timothy. I shall not undertake a detailed analysis of *Institutes* 4. 3, which mirrors the perspective of the Commentary and the Sermons.

## II. *Institutes* 4. 4. 1 – 4. 5.4

Even the most cursory reading of *Institutes* 4. 4. 1 – 4. 5. 4 suffices to convince us that Calvin does not consider post-apostolic practices as a steady decline of the apostolic model. Indeed, he considers them useful for two reasons: one is his wish to show that the Roman model of his own era is an innovation with no good basis. The other, more positive, reason is that he feels it necessary to confront the Genevan model of ecclesiastical organisation, including its notion of

---

[6] RCP I, 3: "Quant à la maniere d'introduire pour ce que les ceremonies du temps passé ont esté tournees en beaulcoup de superstitions à cause de l'infirmité du temps, il suffira qu'il se fasse par un des ministres une declaration en remontrance de l'office auquel on l'ordonne, puis qu'on fasse prieres et oraisons affin que le Seigneur luy fasse la grace de s'en acquitter." Cf. O. S. II, 330-331 (note).

[7] This was noted particularly by Kingdon after Pannier. See Kingdon, "The Episcopal Function," 214-215.

episcopacy, with that of the post-apostolic and post-Nicene early church. Indeed, as we shall see, a good many verbal parallels can be established between the reformer's description of early ecclesiastical organisation in the *Institutes* and the *Ordinances* of 1541. The section of the *Institutes* that we shall examine deals with the offices of bishop, priest and deacon, the education of the clergy and the ordination of ministers with particular emphasis being laid on the question of participation of the people. Calvin's arguments are very carefully supported by references to the *Decree of Gratian*, to patristic literature of the fourth and fifth centuries, and to the *Ecclesiastical Histories* of Eusebius, Socrates, Sozomenes, Cassiodore etc. Calvin is not interested in going back further than that. Cyprian, the only representative of the ante-Nicene church, is made to harmonise with the post-Nicene Fathers.

## A. The Office of Bishop

Calvin's chief authority for the office and function of bishops in the early church is Jerome and more particularly Jerome's commentary on Titus. He notes that Jerome states there that bishops are no different from priests (presbyters) and that before the devil had sown dissensions in the Roman church, and that before people started saying "I am Paul's and I am Peter's," all churches were governed by a common council of presbyters. Later the office was given to one person so that discords would not arise. Calvin comments that just as presbyters know that it is only human custom for them to be subjected to one who sits over them, so bishops should know that they are greater than presbyters due to a human decision rather than by the truth of the Lord's decree and should therefore govern the church collegially.[8] He obviously devoted some attention to studying Jerome on this issue as he notes that the church father does not say the same thing in his letter to Evagrius (in fact, Evangelus[9]) where he insists not on the pragmatic nature of the office of bishop as a remedy to abuses of colle-

---

[8] *Institutes*, 4. 4. 2, OS V, 59: "Atque idipsum pro temporum necessitate fuisse humano consensu inductum, fatentur ipsi veteres. Ita Hieronymus in epistolam ad Titum: 'idem inquit presbyter qui episcopus. Et antequam diaboli instinctu dissidia in religione fierent, et in populis diceretur: ego Pauli, ego Cephae, communi consilio presbyterorum ecclesiae gubernabantur. Postea vt dissensionum semina euellerentur ad vnum omnis sollicitudo est delata.' Sicut ergo presbyteri sciunt se ex ecclesiae consuetudine ei qui praeest subiectos, ita episcopi nouerint se magis consuetudine quam dominicae dispositionis veritate presbyteris esse maiores et in commune debere ecclesiam regere." Cf. Jerome, In Titum 1, 5, MPL 26, 562: "Idem est ergo presbyter qui est episcopus et antequam diaboli instinctu studia in religione fierent et diceretur in populis: *ego sum Pauli, ego Apollo, ego autem Cephae* [1 Cor. 1:12] communi presbyterorum consilio ecclesiae gubernabantur. Postquam vero vnusquisque eos quos baptizauerat suos putabat esse, non Christi, in toto orbe decretum est vt vnus de presbyteris electus superponeretur caeteris, ad quem omnis ecclesiae cura pertineret et schismatum semina tollerentur."

[9] Jerome, Ep. 146, 1; CSEL 56, 310.

giality but on its antiquity, claiming that in the Alexandrian church, the office went right back to the time of Mark the Evangelist.[10]

In fact, if one looks carefully at Jerome's letter to Evangelus, the church father does not defend the antiquity of the office as against its pragmatic function. He still claims that it was only to put an end to schisms and power struggles that the office was instituted. He grants, however, that the tradition of the office went back all the way to the time of Mark, the Evangelist. He also insists that only the right to ordain distinguishes a bishop from any other presbyter (Calvin would not admit that any distinction whatsoever obtains) and that the Roman church is worth no more and no less than any other. [11] On the strength of the evidence which he selects from Jerome's letters and sources such as Eusebius' *Ecclesiastical History,* Calvin portrays the organisation of the early church thus:

Each city had its own college of priests (presbyters) who were both pastors and teachers or doctors. For all had the duty of instructing, exhorting and correcting the people, tasks which Paul enjoined to bishops. In order to leave a posterity behind them they also devoted attention to teaching the younger people who had signed up for the holy militia. Each city had a region allotted to it, which would take its pastors from that city and integrate them into the body of the church. Each *collegium* of priests was under one bishop only for the sake of preserving peace and public order. The bishop presided over them as one might preside over a council of brethren. If the area assigned to a bishop was too large for him to manage alone, priests were appointed in certain places in the area who could do some of his less important business. These were called *chorepiscopi* because they represented the bishop in that particular province.[12]

---

[10] *Institutes,* 4. 4. 2, OS V: 59: "Alibi tamen docet quam fuerit antiquum institutum. Dicit enim, Alexandriae, a Marco Euangelista vsque ad Heraclam et Dionysium presbyteros semper vnum ex se electum in excelsiori gradu collocasse, quem episcopum nominabant."

[11] Jerome, Ep. 146, 1; CSEL 56, 310 (Cf. *Decr. Grat.* 1a pars, dist. 93, can. 24, Friedberg I, 327): "Quod autem vnus electus est, qui caeteris praeponeretur, in scismatis remedium factum est, ne vnusquisque ad se trahens Christi ecclesiam rumperet. Nam et Alexandriae a Marco Euangelista vsque ad Heraclam et Dionysium episcopos presbyteri semper vnum de se et in excelsioro gradu collocatum episcopum nominabant, quomodo si exercitus imperatorem faciant aut diaconi eligant de se quem industrium nouerint et archidiaconum vocent. Quid enim facit excepta ordinatione episcopus quod presbyter non facit? Nec altera Romanae vrbis ecclesia, altera totius orbis aestimanda est…"

[12] *Institutes,* 4. 4. 2; OS V: 59: "Habebant ergo singulae ciuitates presbyterorum collegium qui pastores erant ac doctores. Nam et apud populum munus docendi, exhortandi et corrigendi quod Paulus episcopis iniungit, omnes obibant et quo semen post se relinquerent, iunioribus qui sacrae militiae nomen dederant erudiendis nauabant operam. Vnicuique ciuitati erat attributa certa regio quae presbyteros inde sumeret et velut corpori ecclesiae illius accenseretur. Singula, vt dixi, collegia politiae tantum et pacis conseruandae gratia vni episcopo suberant qui sic alios dignitate antecedebat vt fratrum cetui subiiceretur. Quod si amplior erat ager qui sub eius episcopatu erat quam vt sufficere omnibus episcopi muniis vbique posset, per ipsum agrum designabantur certis locis presbyteri qui in minoribus negotiis eius vices obirent. Eos vocabant chorepiscopos quod per ipsam prouinciam episcopum repraesentabant."

Calvin's source for the information about *chorepiscopi* is Eusebius' *Eccclesiastical History* 7, 30. 10. The passage cited above reveals that Calvin confronted the information provided by Jerome, and, to a lesser extent, Eusebius, with Paul's instructions in the same way as Jerome did in his Commentary on Titus. Indeed, it is not excessive to claim that Jerome's concerns in his Commentary on Titus were not dissimilar to Calvin's. Like the Genevan reformer he adopted a critical stance on the clerical *mores* of his time, finding bishops particularly to be despotic, nepotistic and neglectful of their duty of preaching and exhortation. Like the Genevan reformer, he stressed that neglect of preaching and teaching duties in a bishop was tantamount to going against the Apostle's orders.[13] Both Jerome and Calvin were clear that the bishop was a post-apostolic institution and both insisted on his function as president of a council of brethren.

Jerome's conception of episcopacy, particularly as expressed in his commentary on Titus, served Calvin's needs very well. Firstly, Jerome provided a historical model for taking Paul's instructions as the only foundation. Secondly, he insisted on collegiality while admitting that a limited degree of individual leadership was a historical necessity, even though it constituted a departure from the apostolic model. The Commentary on Titus and Jerome's letters thus provided Calvin with a blueprint of the tolerable limits of deviation from the apostolic model. In the *Institutes* at least, it is not his aim to recapture the organisation of the Apostolic church in its pristine form , any more than it had been Jerome's aim. He is far more interested in using Jerome's authority to show that the Genevan model is grounded in tradition. Using Jerome as the main guarantor was also an apologetic move, but it would not be fair to say that Calvin's recourse to Jerome was motivated first and foremost by apologetic concerns.[14] They did play an important part but so did the genuine conviction that Jerome had in some sense "got it right."

## B. Bishop and Presbyter

The model of the early church is of equal importance in supporting Calvin's view that both ordinary presbyters and bishops have to preach and dispense the sacraments. Although he cites a variety of historical sources in support of the practice, his main doctrinal guarantors are Jerome and Gregory the Great.

---

[13] Jerome, *In Titum* ad 1, 9; MPL 26, 569-570: "Porro si doctrina et sermone fuerit eruditus, potest se caeterosque, et non solum instruere et docere suos, sed et aduersarios repercutere, qui nisi refutati fuerint atque conuicti, facile queunt simplicium corda peruertere. Hic locus aduersus eos facit qui inertiae se et odio et somno dantes, putant peccatum esse si Scripturas legerint, et eos qui in lege Dei meditantur die ac nocte, quasi garrulos inutilesque contemnunt, non animaduertentes apostolum post catalogum conuersationis episcopi etiam doctrinam similiter praecepisse."

[14] See A. N. S. Lane, *John Calvin. Student of the Church Fathers* (Edinburgh: T. & T. Clark, 1999), 32: "Calvin's polemical use of the Fathers usually consists of citing them for his own teaching and against Roman teaching." I prefer to use the term "apologetic" in this context.

Referring to the *Historia tripartite,*[15] he notes that it was only in Alexandria where Arius was disturbing the church that it was decided that a presbyter should not preach. Calvin notes that Jerome's letter to Evagrius (in fact, to Nepotianus) shows that he found non-preaching presbyters an aberration. The reformer, however, omits to add that Jerome criticised not the bishops' reluctance to preach but some presbyters' reluctance to preach in the presence of their bishop "as if he would either get envious or not deign to listen to them."[16]

What Calvin does insist on bringing across is that in Jerome's time it was considered monstrous if someone flaunted himself as a bishop without having the requisite qualities. Moreover—and here Calvin supports his contention with several passages from Gregory the Great—preaching and teaching as the chief duties of presbyters and bishops constituted the norm for a very long time, even during the papacy of Gregory when the church had considerably declined from its early purity.[17] Here, too, it is not the apostolic model as such which is of prime importance to Calvin. He takes it for granted that the apostolic model is the divinely revealed truth. What is important to him is to show how long the apostolic model endured in history.

The section of the *Institutes* which we have just examined provides the theoretical backing for both the vocabulary and the description of the duties of ministers in the Ecclesiastical Ordinances of 1541. It also throws light on certain divergences between the text of the project sketched out by Calvin himself and

---

[15] *Institutes,* 4. 4. 3; OS V: 60: " Sed quantum ad officium attinet de quo nunc agimus, tam episcopum quam presbyteros verbi et sacramentorum dispensationi incumbere oportuit. Nam Alexandriae tantum (quoniam illic Arius ecclesiam turbauerat) institutum fuit ne presbyter concionem ad populum haberet , vt ait Socrates libro 9 Tripartitae Historiae (Hist trip. 9, 38, MPL 69, 1156)."

[16] Jerome, Ep. 52, 7 ; CSEL 54 : 428: "Pessimae consuetudinis est in quibusdam ecclesiis tacere presbyteros et praesentibus episcopis non loqui, quasi aut inuideant aut non dignentur audire."

[17] *Institutes,* 4. 4. 3; OS V: 60: "Quod tamen ipsum Hieronymus sibi displicere non dissimulat (Epist. ad Euagrium=Ep. 52, 7 ad Nepotianum, CSEL 54: 428). Certe instar portenti habitum esset, si quis se pro episcopo venditasset, qui non etiam reipsa exhibuisset verum episcopum. Ea igitur fuit temporum illorum seueritas vt ministri omnes ad implendum munus quale ab ipsis Dominus requirit , adigerentur. Nec vnius tantum aetatis morem refero , siquidem ne Gregorii quidem tempore quo ecclesia iam fere collapsa erat (certe multum ab antiqua puritate degenerauerat) tolerabile fuisset episcopum aliquem a concionibus abstinere. "Sacerdos" inquit ipse alicubi, moritur si de eo sonitus non audiatur, quia iram contra se occulti iudicis exigit, si sine sonitu praedicationis incedit (Greg. I, *Registrum epistolarum* lib. 1, ep. 24, *Monumenta Germaniae Historica* Ep. I 32). Et alibi: quum testatur Paulus se mundum esse a sanguine omnium (Act. 20, 26) in hac voce nos conuincimur, nos constringimur, nos rei esse ostendimur, qui sacerdotes vocamur, qui super ea mala quae propria habemus, alienas quoque mortes addimus; quia tot occidimus quot ad mortem ire quotidie tepidi et tacentes videmus (*Homil. In Ezech.* 11= lib. 1, hom. 11, 10; MPL 76: 910). Tacentes se et alios vocat , quia minus assidui essent in opere quam conueniret. Quum ne iis quidem parcat qui officium dimidia ex parte agebant, quid facturum fuisse putas siquis in totum cessasset? Valuit ergo diu illud in ecclesia vt primae episcopi partes essent, populum verbo Dei pascere, seu aedificare ecclesiam publice ac priuatim sana doctrina."

the final text as incorporated into the Registers of the Company of Pastors. The preliminary text states: "As for pastors, whom the Scripture also calls sometimes bishops (*evesquez*), elders and ministers, their job is to announce the word of God, to indoctrinate, admonish, exhort and chastise both in public and in private, to administer the sacraments and to carry out brotherly reprimands."[18]

In the final text which, as we know, was approved after some revisions by the Council, the word *evesquez* (bishops) has been replaced by *surveillans* (caretakers), which shows that Calvin, who took part in the elaboration of the initial text, was quite happy with the term bishop so long as it covered a function compatible with the tradition of the church transmitted by *Ecclesiastical Histories* and vouchsafed by Jerome and Gregory. The replacement of the word *bishop* by *supervisor*, however, would have probably met with Calvin's full approval as he did not envisage the episcopal function as extending beyond that of a caretaker. Indeed, Jerome makes that very point when he comments on Paul's use of the word *episkopè* in his letter 146 which Calvin knew.[19] More importantly, however, the article, both in its preliminary and in its final form, only makes sense if read against the *Institutes* 4. 4. 3, which provides the doctrinal backing. What does not transpire from the article, as it could not, given its very nature, is the extent of the appeal to the early church that underlies its composition.

## C. Popular Participation in the Ordination of Pastors and Deacons

The *Institutes*—or rather Calvin's conception of the early ecclesiastical organisation they portray—also throw a light on other important points to do with the setting up of the Company of Pastors, such as the issue of popular and magisterial participation in the election of ministers and the question of selection and examination of candidates, including the issue of the laying on of hands. Calvin devotes some time to the practice of the early church in *Institutes* 4. 4. 10-13.

Before we examine these passages, here is a brief reminder of the Genevan ordination practices which are sketched out very clearly by Kingdon in the article I referred to above.[20] The Company of Pastors received applications whenever there was a vacancy in the pastoral corps. It then examined each applicant on his knowledge, his orthodoxy and his moral values. The examination included the preaching of a trial sermon. The successful candidate was then

---

[18] *Projet d'ordonnances*, 1541 ; OS II : 328: "Quant est des pasteurs, que lescripture nomme aussi aulcunefois evesquez anciens et ministres, leur office est dannoncer la parole de Dieu pour endoctriner, admonester, exorter et reprendre tant en publicq comme en particulier, administrer les sacremens et faire les corrections fraternelles avec les anciens ou commis."

[19] Jerome, Ep. 146, 1 ; CSEL 56 : 309: "...audi et aliud testimonium in quo manifestissime comprobatur eundem esse episcopum atque presbyterum: 'pascite qui in vobis est gregem Dei prouidentes non coacte sed spontanee secundum Deum' [1 Petr 5, 2] quod quidem Grsece significantius dicitur *episkopeuontes* vnde et nomen episcopi tractum est."

[20] See Kingdon, "The Episcopal Function", 217-218.

presented to the Council for further examination. If he met with the Council's approval, he was presented to the congregation and if he satisfied the congregation, he would be installed in office. The installation involved the new minister in subscribing to a standard oath of loyalty to the city and its church. This took place at a Council meeting. Finally, he was presented to his new congregation by the minister who was specially assigned to preach in the new minister's church on that particular day.

We note that while the civil authorities played a considerable role in the selection and examination of the new minister, the role of the common lay people was comparatively small. The 1541 preliminary text and the definitive text of the Ordinances specified that the identity of the authorities who were to examine and institute ministers was determined in accord with the practice of the early church, "which was nothing other than the putting into practice of the Scripture."[21] Both documents then specified that it was the ministers' job to select the candidate who was to hold the office. The text in its initial state left things at that. Subsequently, another hand added, "after making it known to their honours" (*layant faict assavoir a la seigneurie*), an addition which was maintained by the definitive text.

The initial text then specified that after his election by the ministers, the candidate should be presented to the Council, which would accept him if it finds him worthy. A later manuscript addition to the original text added: "as it sees fit" (*ainsi que lon verraz estre expedient*), which the definitive text transformed to read: "according to as it sees fit" (*selon quil verraz estre expedient*). Both the preliminary and the final texts then state that on finding the candidate worthy the Council should attest that he is fit to preach to the congregation whose task it was to approve the sermon "so that he may be received by common consent of all the faithful."[22] If the congregation refused its approval, a new election was held. The role of the civil authorities received more emphasis as the project evolved while the role of the common laypeople remained unchanged.

However, in 1560, still in Calvin's lifetime, the Council of 200 decided on an amendment to this particular article as a result of certain abuses:

As regards the reproach made to us by the honourable ministers, that the ordinance on their presentation was not being observed and that those who were

---

[21] RCP I, 2; OS II : 329: "Il sera bon en cest endroict de suyvre l'ordre de lesglise ancienne, veu que ce nest que practique de ce qui nous est monstre par lescripture."

[22] Ibid. "S'ensuyt à qui il appartient d'instituer les pasteurs. Il sera bon en cest endroict de suyvre l'ordre de l'esglise ancienne, veu que ce n'est qu'une pratique de ce qui nous est monstré par l'escripture. De leur election. C'est que les ministres elisent premierement celluy qu'on debvra mettre en l'office, l'ayant faict à scavoir à la Seigneurie, après qu'on les présente au Conseil. Et s'il est trouvé digne, que le Conseil le recoyve et accepte selon qu'il verra estre expedient, luy donnant tesmoignage pour le produire finablement au peuple en la predication affin qu'il soit receu par consentement commun de la compaignie des fidelles. S'il estoit trouvé indigne et demonstré tel par probations legitimes, il fauldroit lors proceder à nouvelle election pour en prendre un aultre."

received by the Council were simply presented in the church without asking the parishioners' approval and that thereby the people and the entire body of the church were deprived of their freedom, it seemed to us too that this constituted a deviation from what had initially been decided. Moreover, given that the ministers drew our attention to the fact that they were not seeking any personal advantage but rather were seeking a shorter leash for themselves and their successors, we decided that the original edict should be observed. And in order to stop similar abuses from occurring and to make sure that all ceremonies in our church were observed truthfully, we decided what follows. When a minister is elected, his name should be proclaimed with the announcement that he who knows things, which might be held against him, should come forth and declare them before the day of the minister's presentation, so that if he is unfit to hold office, a new election might be held.[23]

The abuse which arose suggests that the powers of the civil authorities over clergy were very considerable *already in Calvin's lifetime,* whereas the right of the lay faithful to have a say was reduced to a bare minimum.

If we now turn to the *Institutes* 4. 4. 10-12, we find that those sections provide the doctrinal and historical justification for the Genevan system of ordination. They also account for the limited powers granted to the faithful. What is also worth noting is that in this particular section of the *Institutes* Calvin talks not just about the ordination of ministers in the early church but also about the ordination of bishops without making a sharp distinction between the two. He relies not on the apostolic model but once again on the early post-apostolic church to provide him with the necessary evidence. Starting from the premise that the early church observed Paul's injunctions to Timothy and the example of the Apostles, he takes his reader through a whole range of practices and through some four centuries of history, from Cyprian to Gregory the Great. The actual authorities cited go from Cyprian's letters, through *Ecclesiastical Histories,* letters of Augustine and Leo the Great, to the canons of the doubtful Council of Laodicea. Most of the evidence is thus fairly late and several of the testimonies can be traced to the *Decree of Gratian.* This proves that Calvin has an

---

[23] OS II : 330: "Item sur ce que lesdits spectables ministres nous ont remonstré , que l'ordonnance faicte sur leur presentation n'avoit point esté gardee, d'autant que ceux qui estoyent esleuz et acceptez par la Seigneurie ont esté presentez simplement au temple , sans leur demander si on les approuvoit, et que par cela le peuple et tout le corps de l'Eglise ont esté fraudez de leur liberté, enquoy aussi il nous est apparu qu'on s'estoit destourné de ce qui avoit esté bien estably du commencement: ioint aussi que lesdicts Ministres nous ont remonstré qu'en tout cecy ils ne cherchent point nul avantage pour eux, mais plustost qu'eux et leurs successeurs soyent tenuz en bride plus courte, nous auons aussi arresté que L'Edict ancien selon sa teneur soit deuement observé. Et afin de prevenir tel abus comme il estoit survenu, et qu'il n'y ait point de ceremonie en nostre Eglise sans ce que la vérité et substance y soit coniointe, nous avons prouveu du remede qui sensuit. C'est quand un ministre sera esleu que son nom soit proclamé auec avertissment que celui qui saura à redire sur lui le vienne declarer deuant le iour qu'il devra estre presenté , afin que s'il n'estoit point capable de l'office, on procède à nouelle election."

interest in showing that the church evolved in history, although he tends not to trace most of the developments in detail, indicating the abandonment or change of practices by verbs such as "ceased" (*desiit*) or adverbs of time such as "later" (*postea*).

He notes thus that in the early church the pastors came together to elect ministers, information which he could have gleaned from Cyprian's letters, particularly his letter 55.[24] He also notes that the preliminary examination required that candidates conform to Paul's model, an obvious allusion to a letter of Leo I and to the decision of the fourth Council of Carthage cited by the *Decree of Gratian*. If anything, he adds, they were even more severe than Paul in demanding with the passage of time that their ministers remain celibate.[25] As regards the specific issue of approval of ministers by the people, he notes that the procedure of the early church was not always uniform and points out that sometimes even the minor clergy were elected only once popular approval had been given. His source for this is Cyprian, who apologised (letter 38) for making a certain Aurelius a reader without consulting the rest of the church, while admitting that in doing so he acted against the accepted custom, albeit not without good reason. Calvin takes the opening words of the letter as constituting a proof that the people were regularly consulted on the appointment of all clergy at that time.[26]

It is important to remember that to Calvin the only offices of the early church were those of deacon and presbyter, which bears out his own view of ministers and deacons as the only permanent spiritual offices in the church while granting the dual, temporal and spiritual, nature of the diaconate.[27] The gradual addition of bishops and archbishops as well as *hypo*—or apprentice—*deacons* and archdeacons was simply a measure of expediency and should not be taken to mean that any real hierarchy was instituted. All the other offices, such as readers, acolytes and so on represent, in Calvin's view, simply stages in the training of presbyters. These were necessary since "these holy men," in other words, the early Fathers, were most concerned about the training of

---

[24] *Institutes*, 4. 4. 10 ; OS V : 67: " Quod primum et secundum in ministrorum vocatione esse diximus, quales eligere et quantam religionem in eo adhibere oporteat, in eo Pauli praescriptum et Apostolorum exempla vetus ecclesia secuta est. Solebant enim ad eligendos pastores cum summa reuerentia ac sollicita nominis Dei inuocatione conuenire. (Clem. 44, 3; Cyprian ep. 55, 6 ; CSEL 3, II : 629; ep. 67, 4, CSEL 3, II : 738, 4 sq).

[25] Ibid. "Adhaec formulam examinis habebant, qua eligendorum vitam et doctrinam ad illam Pauli amussim exigebant [Leo I, ep. 12, 2 ; MPL 54 : 67. *Decr. Grat.* I dist. 23, c. 2, Friedberg I, 79]. Tantum peccarunt hic nonnihil immodica seueritate, quod plus requirere voluerunt in episcopo quam Paulus requirat ac praesertim successu temporis coelibatum. Verum in caeteris consentanea fuit ipsorum obseruatio cum Pauli descriptione."

[26] *Institutes*, 4. 4. 10; OS V: 67: "Sic autem praefatur: 'in ordinandis clericis, fratres carissimi, solemus vos ante consulere et mores ac merita singulorum communi consilio ponderare'."

[27] On this point generally, see McKee, *Calvin on the Diaconate*, 152-158.

clergy to assure a future for the church.[28] While acknowledging some differences between the early church and the apostolic model, Calvin shows a great deal of respect for the former. He therefore passes no strictures on developments such as the gradual disuse of the custom of asking the people's consent for the appointment of minor church officers, finding it natural as "there was not much risk attached, seeing as they were taken on for training purposes and not to exercise an important function."[29]

More importantly, Calvin does not criticise the people's gradual abrogation to the bishop and the clergy of the right to decide the suitability of candidates for clerical functions. He finds it satisfactory that they retained their right to approve the election of new bishops and new parochial clergy, with only the congregation concerned being consulted in the latter case.[30] Calvin's source for this last custom is Cyprian's letter 55, which also provided him with the information about the pastors coming together to elect new ministers.

Although Calvin also refers to a canon which, he says, is attributed to Anacletus, the third bishop of Rome after Peter and Linus, he does *not* say that the canon goes much further than Cyprian's letter 55 in granting the people a say in the ordination not only of presbyters but also of deacons.[31] In fact, the so-called canon of Anacletus, if read in its entirety and in its context, does not seem to suit Calvin's purpose at all, which is probably why he does not dwell on it at any length in contrast with the Cyprian passage. The canon says:

> *Priests can only be ordained by a bishop.* Other priests [i. e., other than bishops] are ordained in such a way that citizens and the remaining priests can also give their assent, and they should celebrate the ordination by fasting.

---

[28] *Institutes,* 4. 4. 9; OS V: 65-66: "Haec quae recensuimus veteris ecclesiae ministeria fuerunt. Alia enim de quibus mentionem faciunt ecclesiastici scriptores magis exercitia fuerunt et quaedam praeparationes quam certa munera. Nam sancti illi viri vt ecclesiae seminarium post se relinquerent, adulescentes qui ex parentum consensu et authoritate militiae spirituali nomen dabant, recipiebant in suam fidem ac tutelam atque etiam disciplinam eosque sic formabant a tenera aetate ne rudes ac noui ad obeundum munus accederent (Omnes autem qui eiusmodi tyrociniis imbuebantur generali nomine vocabantur clerici. Vellem equidem aliud nomen magis proprium inditum illis fuisse. Haec enim appellatio ex errore vel certe praua affectione nata est quum tota ecclesia clerus, hoc est haereditas Domini a Petro dicatur."

[29] *Institutes,* 4. 4. 10; OS V: 67: "Verum quia in minoribus illis exercitiis non multum erat periculi, quod ad diuturnam probationem et non magnam functionem assumerentur, rogari consensus plebis desiit."

[30] *Institutes,* 4. 4. 10; OS V: 67-68: " Postea in reliquis quoque ordinibus, excepto episcopatu, plebs episcopo ac presbyteris iudicium delectumque fere permisit vt cognoscerent quinam idonei ac digni forent, nisi forte quum parochiis noui presbyteri destinabantur; tunc enim loci multitudinem nominatim consentire oportuit."

[31] *Institutes,* 4. 4. 10 ; OS V : 68: "Quanquam in presbyteris quoque semper exigebatur ciuium consensus; quod etiam testatur canon primus dist. 67 qui Anacleto tribuitur." (Cf. *Decr. Grat.* I dist. 67, c. 1, Friedberg I, 253).

Deacons should be ordained in the same way. As for the other offices, the testimony of three truthful men and the approval of the bishop is necessary.[32]

The text describes a practice very far removed from what was done in Geneva. Calvin does not distort what it says about the extent of popular participation in the election of clergy but passes over in silence the fact that it also allows popular participation in the election of deacons who are treated on a par with the presbyters.

In fact, as we said, it is the model sketched out in Cyprian's letter 55 that is maintained in the Ecclesiastical Ordinances, which grant the local congregation the right to approve their pastor but do not accord any other popular rights or privileges. The 1560 amendment to the Ordinances does not go beyond confirming the initial decision. It does not extend popular rights; it just makes sure that the original rights of the congregation are reaffirmed. This is a very good instance of the *Institutes* providing a justification for what was actually done by recourse to the early church. On examination, Calvin's appeal to the latter turns out to be highly selective and oriented by considerations of a legal nature.

As if anticipating objections to do with extending popular rights, a procedure justified by the canon of Anacletus, Calvin explains in the same passage in the *Institutes* that it is not at all surprising that the people were not very concerned about not being granted their full right in the process of selecting deacons or in ordaining candidates for the ministry. No one became a *hypodeacon* without a lengthy period of trial in minor clerical orders; no-one was promoted from hypodeacon to deacon unless he had proved himself worthy. The same applied to the step from deacon to presbyter. Thus no one became a minister without being subject to a lengthy scrutiny by the people, sometimes stretching over a period of years. Moreover, strict laws governed the clergy's conduct and all ordinations took place at set times of year so that no candidate escaped popular control. [33]

Calvin is making an oblique reference to the canon of the Council of Sardica of 343 which forbade ordination to the episcopacy of anyone who had not passed through the minor orders. As Ambrose's consecration shows, the canon

---

[32] *Decr. Grat.* I dist. 67, c. 1, Friedberg I, 253: "Sacerdotes ab vno possunt ordinari episcopo. Reliqui sacerdotes aproprio ordinentur episcopo, ita vt ciues et alii sacerdotes assensum praebeant et ieiunantes celebrent ordinationem. Similiter et diaconi ordinentur. Caeterorum autem graduum distributioni trium veracium testimonium episcopi scilicet approbatione sufficere potest."

[33] *Institutes*, 4. 4. 10 ; OS V : 68: " Postquam in eo gradu probatus fuerat, diaconus constituebatur; inde ad presbyterii honorem perueniebat si fideliter se gessisset. Ita nullus promouebatur de quo non re vera multis annis habitum esset sub populi oculis examen. Et erant multi canones ad punienda eorum vitia vt ecclesia malis presbyteris aut diaconis non grauaretur nisi remedia negligeret. Quanquam in presbyteris quoque semper exigebatur ciuium consensus; quod etiam testatur canon primus dist. 67 qui Anacleto tribuitur. [*Decr. Grat.* I dist. 67, c. 1, Friedberg I, 253]. Denique omnes ordinationes ideo statis anni temporibus fiebant nequis clanculum sine fidelium consensu obreperet, aut nimia felicitate absque testibus promoueretur." ( Cf. *Decr. Grat.* I dist. 75 c. 7, Friedberg I, 267).

was not put into operation until later. Calvin is thus referring to a late custom and his direct source could well be not the canon as such but the *Decree of Gratian* which specifies that "orders should be ascended in order, for he who bypasses the different stages and seeks to scale the summit in one go, is heading for a fall."[34] It seems as if canon law of the early—but by no means of the earliest church—provided Calvin with the perfect justification for not presenting to the people candidates for the Genevan office of deacon, thus contributing to its secularisation. Indeed, the corresponding articles of the Ordinances state that candidates for the offices of deacon and elder should be chosen by the ministers and the Council and that their names should be submitted for approval to the Council of 200. They were then asked to swear an oath of loyalty like the ministers.[35]

To return to the appointment of pastors, we saw that it was Cyprian's letter 55, which Calvin refers to in *Institutes* 4. 4. 10, which provides him with the justification for restricting to the congregation concerned the extent of popular approval required for the election of a pastor. We shall now show that *Institutes* 4. 4. 12, which ostensibly deals with the question of the election of bishops in the early church, is found to contain the doctrinal foundation for the rest of the appointment procedure as described in the Ordinances. This foundation, as we shall see, is indeed provided by the practices of the early church, whose authority the article invokes. However, the article does not tell us what it means by the early church. To find out, we have to turn to the Institutes 4. 4. 12. The article imposes the following ordination procedure:

> It is right in this matter to follow the order of the ancient church seeing as it represents the putting into practice of Scriptural precepts. Ministers must first of all elect the right candidate after making it known to the Council . After this, he should be presented to the Council. If he is found worthy, the Council should receive and accept him as it sees fit, attesting that he should appear before the congregation to preach so that he may be accepted by common consent of the assembly of the faithful.[36]

And this is the corresponding passage about the practice of the early church in the *Institutes* 4. 4. 12:

---

[34] *Decr. Grat.* 1a pars, dist.48, c.2, Friedberg 1, 174.: "ordinate ergo ad ordines ascendedum est. Nam casum apetit qui ad summi loci fastigia postpositis gradibus per abrupta querit ascensum."

[35] OS II : 339-340: "Sensuyt le troisieme ordre qui est des anciens…: La maniere de les elire-semble estre bonne telle que messieurs du conseil estroict advisent de nommer les plus propres quon pourra trouver et les plus suffisans et pource faire appeler les ministres pour en communi-quer avec eulx, puys quilz presentent ceulx quilz auront advise au conseil des deux cens , lequel les approuvera. Sil les trouve dignes, quilz facent serment particulier dont la forme se pourra facile-ment dresser…Et au bout de lan…quilz se presentent a la seigneurie affin quilz regardent silz les debvront continuer ou changer…" 341: "Que lelection tant des procureurs que des hospitalliers se face comme des anciens et comys au consistoire…" See Also RCP I: 7.

[36] See note 22 above for original text.

First the clergy alone made their choice. They presented their candidate to the magistrates or to the senate and their leaders. They in turn ratified the election if it seemed just. If it did not seem just, they elected someone else of whom they approved more. Only then was the case brought before the multitude, who, although bound to follow the choice already made, had far less excuse for rowdy demonstrations.[37]

The passage in the *Institutes* was added in 1543, two years after the composition of the Ordinances. We have already discussed Calvin's assimilation of the office of bishop to that of presbyter. Although he also devotes three paragraphs in all (*Institutes* 4. 4. 11-13) to discussing the ordination of bishops in the early church, treating it separately from the ordination of parish ministers, this should not be seen as either a purely polemical stratagem intended to point up the contrast between the Roman procedure of his own day and that of the early church, or a tacit acceptance of the office of bishop on Calvin's part. Were his aim merely to show the Roman church that their practice of appointing bishops was completely aberrant in relation to tradition, it is doubtful that the description of the early church practice would have resurfaced in the Ordinances, which was a legal and not a polemical text. Then again, had Calvin wanted to openly approve the hierarchical office of bishop, it is very doubtful that the passage would have occurred in the Ordinances in the article on the ordination of *ministers*. Finally, what comes through in the *Institutes* and what is completely absent from the Ordinances is an awareness of the dangers of popular uprising if the choice of a suitable candidate is delegated to the multitude.

Calvin's object in the Ordinances and in the Institutes passage is in fact to keep as close as possible to the practice of the early church of the 4th to 6th centuries, with Cyprian constituting the sole exception. He cites several authorities, including Leo' s letters, Theodoret and Augustine, which are intended to prove that the people maintained for a long time their right to have a limited say in the election of bishops. He also cites the famous example of Nectarius of Constantinople, drawn from Theodoret, whom the Council refused to confirm without popular approval.[38] Calvin is not the first reformer to have such exten-

[37] *Institutes*, 4. 4. 12 ; OS V : 69: "Primum enim soli clerici eligebant; quem elegerant, offerebant magistratui vel senatui ac primoribus. Illi habita deliberatione, electionem si iusta videbatur, consignabant. Sin minus, eligebant alium quem magis probarent; tum ad multitudinem res deferebatur, quae tametsi praeiudiciis illis non alligaretur, minus tamen tumultuari poterat."

[38] I*nstitutes*, 4. 4. 11 ; OS V : 68-69: "In eligendis episcopis diu sua populo libertas fuit conseruata nequis obtruderetur qui non omnibus acceptus esset. Hoc igitur in Concilio antiocheno vetitum est nequis inuitis ingeratur. Quod et Leo primus diligenter confirmat. Hinc istae sententiae: is eligatur quem clerus et plebs aut maior numerus postularint. Item: qui praefaturus est omnibus ab omnibus eligatur. Qui enim ignotus et non examinatus praeficitur, necesse est vt per vim intrudatur. Item: is eligatur qui a clericis electus a plebe expetitus fuerit et a prouincialibus cum metropolitani iudicio consecretur (Epist. 90, cap. 2). Adeo autem cauerunt sancti patres ne vllo pacto imminueretur haec populi libertas vt quum synodus vniuersalis Constantinopoli congregata Nectarium ordinaret, id facere noluerit sine totius cleri et populi approbatione, vt sua ad synodum Romanam epistola testata est. Proinde quum episcopus quispiam successorem sibi designaret non

sive recourse to the practices of the early church nor is his knowledge of its writings encyclopaedic. After all, Martin Bucer's knowledge of and interest in canon law was as great if not greater.

However, a quick comparison with Bucer's *Florilegium patristicum,* which remained unpublished until very recently,[39] shows only superficial similarities. It is not part of my purpose here to establish a detailed comparison. A selection of examples suffices to make the point. Like Calvin, Bucer does not distinguish with particular care between the office of presbyter and that of bishop, citing Jerome's letter to Evangelus to show that the office of bishop was a simple expediency instituted to stop internecine quarrels.[40] He is as concerned as Calvin to show that both bishops and presbyters were elected with the approval of the people, but he does not use the same supporting texts as Calvin.

Furthermore, Bucer does not take Cyprian's letter 55 as a model for the consultation of the congregation subsequent to the election of a presbyter by the clergy and the civil authorities. More significantly still, he does not go into the issue of why it was found expedient to consult the people only subsequently to the ordination of both bishops and parish clergy, something that preoccupies Calvin a great deal. Indeed, Calvin, after citing a variety of $4^{th}$ to $6^{th}$ century authorities for people being granted their full say in the election of bishops, expresses open approval of the canon of the "council of Laodicea" (in fact he means the $4^{th}$ century canons of Laodicea put together from several councils, including Nicaea) which forbade the people to participate in the ordination of presbyters.

Calvin's source for this canon is once again the *Decree of Gratian.* Significantly, it occurs in the *Decree* in the section on bishops and equally significantly it is not cited by Bucer in his *Patristicum florilegium.* The canon states: "the populace is not allowed to be admitted to elect those who are to be elevated to the priesthood."[41] In his comment Calvin points out that too many heads rarely come up with the right solution and that the populace is fickle, blowing this way and that.[42] The perfect remedy for the problem was the adoption of the system of

---

aliter ratum est quam si totus populus scisceret. Cuius rei non modo exemplum sed formulam quoque habes apud Augustinum in nominatione Eradii (epist. 110). Et Theodoritus quum refert Petrum ab Athanasio successorem nominatum, continuo adiungit sacerdotalem ordinem ratum id habuisse, magistratum et primores populumque vniuersum sua acclamatione approbasse (habetur apud Theodor. Lib. 4, cap. 20 =Theodoret, Hist. eccl. 4, 20).

[39] Martin Bucer et Matthew Parker, *Florilegium patristicum,* ed. Pierre Fraenkel (Leiden: Brill, 1988).

[40] Bucer, *Florilegium Patristicum,* 95.

[41] *Decree of Gratian,* 1a pars, dist. 63, c. 6, Friedberg I, 236: "Non est permittendum turbis electionem eorum facere qui sunt ad sacerdotium promouendi."

[42] *Institutes,* 4. 4. 12; OS V: 69: "Est quidem et illud (fateor) optima ratione sancitum in Laodicensi concilio ne turbis electio permittatur. Vix enim vnquam euenit vt tot capita vno sensu rem aliquam bene componant et fere illud verum est: 'Incertum scindi studia in contraria vulgus'. Verum huic periculo adhibitum erat optimum remedium."

having the clergy make the initial choice, then submitting it to the civil rulers and the magistrate and only then having it validated by the people. This, as we saw, was the system outlined in the Ordinances.

Calvin cites two letters of Leo the Great as a historical source for the practice. In letter 10 (cited by Calvin as letter 87) Leo says: "we should like to have indication of the wishes of the citizens, the testimony of the people, the judgement of public officials and the election by the clergy." [43] In letter 167 he asserts: "we must have the testimony of public authorities, the agreement of the clergy and a consensus of the clergy and the people; there is no other way of proceeding." [44] This system in Calvin's view provides the perfect compromise solution to the issue: the people are not ignored but they are not allowed to be the main electors. Together with Cyprian's letter granting consultation rights to individual congregations on the election of parish clergy, the letters of Leo I and the canon of Laodicea provide Calvin with a model for the text of the Ordinances. As if to put himself above any suspicion of ignorance of tradition, he notes that this system of election was still operative in Gregory the Great's time and after, and that both Gregory's letters and the *Decree of Gratian* show that in Rome the election of the bishop by the clergy and the people had to be ratified by the emperor. [45] Throughout this section of the *Institutes* Gregory's reign has an emblematic value for the reformer as instantiating the beginning of the period of major decadence. For this very reason he takes care to point out, wherever he can, that even Gregory took care to remain close to the apostolic model. He thus establishes implicitly an unfavourable comparison between the Roman church of his day and Gregory, one of its chief authorities.

---

[43] *Institutes* 4. 4. 12; OS V: 69: " Hunc ordinem ponit alibi Leo quum dicit:expectanda sunt vota ciuium , testimonia populorum, honoratorum arbitrium, electio clericorum [Epist. 87; Leo I, ep. 10, 4, MPL 54, 632]."

[44] Ibid. " Item: teneatur honoratorum testimonium, subscriptio clericorum, ordinis consensus ac plebis; aliter (inquit) fieri nulla ratio sinit. [Leo I, ep. 167; MPL 54: 1203]."

[45] *Institutes*, 4. 4. 14 ; OS V : 70, 71: " Haec eligendi ratio adhuc aetate Gregorii valebat et verisimile est diu postea durasse. Extant apud eum plurimae epistolae quae luculentum huius rei testimonium dant. Quoties enim de creando alicubi nouo episcopo agitur, scribere solet ad clerum, ordinem et plebem, interdum etiam ad ducem prout est regimen ciuitatis constitutum. [Greg. I, Reg. Ep. 58, MGH Ep I , 81etc.]… Romae autem tantum olim valuit imperatoris authoritas in episcopo creando vt Gregorius se ipsius iussu in ecclesiae gubernaculis constitutum esse dicat, quum tamen solenni ritu a populo fuisset expetitus [Epist. 5, lib. 1; MGH Ep I 6]… Hoc autem moris fuit vt quum aliquem designassent ordo, clerus ac populus, ad imperatorem statim referret ille vt vel scisciceret electionem sua approbatione vel improbando abrogaret [*Decr. Grat.* Dist. 63, c. 18, Friedberg I, 239]. Neque huic consuetudini repugnant decreta quae a Gratiano colliguntur vbi nihil aliud dicitur quam nullo modo ferendum esse vt sublata canonica electione, rex pro sua libidine episcopum constituat et a metropolis non esse consecrandum qui per violenta imperiasic fuerit promotus [*Decr. Grat.* Dist. 63, c. 1-8, Friedberg I, 234]. Alius enim est spoliare ecclesiam iure suo vt totum ad vnius homnis libidinem transferatur; aliud hoc honoris regi aut imperatori dare vt sua authoritate legitimam electionem confirmet."

In fact, as we saw, Calvin's model for the election of clergy had the obvious drawback of privileging the role of civil authorities while effectively reducing the congregation's role to that of almost total passivity. This is in fact what happened in Geneva between 1541 and 1560, making the 1560 amendment to the Ordinances indispensable. How, and if, the amendment was applied is another matter, which I do not propose to go into here.

## D. Ordination Ritual and Imposition of Hands

As we saw, the question of the imposition of hands created a certain amount of embarrassment, and the text of the initial draft of the Ordinances was revised quite substantially before it was accepted as definitive. If we look at the two versions, we see that the draft reveals greater concern than the final version about abolishing what was an apostolic custom. The corresponding passages in the *Institutes* (4. 4. 14-15) are found to be in support of the imposition of hands. Calvin wants to show above all how and to what extent the early church maintained the apostolic nature of the entire ritual without conceding undue powers to the bishop. He does not dwell, as he might have done, on its biblical simplicity and purity, or on the symbolic nature of the imposition of hands, as he will do in his comments on Acts 6: 6.

Calvin's main sources for the ordination ceremony and for the practice of the imposition of hands are the canons of the first Council of Nicaea and the letters of Cyprian. These two sources provide the reformer with evidence of ordination being practised by a collective. He draws attention to the fourth canon of the Council of Nicaea which requests that the metropolitan together with all the bishops of the province be present at the ordination ceremony. If the length of the journey, illness or other valid reasons prevent some of them from attending, at least three should be present and those who cannot attend should indicate their consent in writing.[46] He is aware that the canon was also proclaimed by several later Councils whenever it was felt that it had been neglected.[47] In Calvin's view the presence of the largest possible number was

---

[46] *Institutes,* 4. 4. 14; OS V: 71: " Extat autem decretum Nicaeni Concilii vt Metropolites cum omnibus prouinciae episcopis conueniat ad eum qui electus fuerit ordinandum. Si autem itineris longitudine aut valetudine, aut alia necessitate pars impeditur vt tamen tres minimum conueniant, qui autem absunt, suam consensionem per litteras testentur." This is a literal quotation from the canon, which states: "Episcopum conuenit maxime quidem ab omnibus qui sunt in prouincia episcopis ordinari. Si autem hoc difficile fuerit aut propter instantem necessitatem aut propter itineris longitudinem, modis omnibus tamen in id ipsum conuenientibus et absentibus episcopis pariter decernentibus et per scripta consentientibus tunc ordinatio celebretur. Firmitas autem eorum quae geruntur per vnamquamque prouinciam, metropolitano tribuatur episcopo." See *Conciliorum oecumenicorum Decreta,* ed. G. Alberigo et alii, Basel: Herder, 1962, 6-7. Cited herafter as: *Decreta.*

[47] *Institutes,* 4. 4, 14 ; OS V : 71: " Atque hic Canon quum desuetudine obsolesceret, pluribus deinde synodis renouatus fuit." The editors of OS cite the examples of the third Council of Carthage and of the second Council of Nicaea.

necessary to ensure that the examination of the ordinand's doctrine and morals was carried out with the maximum of rigour, as it was an indispensable part of the proceedings.

The reformer is alluding to the ninth canon of the Council of Nicaea, but he goes beyond it. The canon in question simply states that no one can be ordained without a preliminary examination; it does not say what the examination should consist of, nor does it advocate the presence of the largest possible number of presbyters and bishops to ensure rigour.[48] The second canon of the Second Council of Nicaea, which reaffirms the ninth canon of the first Nicene Council specifies the content of the examination to be undergone by a candidate for episcopal consecration along the lines sketched out later in the Geneva Ordinance; but it says nothing about the greatest possible number of the clergy being present and states explicitly that the examination should be carried out by the metropolitan. Cyprian's letter 67, which Calvin quotes, does advocate, like the first Council of Nicaea, the presence of the episcopal corps at ordinations but does not say that this is to ensure the rigour of the examination.[49]

On turning to the Ordinances of 1541, we note that they place great stress on the examination of the candidate's doctrine and morals. They specify that the examination is in two parts. The doctrinal part tests the candidate's knowledge of Scripture and his capacity to communicate its message. He is then asked to declare that he subscribes to the Genevan church's teaching. Finally he is to be interrogated on his doctrine and asked to talk about it in private. In the second part of the examination on the candidate's morals, the Ordinances recommend that St. Paul's rule should be observed.[50] It is quite clear that the

---

[48] Ibid. "Omnes autem, aut saltem quicunque excusationem non haberent, ideo adesse iubebantur quo grauius de doctrina et moribus ordinandi haberetur examen, neque enim sine examine res peragebatur. Et apparet ex Cypriani verbis, non post electionem vocari sed electioni interesse olim solitos atque in eum finem vt essent quasi moderatores, nequid in ipsa turba fieret turbulenti." The ninth canon of the first Council of Nicaea states : "Si qui presbyteri sine examinatione sunt promoti vel cum discuterentur, sua peccata confessi sunt et homines moti contra canones confessis manus imponere temptauerunt, tales regula non admittit, quia quod in reprehensibile est catholica defendit ecclesia." See *Decreta* (1962), 9-10. The second canon of the second Council of Nicaea states that candidates for episcopal consecration should undergo an examination on their knowledge of Scripture, on their ability to teach and on their morals but it specifies that the examination should be carried out by the metropolitan and says nothing about the largest possible number of the clergy being present. See *Decreta* (1962), 115-116.

[49] See Institutes, 4. 4. 14; OS V: 71-72.

[50] OS II : 329: "Lexamen contient deux parties, dont la premiere est touchant la doctrine, assavoir si celluy, quon doibt ordonner , a bonne et saince cognoyssance de lescripture. Et puys sil est ydoine et propre pour la communiquer au peuple en edification [the project adds: 'estant premierement appres lexamen fayct presente a la seigneurie' ]...Aussi...il sera bon quil proteste de recevoir et tenir la doctrine approuee en lesglise. Pour cognoistre sil est propre a enseigner, il faudra proceder par interrogations et par l'ouyr traicter en prive la doctrine du seigneur. La seconde partie est de la vie...La reigle dy proceder est tresbien demonstree par sainct Paul, laquelle il fauldra tenir." See RCP I: 2.

examination was carried out by the ministers only and that the candidate was presented to the Council only if successful.[51]

It is equally clear that in *Institutes* 4. 4. 14 Calvin intends to present the Nicene canons and Cyprian's letter 67 as models for the Genevan practice. At the same time he implicitly attacks the Roman Catholic practice by showing that the procedure described in the Ordinances not only had the backing of the apostle Paul but was also ratified by the Council of Nicaea and validated by later church councils. It was first and foremost collegiate, assuring that the candidate about to be consecrated was examined by a group of his peers and not by just one person in private. Moreover, the examination was conducted in the place where the ordinand would serve if he passed all the tests.

Two major abuses corrupted this practice in Calvin's view. The first was for the ordinands to travel to be ordained by the metropolitan bishop; the second, even worse, was for all Italian bishops to seek consecration from the bishop of Rome. As for the ceremonies attendant upon ordination, Calvin notes that before abuses crept in, only imposition of hands and a special vestment for the bishops were tolerated so as to distinguish them from other priests. Bishops, presbyters and deacons alike were ordained by imposition of hands, and bishops accompanied by their *collegium presbyterorum* ordained the presbyters in their diocese. He stresses that there was no real hierarchy, but the bishop was said to be the only one to have ordination powers because he presided over the ordination. The collegiality of the practice of imposition of hands as described by Calvin is borne out by the *Decree of Gratian*.[52]

In his description of the early ordination rituals, Calvin very deliberately blurs the distinction between presbyter and bishop, his constant practice in the *Institutes*. At the same time he acknowledges the bishop's importance as overseer or *surveillant* within the *collegium*. He says nothing about the apostolicity of imposition of hands but obviously has nothing against the early custom of presbyters receiving imposition of hands from their bishop or *surveillant*. Calvin's use of the early church here as throughout *Institutes* 4. 4 is normative (in the sense of providing legal justification for the practices adopted in Geneva) and not just apologetic. Had it been purely polemical, he would have either pulled the early church into line with the Genevan practice showing that imposition of hands was practised sporadically or argued against the early church rituals as deviating too far from the apostolic model. In fact, he does neither. Here as in the rest of this section of the *Institutes*, the early church is seen as providing

---

[51] See OS II : 329 ; RCP I : 2: "C'est que les ministres elisent premierement celluy quon doibvra mettre en loffice. Apres quon le presente au conseil." See also note above for addition to the draft after "edification" which makes the point even more clearly.

[52] See *Institutes*, 4. 4. 15; OS V: 72-73. The editors of the OS cite *Decr. Grat.* I, dist. 23, c. 8. 11, Friedberg 1, 82: "presbiter cum ordinatur, episcopo eum benedicenteet manum super caput eius tenente, etiam omnes presbiteri, qui praesentes sunt, manus suas iuxta manus episcopi supe caput illius teneant."

authoritative support for what was done in Geneva or for what could have been done, had Roman abuses not made it necessary to deviate from rituals and practices, which were legitimate or apostolic in origin.

### III. Calvin's Commentary on Acts and Sermons on 1 Timothy

The apostolic model seems thus to be absent from the *Institutes* 4. 4. 1 – 4 and 5. 4 where Calvin makes a concerted appeal to legal documents of the 3rd to 6th century church (either directly or via the *Decree of Gratian*) so as to justify either actual or possible Genevan practices, as set out in the Ordinances. The contrast with what Calvin says in his Commentary and Sermons on Acts could not be greater. There he makes no mention of the early church as a propagator of the apostolic doctrine or of the evolution of the church in history. On the contrary, he insists that the apostolic church is God-given and should serve as an example and a direct source of inspiration to all pastors. Indeed, Calvin's Sermons and Commentary on Acts bear out the view expressed by Kingdon and others that the reformer believed he was recreating the apostolic church in its pristine purity.

What is to be made of what seems to be a contradiction in Calvin's doctrine of the church? In an attempt to answer this question, I shall examine the relevant passages from his Commentary and Sermons. First, however, it might be useful to remember that what the reformer does in the *Institutes* is to situate his notion of church organisation within existing legal frameworks. We might argue that, unlike Bucer and mediaeval canonists[53] who attributed an intrinsic worth to each canon in the Canon law corpus, Calvin views it as a collection of legal documents which could provide support for continuing or discontinuing a given practice. This is why he makes such an extensive use of it in, for example, justifying the limits of popular approval necessary for the election of pastors. In many ways, as we saw, the *Institutes* provide the explanation for the Ordinances, and Calvin was a realistic enough pastor and a good enough lawyer to see that it was neither practicable nor orthodox to use the New Testament as a code of church organisation. As a sacred text, however, it could and did provide the only conceivable foundation for such a code. I shall therefore argue, using Acts as an example, that Calvin's biblical works should be seen as an exposition of the foundation for a tradition-based code of church organisation which is developed in the *Institutes* and in the Ordinances in keeping with the legislation of the early church.

This is why Calvin emphasises the divine nature of the church and of vocation to the pastorate in his Commentary on Acts,[54] and this is why he places empha-

---

[53] On this see Robert Stupperich, "Martin Bucers Gebrauch des kanonischen Rechts" in Marijn de Kroon and Marc Lienhard (eds), *Horizons européens de la réforme en Alsace* (Strasbourg: Istra, 1980), 241-252.

[54] The first part of Calvin's commentary on Acts covering chapters 1-13 was published in Geneva by Jean Crespin in 1552, and the second in 1554. I shall be referring to Helmut Feld's edition: *Commentariorum In Acta Apostolorum liber primus[-secundus]*, in *Joannis Calvini Opera omnia denuo recognita*. Series II, vol. 12: 1; 12: 2, Geneva: Droz, 2001.

sis on God's role in the setting up and continuation of his institution. Needless to say, Calvin does not dwell on organisational details except for the very minimum which find direct support in the biblical text. Several references to necessary points of difference between the apostolic and the later church would further bear out the argument that Calvin does not see it as either feasible or advisable to recreate the apostolic church in its pristine purity. Thus talking about the election of ministers in Acts 13: 1-3 he emphasises, *à propos* of the election of Barnabas, that the only legitimate election of pastors is one which is decided by God. When God ordered pastors and bishops to be elected by the church, he did not allow it the liberty of doing without himself as Moderator. Here Calvin draws a distinction between apostolic and historical election. The latter differs from the election of Paul and Barnabas because, as they were going to be Apostles to the Gentiles, it was necessary to have God's own testimony. This, according to Calvin, is absolutely not necessary in a normal election of pastors. Ordinary pastors do, however, have one thing in common with the apostles: they are divinely elected before being submitted to any human election and ordination procedure. However, he adds, the Holy Spirit does not shout to us from on high that a candidate for ordination has been chosen by God. He hands down to the church automatically those who have the necessary gifts.[55]

Calvin makes a similar point commenting on Acts 20: 28 ("the Holy Spirit appointed bishops") where he insists on what is divine and what is human in their appointment. He notes that although the Lord from the very beginning wanted the ministers of the Word to be elected by human votes, he nonetheless abrogates to himself the government of the church, not just so that we recognise that he is its only head but also so that we know that he is the sole source of salvation. As for the word "bishop," it provides Calvin with the Scriptural basis for the doctrine developed in *Institutes* 4 and in the Ordinances. He points out that all priests at Ephesus were called that by Paul. From this it is plain, according to Calvin, that according to the usage of the Scripture, there was no difference between priests and bishops and that vice and corruption brought it about that those who occupied the top rank in single cities began to be called bishops. However, he hastens to add, the Scripture does not say, and it is indeed not the case, that it is bad for one man to be superior to others in a particular *collegium*. What is intolerable is when men modify the language of the Holy Spirit by twisting the words of Scripture.[56]

There is no contradiction between Calvin's understanding of the word *episkopos* here, in the *Institutes* and in the Ordinances. Scriptural usage is seen to provide the basis for what happened in the early church and for what should be done in the Genevan church. Calvin obviously does not see it as a part of the function of Scripture to provide information on details of ordinands' examina-

---

[55] Calvin, *In Acta*, I: 363-364.

[56] Calvin, *In Acta*, II: 187-188.

tion, the degree of popular participation in their election or on issues such as passage through minor orders as a way of training the clergy. All these details can be settled and modified by a careful scrutiny of what happened in the early church.

Imposition of hands proves more of a problem as it is recommended *expressis verbis* in Acts 6: 6 and in Acts 9: 17. Calvin does not evaluate the importance or rather unimportance of the ceremony in quite the same way in his exegesis of these two passages. He thus makes Scripture (which, as we noted, he sees as providing the foundation for church organisation) say something it does not so as to allow him to account for both the maintaining of the ritual (which, as we saw, he considered legitimate in the context of the early church) and for its suppression (particularly in the case of deacons). In his exposition of Acts 6: 6 (*precati, imposuerunt illis manus* – after praying, they laid hands on them) he takes the prayer offered up before the imposition of hands to be the normative ritual. After pointing to the Old Testament origins of the imposition of hands, he notes that the Apostles practised it on deacons as a sign of their being offered up to God. However, according to Calvin, it was the prayer accompanying the imposition of hands which constituted the ceremony proper as it was the only way that the help of the Holy Spirit could be invoked. The actual laying on of hands was as meaningless as any other ceremony.[57]

In other words, for Calvin the Bible provides no concrete rules on how deacons should be elected. All the Bible does provide is a firm indication that their office is spiritual. In fact, as we saw, Calvin relies on the legislation of the early church to give him concrete guidance on the election of deacons. In the corresponding passage in the *Institutes* he cites the decree of the Council of Sardica and the ecclesiastical canon that specifies that orders should be ascended gradually. We saw that he took this to mean that deacons in the early church were among the people anyway so that there was no need to have their election ratified by the congregation. This gave him the freedom to have their election conducted along lines that differed from those of the parish ministers. Had Calvin seen the Bible as providing a blueprint for the election of deacons, he could not but have them elected by the people as this is what happened in Acts 6: 6. However, he does not even advert to the matter in his commentary on the passage.

Acts 9: 17 deals with the imposition of hands not on deacons but on ministers, as symbolised by Ananias laying hands on Paul. Calvin refers to what he

---

[57] Calvin, *In Acta*, I: 168: " [In Act. 6, 6: *precati imposuerunt illis manus*]. Impositio manuum solenne consecrationis symbolum erat sub Lege. In hunc finem nunc apostoli manus diaconis imponunt vt se offerri Deo agnoscant. Quia tamen inanis per se esset caerimonia, simul additur precatio qua fideles Deo commendant quos illi ministros offerunt. Refertur quidem hoc ad Apostolos. Neque enim totus populus diaconis manus imposuit. Sed cum Apostoli preces ecclesiae nomine conciperent, alii etiam sua vota addiderunt. Hinc colligimus manuum impositionem quum Apostolis in vsu fuerit, ritum esse ordini et decoro congruentem , nec tamen quicquam habere per se efficaciae aut virtutis, sed vim et effectum a solo Dei spiritu pendere. Quod etiam generaliter de omnibus ceremoniis statuendum est."

had already said in Acts 6: 6 about the imposition of hands going back to the Old Testament. However, he does not portray it as an empty ceremony here. He explains that the apostles took over the Jewish custom to indicate either the conferring of visible, spiritual grace or ordination to the ministry. Ananias in fact was doing both. Calvin is concerned chiefly with the rank and identity of him who lays on hands, referring the reader to his exposition in Acts 10 on the usefulness of those ceremonies that are sanctified by God. As for Ananias having the authority to lay on hands, Calvin refers the reader to Acts 22: 14 where Paul's words show that Ananias not only had the authority to preach but also to administer baptism. Calvin considers this to be arguing conclusively against the Roman practice of entrusting ordination to the bishop only. It is obvious that here he takes the word "bishop" in its most negative connotation which has nothing to do with the *surveillant* who can be any member of the pastoral body.

We saw that in the *Institutes* Calvin above all wanted to show that the early church maintained the simplicity of the custom without conceding undue powers to the bishop. However, at no stage, not even in the Ordinances, does he show any opposition to the imposition of hands as such. His exegesis of Acts 9: 17 is not conclusive and provides no clues about whether imposition of hands should in fact be part of the ordination ritual. What it does admit is the legitimacy of the rite if practised by an ordained minister on an ordinand. Once again it is only Calvin's discussion of the usage of the early church which provides us with the doctrinal background for the Genevan ordination practice.

Calvin does not feel that he has to establish an organic link between what the Scripture says, what the early post-apostolic and post-Nicene church did and what should be put into operation in Geneva. To Calvin Scripture is always the source of divine wisdom and revelation. It is also the source of knowledge about the role of the earliest church with respect to God's design. However, he does not think that it is possible or necessary to recreate the earliest church in 16th century Geneva, and he does not see Scripture as a source of legislation on ecclesiastical organisation. This is why he devotes so much attention to discussing the practices of the early church in the *Institutes*, and that is why this discussion throws much more light on the organisation and legislation pertaining to the Company of Pastors than Calvin's commentary on Acts.

What of Calvin's Sermons on 1 Timothy? Can they not be taken as a paradigmatic instance of Calvin's literal application of apostolic precepts to the ministerial office in the Genevan church? The answer is: "Yes—but only in as much as Paul's precepts convey a particular moral code, which is directly applicable to any minister of God anywhere." I have tried to show in a recent work that although Calvin never completely forgot principles and concepts of pagan ethics—even to the extent of maintaining the use of certain concepts such as happiness, virtue, wisdom etc—he thought nonetheless that pagan ethical concepts should be reworked to fit into the Christian ethical framework, which was based on the Bible. Thus happiness is not the absence of pain but suffering in the name of Christ, wisdom is not abstaining from emotion but giving in to strong emotion, if ordered by God. [58]

Calvin uses Scripture as a moral code in a way in which he would never dream of using it as a code of church organisation and legislation. Paul's definition of a model bishop or pastor in 1 Timothy 3: 1-7 is thus a moral definition so far as Calvin is concerned. Throughout the Sermons, his object is to fill in gaps in Paul's rather succinct definition in such a way that pastors have a code to appeal to. To take just one example, he explains over several pages what exactly Paul means when he says, "married to one wife". According to Calvin's interpretation Paul is not saying , "he cannot have been married more than once"; neither is he saying, "he must be loyal only to the church". What the apostle is forbidding is polygamy and what he is asking for is that a bishop, in the sense of pastor, be a man of unimpeachable private life.[59]

Just in case anyone is still in doubt, Calvin extends the applicability of Paul's declaration beyond the office of pastor. Calvin repeats after Paul: How can a man who cannot manage his own household hope to accede to public office? Calvin adds that this applies not just to ministers of God but to all who aim for public office.[60] He then builds an intention into Paul's pithy statement: the Apostle, who is God's instrument, is asking that each minister undergo an inquiry into his private life prior to his appointment.[61] Calvin thus offers a biblical justification for the morals test which figures in the Ordinances, in a way in which he never offers for popular participation or for the ministerial election procedure as a whole.

However, Calvin is well aware that although the Bible can act as a code of morals if interpreted correctly, it also contains passages that lend themselves to a radical misinterpretation. Passages on the personal morals of the Old Testament Patriarchs are very much a case in point. Obviously realising that polygamous ministers of his own era could invoke Abraham or Jacob as an example, Calvin insists that it is their example, subsequently copied by their descendants, which led Paul to issue his injunction to the ministers in particular.[62] Any minister, after becoming acquainted with Calvin's Sermons on 1 Timothy, would know exactly what standard of private morals was expected of

---

[58] On this see Irena Backus, *Historical Method and Confessional Identity in the Era of the Reformation* (1378-1615) (Leiden: Brill, 2003), 71-83.

[59] *Calv. Opp.* 53, 243-244.

[60] *Calv. Opp.* 53, 243: "Or ceci n'est point seulement pour les ministres de la parole mais nous avons à receuillir une doctrine generale, c'est quand on doit appeler quelques gens en estat public, qu'on regarde en premier lieu qu'ils ayent conversé honnestement entre les hommes…"

[61] *Calv. Opp.* 53, 244: "Et pourtant retenons bien quelle est l'intention de S. Paul: c'est que quand on appelle quelqu'un pour annoncer la parole de Dieu, il faut qu'auparauant il ait esté esprouvé. Et comment? En sa personne et puis en son message…"

[62] *Calv. Opp.* 53, 245-246.

him. By contrast, it cannot be said that all ministers who read Calvin's commentary on Acts would find it mirroring the Genevan system of church organisation. For that they had to consult the account of organisation of the early church as outlined in *Institutes* 4.

## IV. Conclusion

It would seem from the foregoing investigation that Calvin was not labouring under any illusions about the sort of church he was setting up in Geneva. He did not set out to recreate the God-given apostolic church in its pristine purity, and he did not think that this was possible or even advisable. While he saw the Bible as the ultimate source of truth and revelation, he was very aware of the distance separating the directly inspired apostolic church from the church as it developed in history. Scripture as the absolute foundation could not and did not provide all the details of ecclesiastical organisation and the election of ministers in particular. For this an appeal had to be made to the organisation of the post-apostolic early church with a view to reviewing, selecting and adapting its practices.

Calvin's appeal to the post-apostolic and post-Nicene early church accounts in a large measure for the power which the Genevan civil authorities exercised over the clergy from very early on. It also sheds light on why the faithful had so little say over the appointment of their pastors. Finally, it elucidates Calvin's conception of the *episcopè* which, as we saw, was inspired by Jerome. Scripture could and did act as a reliable guide to the reformer when it came to outlining the setting up of the New Testament church. It also provided a blueprint for the morals of the clergy. However, as is shown by the discrepancy between the amount of biblical testimony in *Institutes* 4. 3 and *Institutes* 4. 4 – 4. 5, Calvin never thought that the Scriptural model of the church could be applied to his own era without any variants. We also saw that he thought that even its pronouncements on the morals of the clergy had to be interpreted.

The particularity of Calvin's position comes across better if we compare him with Heinrich Bullinger, the Zurich reformer. In his commentary on Matthew, Bullinger sees the entire Zurich system of church organisation as stemming directly from the Gospel. He points out that a church where theology and teaching flourish inevitably contains a certain amount of pseudo-believers or bad Christians who pretend to practice true faith while doing nothing which is worthy of it. As they do not respond to being admonished, the church needs not just ministers and teachers but also elders and magistrates to restrain obstinate sinners. The magistrates must be good, pious, temperate and holy men who are capable and willing to do their duty. This, he continues, is the whole point of the office and election of the magistrates. This is also the point of sumptuary laws, laws on marriage, divorce and adultery, laws on education, as well as laws on public order, laws against usury, mercenary service, poor laws and laws on church goods.[63] So as not to leave his reader in any doubt that all these institutions are actually prescribed by the Gospel in so many words, Bullinger concludes:

> I wanted to outline these things briefly and to glance rapidly over apostolic teaching, that is the teaching of truth, and its ministers, in other words, pupils, doctors, teachers, preachers and the holy senate of the church. I could find nothing in the apostolic writings about cantors or singing in church. Paul orders his congregation to sing with their mind and with their spirit. Therefore it is enough for a righteous church if it offers pure prayers to the Lord in true faith through Christ.[64]

Now, obviously there is not a single passage in the Gospels or in any apostolic writings which outlines Zurich church organisation and ecclesiastical discipline as Bullinger has described it. There is, therefore, no question of the Gospels providing literally a blueprint for Christian life as lived in Zürich in the mid-16th century. What Bullinger is saying is that the multiple laws, regulations—in fact the entire organisation of the Zurich church—can be traced back to the Gospels if the Gospels are read in a particular way. Calvin for his part always sees a gap between the Scripture as a standard and the putting of it into practice. That gap can be bridged partly by careful study of the practices and legislation of the early post-apostolic and post-Nicene church. It was this church that provided Calvin with much practical information about how to set up and run the Company of Pastors.[65]

---

[63] *In sacrosanctum Iesu Christi Domini nostri Euangelium secundum Matthaeum Commentariorum libri XII per Heinrychum Bullingerum* (Zürich: Froschouer, 1542), aaa 5v.-aaa 6r. .

[64] Bullinger, *In … Mattheum.*, aaa 6r.: " Haec autem obiter indicare ac in transcursu perstringere volui de doctrina apostolica, vel veritatis, et ministris eius, hoc est de discentibus, doctoribus, professoribus, praedicatoribus et senatu ecclesiae sancto. De cantoribus et cantu ecclesiastico nihil possum dicere ex institutione apostolica. Paulus suos spiritu et mente iubet canere. Sufficit ergo iustae ecclesiae, si in vera fide puras alioqui preces Domino offerat per Christum."

[65] The present version of the paper takes account of A. N. S. Lane's point to do with the role of *Institutes*, 4. 3. I take this opportunity to thank him for his very helpful observations.

# A Response to "*These Holy Men:* Calvin's Patristic Models for the Setting Up of the Company of Pastors"

*Anthony N. S. Lane*

It is a great pleasure for me to respond to Irena Backus. We have known each other for many years now and have for most of that time shared a common interest in the relation between the Reformation and the Fathers and have met to discuss this theme at many conferences. A number of my own published works have been considerably improved by her helpful comments on earlier drafts, and I am very grateful for this.

Her paper rightly offers a corrective to the idea that Calvin sought to base the Genevan model of ecclesiastical organization on Scripture alone. She points very effectively to the discrepancies between the Genevan and apostolic patterns and also to Calvin's appeal to post-apostolic practice in the *Institutio.* As always, her paper is very carefully and clearly argued, and I do not have many points to raise, although she has kindly left one or two small loose ends for me to grasp. My main query is to ask whether the case might perhaps have been slightly overstated. To that end I have two points to raise.

*First,* there is a surprising lacuna in the paper. Calvin's material on the Fathers in *Institutio* 4.4.1 – 4.5.4 is compared with his teaching in the Acts commentary and the I Timothy sermons. The surprising omission is Book 4, chapter 3 of the *Institutio* which considers "The Doctors and Ministers of the Church, Their Election and Office." This chapter is based on Scripture with hardly any reference to the Fathers. I do not think it is mentioned anywhere in the paper. I have no doubt that Irena Backus had it in mind when she wrote the paper. But the impression given to the reader who may not remember all of the details of Book 4 and does not perhaps refer back to the text of the *Institutio* will be that the teaching on the ministry in the latter is based upon the Fathers, while in the sermons and commentaries it is based on Scripture. In fact much (though not, of course, all) of what is said in the commentaries is also found in 4.3. Indeed, the *Institutio* appears to keep closer to Scripture than the commentary (6:6, 9:17) on one key point in that it takes a stronger line on the use of the laying on of hands in ordination:

> Although there exists no set precept for the laying on of hands, because we see it in continual use with the apostles, their very careful observance ought

to serve in lieu of a precept. And surely it is useful for the dignity of the ministry to be commended to the people by this sort of sign ...[1]

Thus the contrast between the *Institutio* and the exegetical works on the issue of pastoral ministry is not that the latter are based on Scripture and the former on the Early Church, but that the former (the *Institutio*) is based on Scripture *and* the Early Church. None of this is denied in the paper, but it is the impression that the unwary reader could gain—and I admit to having been one such unwary reader until I went back to the text.

But let me make it clear that I do not at all question the statement that Calvin did not aim to "recapture the organization of the Apostolic church in its pristine form." He was not an Anabaptist biblicist and had no problems with subsequent developments like the state church. Given this, it is not surprising that he is interested in the developments that took place in the Early Church.

*Secondly,* I have a problem with the claim that "Calvin's object in the Ordinances and in the *Institutes* passage is in fact to keep as close as possible to the practice of the early church of the 4th-6th centuries." I am far from convinced that Calvin gave such a great authority to the Early Church—especially since it is the point of the paper that he did not give such unqualified authority even to the New Testament on this issue. Would it not be more accurate to say that his concern was to be able to *claim the support of* these fathers (and of Cyprian)? And, furthermore, that this claim was based on a highly selective selection of evidence?

Observant readers will at this point note that I am returning to a hobby horse of mine—the mainly (but *not* exclusively) polemical nature of Calvin's use of the fathers. "Polemical" here I understand not just in the negative sense of opposing the views of others but also in the more positive sense of defending one's own view. It might have caused less misunderstanding if in my writings on this theme I had used the word apologetic instead of polemical.[2] To talk of Calvin's apologetic use of the fathers makes the point that it comes in the context of controversy, but without implying such a negative emphasis.

I certainly do not for a moment question that Calvin looked upon the early centuries as a source of guidance from which one could learn and that he quite often cites the fathers in this way. But he did not regard them as a final authority that had always to be followed, on this or on any other issue. *More* often (and we are talking here in statistical terms of what constitutes the majority of his patristic citations) he cites them for support: positive precedent for his own position and negative evidence against his opponent's position. I would, therefore, be prepared to state that Calvin *cited* (not necessarily *read*) the Fathers in

---

[1] *Institutes,* 4.3.16. As the final footnote in Prof. Backus' paper indicates, these comments were made in response to the paper as delivered.

[2] For my use of "polemical" and related words, cf. e.g. *John Calvin: Student of the Church Fathers* (Edinburgh: T & T Clark, 1999, and Grand Rapids: Baker, 2000), 3, 11, 26, 28-29, 31-33, 46, 49-52. I am grateful to Irena Backus for prompting me here (cf. note 14 of her paper).

the same way that a drunk uses a lamp-post — more for support than illumination. But in this case the word "more" simply means that there are more citations of the one sort than the other. Both are there — but there are more of the apologetic than the other citations.

Let us return to the claim that "Calvin's object in the Ordinances and in the *Institutes* passage is in fact to keep as close as possible to the practice of the early church of the 4th-6th centuries." I have to confess that I find this hard to believe. I see no indication that Calvin wished to emulate the sacerdotal concept of ministry found from the time of Cyprian, that he wished to encourage the practice of clergy living together in celibate communities, that he approved of the increasingly hierarchical approach to the ministry during the fourth to sixth centuries, etc. Consider the two key points where Calvin is said to depart from apostolic practice. The abolition of the imposition of hands in ordination is hardly evidence of seeking to emulate "the practice of the early church of the 4th-6th centuries." Calvin's "disinclination to discredit completely the episcopal nomenclature and the office of bishop" falls far short of the patristic theory and practice, which regarded episcopacy as normative. I would suggest that Calvin's acceptance of ordination without laying on of hands and his toleration of episcopacy had more to do with practical and political considerations than a desire to model the ministry on the late patristic pattern.

Finally, a few words about a theme which lies not far beneath the surface of this paper: the question of *sola scriptura*. The actual slogan did not emerge until after the Reformation but, rightly understood, it describes the stance of the Reformers.[3] Their attitude was not one of dogmatic biblicism. They did not claim that Scripture was all that we need nor that it was the only authority. They were willing to accept the authority of the Fathers, but subjected it to the final authority of Scripture. They were also willing to adapt apostolic practice to the demands of changing circumstances, as Irena Backus's paper has ably illustrated.

---

[3] For a discussion of this, cf. A. N. S. Lane, "Sola Scriptura? Making Sense of a Post-Reformation Slogan," in P. E. Satterthwaite and D. F. Wright, eds. *A Pathway into the Holy Scripture* (Grand Rapids: Eerdmans, 1994), 297-327.

# The *Congrégation*: An In-Service Theological Training Center for Preachers to the People of Geneva

*Erik A. de Boer*

*I know there are pious men here who, having no reason to be humble about their learning, would rather miss two sermons than one exposition of Scripture like those heard here.[1]*

John Calvin

## I. Introduction

The purpose of this study is to define the nature, contents and functions of the ecclesiastical institution called *la congrégation* in Geneva, and, along the way, to compare its character to similar institutions in the Reformation, such as the *Prophezei* in Zurich. The purpose of the *congrégation* is described in the Genevan church order as "to maintain purity and unity in doctrine" (*pour conserver pureté et concord de doctrine*). The method of working in the *congrégation* seems, when we look at the documents, to be no more than training in exegesis. In the following historical description of the *congrégations* in Geneva I try to answer the question: how does the emphasis on doctrine correspond to the working method of expounding biblical books? Or, to narrow my question down to one word: is my translation of the term *congrégations* as "Bible study meetings" accurate?

The secondary literature on the Genevan Reformation and on Calvin's life and work offers every now and then a glimpse of the nature of the *congrégations*, especially when the case against Jerome Bolsec (1551) is considered. Two publications in the early 1960s stimulated further research into this unique institution: the edition of the *Registers of the Company of Pastors*[2] and of Calvin's *Deux*

---

[1] CO *13: 434:* Scio hic esse pios homines et eruditionis non poenitendae, qui sibi duas conciones adimi malint quam unam scripturae tractationem quales audiuntur *(letter no. 1294 of 22 October 1549).*

[2] *Registres de la Compagnie des Pasteurs de Genève au temps de Calvin,* vol. I (1546-1553), ed. Jean-François Bergier (Genève: Librairie Droz, 1964); vol. II (1553-1564), ed. Jean-François Bergier and Robert M. Kingdon (1962); vol. III (1565-1574), ed. O. Fatio and O. Labarthe (1969); vol. IX (1604-1606), ed. G. Cahier, M. Campagnolo and M. Louis-Courvoisier (1989); vol. X (1607-1609), ed. G. Cahier, M. Campagnolo, M. Louis-Courvoisier (1991). English translation by Philip E. Hughes of the first two volumes in: *The Register of the Company of Pastors of Geneva in the Time of Calvin,* Grand Rapids, William B. Eerdmans Publishing Company, 1966. Most translations, given below, are my own.

*congrégations et exposition du Catéchisme.* The Strasbourg scholar Rodolphe Peter pulled this ecclesiastical institution out of obscurity by the publication of a 16th century edition of two of Calvin's contributions on Galatians. It is preceded by a lucid introduction of twelve pages which summarizes our knowledge of the Bible study meetings at that time.[3] It is my purpose to study this ecclesiastical institution in close detail.

How accurate is the picture of the congrégations presented in the secondary literature? We find some very unclear definitions of these Bible study meetings. Robert M. Kingdon labeled it as "a type of adult Bible class."[4] Other authors regard the *congrégations* as a kind of church service (Heyer, Holtrop) in which a sermon was presented (Neuser).[5] Bernard Cottret gives the following definition: "These *congrégations* involved preaching and what we would call today a Bible-reading society, permitting an exchange of views."[6]

Statements like this indicate that a fuller study of the *congrégations* in the manner of Rodolphe Peter may have its merits. The present essay may serve as an introduction to a future, more comprehensive study.

## II. Bible Studies or Prophecy?

When the former bishop, Pier Paolo Vergerio, visited Geneva in 1550, he wrote a report of his impressions of the reformed city.[7] This "letter" was published by Conrad Badius, the printer whom Vergerio may have met in the Bible study meetings. One of the jubilant passages concerns his attendance of the *congrégation* in St. Pierre and reads as follows:

---

[3] Jean Calvin, *Deux congrégations et exposition de Catéchisme,* ed. Rodolphe Peter (Paris: Presses Universitaires de France, 1964), p. IX-XX. Other literature on the Bible studies: Wulfert de Greef, *Johannes Calvijn. Zijn leven en werk* (Kampen: De Groot Goudriaan, 1989) 108-111; J. Plomp, *De kerkelijke tucht bij Calvijn* (Kampen: J.H. Kok, 1969), 265, 283-288; Roger Stauffenegger, *Église et société. Genève au XVIIe siècle. Texte* (Travaux d'Histoire Éthico-politique, vol. 41) (Genève : Librairie Droz, 1983), 217-220.

[4] R.M. Kingdon, "Popular Reactions to the Debate between Bolsec and Calvin," in *Calvin: Erbe und Auftrag. Festschrift für Wilhelm Neuser zu seinem 65. Geburtstag,* ed. W. van 't Spijker (Kampen: Kok Pharos, 1991), 139.

[5] Henri Heyer, *L'Église de Genève 1555-1909. Esquisse historique de son organisation* (reprint Nieuwkoop : B. de Graaf, 1974), 65 ; Philip C. Holtrop, *The Bolsec Controversy on Predestination from 1551 to 1555,* vol. 1, book 1 (Lewiston : The Edwin Mellen Press, 1993), 53 ; Wilhelm H. Neuser ed., *Ioannis Calvini opera omnia (COR),* series III, vol. 1: De *aeterna dei predestinatione* (Genève: Librairie Droz, 1998), XII.

[6] Bernard Cottret, *Calvin. A Biography* (Grand Rapids: William B. Eerdmans Publishing, 2000), 209f. On p. 296f: "... this resembled what occurred in a university seminar or Bible-study class."

[7] In November, 1549, Gribaldi sent a letter of introduction to Calvin (CO 13: 448, no. 1304), but the Italian bishop did not show up. In the meantime, Vergerio contacted Calvin for a preface to the booklet on the history of Francesco Spiera.

Every week, on Fridays, a conference is held in the largest church [St. Pierre] in which all their ministers and many of the people participate. Here one of them reads a passage from Scripture and expounds it briefly. Another speaks on the matter what to him is according to the Spirit. A third person gives his opinion and a fourth adds some things in his capacity to weigh the issue. And not only the ministers do so, but everyone who has come to listen. Thus is being followed what Paul found in the Church of Corinth, and on which he said that, when the brothers gathered, every one of them could say what the Spirit revealed to him; then he was silent, sat down and another began to speak [1 Cor. 14:29-30].[8]

Several elements of this impression of the *congrégation* are worth noting. The first is the prominence of the ministers and their various contributions. The second is the participation of lay members in these Bible studies. A third element to be noted is the clear allusion to Paul's First Letter to the Corinthians, Chapter 14, and to the gift of prophecy. Did Vergerio present an adequate impression of these Genevan Bible studies?

## A. The *Prophezei*

I find Vergerio's allusion noteworthy because the Genevan form of Bible study was called the *congrégation, conférence des Escriptures*, or *colloque*, but never *la prophétie*. In Zurich, in 1525, the *Prophezei* was instituted.[9] The name of this institution is derived from 1 Corinthians 14:29-32. According to Huldrich Zwingli every preacher has the task of a prophet. Knowledge of the biblical languages was deemed necessary to expound and apply the Scriptures prophetically.[10] In German the word *Offenbarung* is used for "preaching." The *Prophezei* evolved into the theological faculty.

In Strasbourg Martin Bucer and his colleagues instituted a related form of Bible lectures. In 1526, Bucer proposed to the magistrate that the canonical services be transformed into a *Prophezei*. That is why some form of service around the biblical lectures was maintained. Every morning and evening a service was held with half an hour of singing the Psalms and half an hour of *prophecy* or *christliche Übung* and prayer.[11] The place of the canons in these services was

---

[8] Pier Paolo Vergerio, *Epistola del Vergerio, nella quale sono descritté molte cose della Citâ, è della Chiesa di Geneva*, 15 July 1550 (J.-Fr. Gilmont, *Bibliographie des editions de Jean Crespin 1550-1572*, vol. 1 (Verviers: Librairie P.M. Gassen, 1981), 7 (50/11).

[9] Heinrich Bullinger, "Wie vnd wenn man Zuriych angehept die Biblisch Lection in dryen sprachen läsen," in Fritz Büsser, *Die Prophezei. Humanismus und Reformation in Zurich* (Bern e.a.: Verlag Peter Lang, 1994), 7-9; Gottfried W. Locher, *Die Zwinglische Reformation im Rahmen der europäischen Kirchengeschichte* (Göttingen – Zurich: Vandenhoeck-Ruprecht, 1979), 161-163.

[10] Cf. Locher, *Die Zwinglische Reformation im Rahmen der europäischen Kirchengeschichte*, 161f; W.P. Stephens, *The Theology of Huldrych Zwingli* (Oxford: Clarendon Press, 1986), 39f, 137f, 278.

[11] *Martin Bucer Deutsche Schriften*, ed. Robert Stupperich, vol. 2 (Gütersloh – Paris, 1962), 520f.

taken by preachers, schoolmasters, K*irchenpfleger*, and pious people who wanted to be taught the Scriptures. The synod of 1533 and the *ordonnance* of 1534 codified the *Convent ecclesiastique*.[12] During Calvin's years in Strasbourg these Bible studies were poorly attended.[13] But the name, which in the French speaking congregation must have been *la prophétie*, was not transferred to the Bible studies held in Geneva.

## B. 1 Corinthians 14

When Vergerio made the connection between the Bible studies which he witnessed in Geneva, and the passage on prophecy from 1 Corinthians 14, he also must have had some knowledge of this institution as it was established in Zurich through Bullinger or in Strasbourg. Did the ministers of Geneva also apply this passage to their Bible studies? The *Ordonnances ecclésiastiques* do not mention 1 Corinthians 14 or reflect its wording.

I know of only one instance in which an allusion to 1 Corinthians 14:29-32 was made: in the case of censure against Philippe d'Ecclesia, one of the Genevan ministers. In 1549 a dossier on d'Ecclesia was opened. He was reprimanded for having raised unedifying issues and senseless questions. A file of such lapses had been kept and d'Ecclesia was confronted with it. The Registers tell us that his colleagues decided "that he should be warned not to speak at the Bible studies at all, neither after the one who had expounded, nor when his own turn came round to expound, until the next day of censures." In a marginal note the secretary of the Company of Pastors added: "The ground [for this] was cited to him from St. Paul: that he who brings nothing of edification ought to keep silent in the church."[14] This note clarifies that the ministers saw a connection with the Pauline prescriptions regarding prophecy. Still, it considers only the negative part, that is, the imposition of silence. A positive application of 1 Corinthians 14 with regard to the *congrégation* is missing.

What was Calvin's understanding of prophecy as one of the New Testament gifts of the Spirit to the Church? With regard to the Bible study meetings it is necessary to include the Reformed view of the gift of tongues. Both the Zurich and Genevan theologians saw the Pentecost miracle of Acts 2 as the gift of communicating the Gospel in foreign languages.[15] It was applied to the situation of

---

[12] François Wendel, *L'Église de Strasbourg. Sa constitution et son organisation, 1532-1535* (Paris: Presses Universitaires de France, 1942), 102f, 196-198. On the responsibility of the Convent in matters of preaching, see p. 204.

[13] Philippe Denis, "La prophétie dans les Églises de la Réforme au XVIe siècle," in *Revue d'Histoire Ecclésiastique* 72 (1977), 292-295.

[14] *RCP* I: 47.

[15] Leonard Sweetman, "The Gifts of the Spirit: A Study of Calvin's Comments on 1 Corinthians 12:8-10, 28; Romans 12:6-8; Ephesians 4:11," in David E. Holwerda ed., *Exploring the Heritage of John Calvin* (Grand Rapids: Baker Book House, 1976), 291-297.

the Church in the 16th century and the knowledge of the newly discovered biblical languages, Hebrew and Greek. In his commentary on 1 Corinthians (1546) Calvin explained 14: 29-32 without any reference to the Bible studies in Geneva. However, he did apply some features of the text to the situation of the church. On verse 27 he remarks that "the Church can do without tongues and suffer no inconvenience, except where they are helpful for prophesying, as for example Hebrew and Greek are today." On verse 29 Calvin commented on the limitation of the number of people prophesying: "In the discourse, the interpreter took the place of the prophet, and so that was the chief, and the more frequent, way in which languages were employed."[16] The interpretation of "language" is the interpretation of prophecy.

What then is the character of prophecy after the time of the New Testament church? Calvin comments: "I bracket revelation and prophesying together, and I think that prophesying is the servant of revelation." Teaching, however, is associated with knowledge: "Teaching is the way to pass on knowledge." Calvin's definition of prophecy states: "prophesying does not consist in the simple and bare interpretation of Scripture, but also includes the knowledge for making it apply to the needs of the hour, and that can only be obtained by revelation and the special influence of God."[17] According to Calvin prophecy begins as interpretation of Scripture, but only rises to the level of New Testament prophecy in the inspired application to the situation of the church. In Calvin's view of biblical prophecy the element of predicting future events is also an essential part. But this feature reached its fulfilment in the coming of Christ who was the greatest prophet of God.[18]

Thus Calvin would stress "that teachers, in their interpretation of Scripture, should focus on the preservation of sound doctrine, while prophets have the task of applying Scripture to the present situation."[19] This may explain why in

---

[16] CO 49: 528-529. Cf. *Institutes*, 4. 1.12 on 1 Corinthians 14:30: "If a better revelation is made to another sitting by, let the first be silent." From this it is clear that every member of the church is charged with the responsibility of public edification according to the measure of his grace, provided he perform it decently and in order'. Cf. *Institutes*, 4.8.9.

[17] CO 49: 519.

[18] Wulfert de Greef, "Calvin on Prophecy," in Wilhelm H. Neuser, Herman J. Selderhuis ed., *Ordentlich und fruchtbar. Festschrift für Willem van 't Spijker* (Leiden: Uitgeverij J.J. Groen en Zoon, 1997), 113-118 (111-128).

[19] De Greef, "Calvin on Prophecy," 123f. Calvin's exposition of the Old Testament texts, referring to "schools of prophets," does not have any allusion to the *congrégations* either. In a *congrégation* on Isaiah 1, Calvin said : "Or les prophetes là ont eu don de reveler les choses advenir, comme il est assez notoire. Mais leur office n'estoit seulement de predire ce qui estoit incognu aux hommes, mais de c'estoit de l'applicquer à l'instruction du peuple" (E.A. de Boer, « Jean Calvin et Ésaïe 1 (1564). Édition d'un texte inconnu introduit par quelques observations sur la différence et les relations entre congrégation, cours et sermon, *Revue d'Histoire et de Philosophie Religieuses* 80 (2000), 382 (371-395)).

Geneva the phrase *conférence des Escriptures* was favored, and not *la prophétie*. Both the interpretation of Scripture and the formulation of doctrine were the focus of the *congrégation*.

## III. Regulations and Structure

The Bible study meetings are poorly documented in the sources, although their aim has been clearly described in the church order. However important the first two volumes of the *Registres de la Compagnie des Pasteurs* are, they do not contain any direct information on or documentation of the Bible studies. That should not surprise us, since a weekly procedure of oral discussion soon became a normal feature in the Company of Pastors, leaving hardly any written traces. It is only when the weekly routine is broken by an incident that the *congrégation* as such and the issues discussed surface in the records and correspondence.

There are also very few transcripts of the contents of the Bible studies. Since the recording of Calvin's lectures and sermons started in 1549, the scribe, Denis Raguenier, also seems to have seen it as his task to make a verbatim report of the *congrégations*, just as he was hired to preserve Calvin's sermons in writing. On the basis of such transcripts four texts were published in the 16th century (one on John 1, two on Galatians 2, and one on election), while the manuscripts of five full expositions survived (four by Calvin: on Exodus 1:1-8, Joshua 1:1-5, Joshua 11 and Isaiah 1:1-3; one on Joshua 1:6-11 by Michel Cop), together with a body of nineteen texts on Joshua on which Calvin and Beza gave additional comments in the Bible studies. That gives us a total of twenty-eight texts for a period of fifteen years. In the course of fifteen years the ministers would have held some 780 study meetings. The fact that less than thirty texts survive means that we only have a partial transcript of one in every thirty meetings. And even that average number is highly misleading, since the body of texts on the book of Joshua account for twenty-one of the manuscripts (that is, three full expositions and eighteen additional comments), all of which were recorded in the eight months between June 1563 and January 1564.

The first impression in investigating these Bible studies in Geneva is that the role of John Calvin, the moderator of the Company of Pastors, seems to have been dominant. The texts—some in print, more in manuscript—are almost all transcripts of Calvin's spoken words. The *Vita Calvini* paints the following picture. The first version by Theodore de Bèze (1564) describes Calvin's role in the Bible studies, within the contexts of his weekly activities, in one dash of the pen: "he presented ... nearly a full lecture on every Friday in the conference on Scripture, which we call the *Congrégation*, and has so kept up this routine without interruption until his death that he never failed to be there one single time, except when extremely ill."[20] Beza wrote this in the preface of the commentary

---

[20] CO 21 : 33. In his version of 1575, Beza followed his own version: *diebus Veneris in communi collatione scripturae, quam Congregationem vocamus, iustam paene lectionem habebat* (CO 21: 132). He took up the line on Calvin's perseverance in the account of 1564 (CO 21: 160).

on Joshua shortly after Calvin's death. The gaps in the series of *congrégations* on Joshua in 1563 tell us of Calvin's absence.

This general impression is elaborated in some detail in Beza's second *Vita*, in which he used information from Nicolas Colladon. He is more accurate in describing Calvin's part in the Bible studies, again in the context of the reformer's workload: "on every Friday in the conference on Scripture, which we call *la Congrégation*, what he added in explanation after the expositor was like a lecture."[21] Beza proceeds a few pages further, when he tells of the beginning of the recording of Calvin's sermons and lectures in 1549: "That is why I will point out hereafter, following the order of time, what books he explained in lectures or sermons, next to what he composed either in the form of a commentary or otherwise, and also what was treated in the *congrégations* on Friday."[22]

It is through this source that we know the sequence of biblical books which were studied by the Company of Pastors since 1549, starting with Hebrews. Beza's source must have been Colladon. Together with his parents and uncle, Nicolas Colladon arrived in Geneva in 1550.[23] As a student at the Collège de Rive he was present in the *congrégation* of 16 October 1551, in which the Bolsec affair on predestination started. As a devoted student and, later, a trusted colleague of Calvin, he may have kept his own notes on the Bible studies. But the context of this passage on the sequence of biblical books, treated on Friday mornings, points to the work of Denis Raguenier, the scribe of Calvin's sermons. Colladon may have checked the records of the scribe to verify his information.[24] While Beza's praise of Calvin's contribution to the biblical studies is general, Colladon's account seems a detailed and reliable source. They both testify that Calvin's contribution, even if he did not present the exposition proper, was "like a lecture."

---

[21] CO 21: 66: *tous les Vendredis en la conference de l'Escripture, que nous appellons la Congregation, ce qu'il adioustoit apres le proposant pour la declaration estoit comme une leçon.* Denis Crouzet took this line and wrote on the Bible studies as if John Calvin alone spoke; see Denis Crouzet, *Jean Calvin. Vies parallèles* (Paris: Fayard, 2000), 261-263, 279, 315.

[22] CO 21 : 70f.

[23] Nicolas Colladon, son of the lawyer Léon Colladon, studied in Lausanne (1549) and, after his father Léon and his uncle Germain fled to Geneva in 1550, at the College de Rive (exam in 1552). He became minister in the village Vandoeuvres in 1553, filling the vacancy after the dismissal of Philippe d'Ecclesia (RCP I:160), and was later transferred to the city, probably in the same year. His name is found in the list of witnesses for the trial against Jerome Bolsec (CO 8: 185f). Cf. on Colladon's involvement in the second edition of the *Vita Calvini* Rodolphe Peter – Jean-François Gilmont, *Bibliotheca calviniana. Les oeuvres de Jean Calvin publiées au XVIe siècle*, vol. III, *Écrits théologiques, littéraires et juridiques 1565-1600* (Genève : Librairie Droz, 2000), 34.

[24] The question whether all or at least all of Calvin's contributions to the Bible studies were transcribed must be dealt with elsewhere. Raguenier's catalogue does not include any volume on the *congrégations* (*SC* II: XVf), but volumes like ms.fr. 40a, 40b, and 40c do exist, even though they were omitted from the catalogue.

Another eyewitness testimony to the *congrégations* comes from Conrad Badius. The printer-publisher, who was probably a regular visitor at the Bible studies, gave the following description of these meetings in the preface of the volume *Plusieurs sermons* in 1558. The *congregation* is

a certain assembly of the Church which takes place on one of the weekdays, where each one of the ministers, in turn, explains some passage of Scripture, more by way of a lecture than a sermon. This being done, if there is one of the other ministers to whom the Spirit of God has revealed something which contributes to the understanding and clarification of what had been set forth, he is free to speak.[25]

While Beza highlighted Calvin's prominence, Badius concentrated his description of the *congrégations* on the role of the ministers. In fact, all ministers, including Calvin, had an equal obligation to speak in these Bible studies, so that each colleague had a turn approximately every three months.

## A. The Genevan Practice

The first indication of the institution of the Bible studies is dated November 1536 [26]. The Genevan ministers wrote to Lausanne, to the north of Lac Leman: "Through Christ we have established colloquies."[27] The neighbouring colleagues from the Pays de Vaud were invited to participate on the basis of full equality. The common cause of reformation led to the plan of a broad platform of regular meetings and discussions, in which unity of doctrine was the primary aim.

I suggest that it was through the influence of Guillaume Farel that the idea of Bible studies, as they were practiced in Zurich, was transported to Geneva. Farel's letters to Christoph Fabri (also called Libertet, a colleague in Thonon) inform us of some events related to the early phase. A man by the name of Dionysius (identified by A.-L. Herminjard as Denis Lambert), also nicknamed

---

[25] *Plusieurs sermons* is a collection of sermons, preceded by the publication of Calvin's introductory exposition to the Gospel of John: *Or par ce mot de Congregation j'enten une certaine assemblée de l'Eglise qui se fait un des jours de la sepmaine, où un chacun des Ministres en son ordre expose quelque passage d'Escriture, plus par forme de leçon que de predication; et cela fait, s'il y a quelqu'un des autres à qui l'Esprit de Dieu ait revelé quelque chose faisant à l'intelligence et esclairissement de ce qui a esté proposé, il luy est libre de parler* (CO 35: 591f).

[26] Maybe Farel's work in Neuchâtel included some form of the *congrégation*. Farel promoted the conference in a letter of 4 April 1537 to Christoph Fabri in Thonon; see A.-L. Herminjard, *Correspondance des Réformateurs dans les pays de langue française* (Genève: H. Georg, 1872), vol. 4, 220. In the *classis* of Thonon, the *congrégations* seem to have been instituted after the example of Geneva (Herminjard, *Correspondence*, vol. 4, 272 n. 6; 299 n. 11). In 1608, when a change in the structure of the *congregation* was contemplated, its institution was recalled: *La continuation d'iceluy depuis 70 ans ou environs, ayant apporté un singulier ornement à ceste Eglise, que tous changements et nouveautez doibvent ester à très bon droit suspectes, et surtout en matieres ecclesiastiques* (RCP X : 88).

[27] CO 10b: 73 (no. 40, 21 November 1536; Genevan ministers, *Ex coetu nostro*, to colleagues in Lausanne); Herminjard, *Correspondance*, vol. 4, 107 (no. 581).

"Bacchus" for his diet of wine, disturbed the Bible conferences. A former monk, Lambert had become a pastor in the Bernese territories and demanded to be recognized as such in Geneva. However, he was asked to resign because of undignified behaviour towards his colleagues: "He was admonished by Calvin and asked in the name of the brethren to leave the ministry."[28] This Dionysius even took his wife, who was not without reproach either, to the *congrégation* to plead for her husband.

These Bible studies developed in the surrounding Bernese territories as well. The second synod of Lausanne, held on 14 May 1537, stipulated that the ministers of each of the seven *classes* should meet once a week for mutual exhortation and Bible study.[29] The structure and terminology are very similar to the Genevan practise. In early 1538, Bern managed to sever relations between Geneva and Lausanne: "Our colloquies are forbidden to the brethren, and theirs to us," as Farel wrote.[30] The crisis of 1538, resulting in the dismissal of Farel and Calvin, was building. "Bacchus" seems to have played a role in disturbing the relations between Geneva and Lausanne.[31] From that date participation in the Bible studies was confined to Geneva and its territories.

## B. The Church Order of Geneva

The *Ordonnances ecclesiastiques* of 1541 (following the draft of John Calvin) contain the following paragraph, connected with the oath of office of newly elected ministers:

> Now as it is necessary to examine the ministers well when they are to be elected, so also it is necessary to have the right order to keep them in their duty. To this end it will be expedient in the first place that all ministers, in order to preserve purity and concord of doctrine among themselves, gather on a set day of the week to hold a conference on the Scriptures.

The following paragraph concerns attendance:

> No one should be absent without a legitimate reason. If anyone is negligent in this respect, let him be admonished. As for those who preach in the villages, subordinate to the Seigneury, they are to be exhorted [1561: our min-

---

[28] CO 10b: 76 (no. 43, Farel to Libertet, 6 Dec. 1536); Herminjard, *Correspondance*, vol. 4, 121-124 (no. 588).

[29] Henri Vuilleumier, *Histoire de l'Église Réformée du Pays de Vaud sous le régime Bernois*, vol. 1, *L'Âge de la Réforme* (Lausanne: Éditions la Concorde, 1927), 285-287; Jean Barnaud, *Pierre Viret. Sa vie et son oeuvre (1511-1571)* (Nieuwkoop: B. de Graaf, 1973), 167.

[30] CO 10b: 145 (no. 88, Farel to Libertet, 14 Jan. 1538); Herminjard, vol. 4, 350-352 (no. 678). Also in Calvin's letter to Martin Bucer of 12 January, CO 10b: 144; Herminjard, *Correspondence*, vol. 4, 349 (no. 677).

[31] CO 10b: 78 (no. 44, Farel to Libertet, 16 Dec. 1536); Herminjard, *Correspondance*, vol. 4, 135f (no. 592).

isters of the city should go and exhort them] to come as often as they can. However, if they default an entire month, it is to be regarded as a very great negligence, unless it is a case of illness or another legitimate hindrance.

In the revision of 1561 a passage was inserted on the conference as a means of keeping an eye on each colleague and his duty to study the Scriptures:

> In order to recognize how diligent everyone is in his studies and that no one grows lax, each member shall expound by turns the passage from Scripture that comes next [1576: on the day of the *Congrégation*]. When finally the ministers have retreated [1576: separately to the place where they meet][32], each member of the Company shall admonish the one who propounded on what needs contradiction, so that such critique serves him as correction.

The prescriptions of 1541 proceed with a final paragraph—maintained of course in 1561—on conflicts over doctrine. A closed session of the *Compagnie des Pasteurs*, following a conference, is the first platform to deal with such cases:

> If there appears a difference in doctrine, let the ministers come together to discuss the matter. Afterwards, if need be, let them call the elders and those commissioned by the Seigneury to assist in composing the contention. Finally, if they are unable to come to friendly agreement because of the obstinacy of one of the parties, let the case be referred to the magistrate to be put in order.[33]

A few remarks on terminology are in order. The word *congrégation*, a gathering or meeting, is rather vague. A more adequate term for these Bible studies, *conférence des Escriptures*, is seldom used. In some letters, we encounter the term *colloque*[34] or, in Latin, *colloquium*. When *congrégation* had become an established term, Beza referred to Bolsec's appearance *in congregationis coetu*.[35] The term *congrégation* is also used in the transcripts as the title of the introductory expositions and in the few samples that were published in the 16th century. In these instances the meaning of *congrégation* is the written or published text of *la proposition* (here rendered as "exposition").

The conference for Bible study, where interested members of the Church were present, was followed by a closed session of the ministers in which they discussed various practical matters of ministry. This session is most frequently also

---

[32] The *Ordonnances* of 1576 put it more clearly: *se seront retirés à part, là où ils s'assemblent* (cf. Jean Calvin, *Deux congrégations*, ed. R. Peter, p. X n. 18, referring to the text of Heyer, *L'Eglise de Genève*, 281).

[33] CO 10a: 18 and RCP I, 3 (text of 1541); CO 10a: 96 and OS II: 332 (text of 1561).

[34] In the *Leges Academiae* of 1559 we find this double terminology in an article concerning the presence of the professors "*à la congregation et au Colloque des Ministres*" (CO 10a: 85). The term *colloque* seems to be applied to the session, following the Bible conference.

[35] CO 21: 143f (twice).

called *la congrégation* in the minutes of the *Compagnie des Pasteurs*.[36] Censure of doctrine and morals had a place in the quarterly sessions which were called *congrégations generalles*[37] (held before each celebration of the Lord's Supper[38]). It should not surprise us that the ministers did not always make a clear distinction between the Bible studies and the following session of the Company of Pastors. In general, the term *congrégation* could be used as an equivalent of the Company of Pastors itself. Following the transcript of the Church order of 1541, the first volume of the Registers begins with a list of regulations from 1546. All ministers signed the document, following the line: *Passé par la congregation des freres assemblee le vendredi …*[39]

## C. The Lausanne *Classis*

The neighbouring Lausanne *classis* (a regional assembly of Churches), in the Pays de Vaud, also had weekly colloquies for the ministers and the people, held on Wednesdays. The Synod of 1537 had instituted the various *classes* in the territory of Bern, which were subdivided into colloquies in 1539.[40] In the second half of 1549 a huge conflict arose between the ministers of Lausanne and the Council of Bern on the effect of these colloquies. Conflicts, in which Viret and Zebedee were the main persons, seem to have annoyed the Bernese Council so much that they decided to restrict the colloquies to four times per year.[41]

At Viret's request, Calvin wrote to Wolfgang Musculus on the matter and strongly advocated the reinstitution of weekly colloquies because everyone of the preachers is heard, stimulated, and corrected so that he is equipped to explain the Scriptures to the people: "This is also the best bond to retain consensus in doctrine."[42] Furthermore, interested laymen were now deprived of a

---

[36] Emil Doumergue confused the terms when he described the *conférence des Escriptures* as follows: « Cette conférence pastorale devait devenir célèbre dans l'histoire de Genève sous le nom de *Vénérable Compagnie des pasteurs* » ; however, he rightly added « et ne doit être confondue avec le Consistoire » (*Jean Calvin. Les hommes et les choses de son temps* (Lausanne : George Bridel, 1917), vol. 5 : 108).

[37] RCP I: 145.

[38] RCP I: 56-58. For other examples of the use of *congrégation* for the session following the Biblical studies, cf. Dourmergue, *Jean Calvin*, vol. 5: 62, 73. After 1553, the term *congrégation* seems to disappear from the minutes of the *Compagnie des Pasteurs*. It is found once in 1554 (*RCP* II: 57), twice in 1555 (*en notre congregation ou colloque*) for the session on the ministers' work (*RCP* II: 62, 65).

[39] RCP I : 21.

[40] Jean Barnaud, *Pierre Viret. Sa vie et son oeuvre (1511-1571)* (1911 ; reprint, Nieuwkoop: B. de Graaf, 1973), 167; Vuillemier, *Histoire*, 286.

[41] Barnaud, *Pierre Viret*, 351-361; Vuilleumier, *Histoire*, 287-289, 660. No minutes of the *classes* prior to 1573 have survived.

[42] Calvin's letter to Wolfgang Musculus, 22 October (no. 1294, CO 13: 433f).

most cherished possibility of studying the Bible. This letter is a unique defense of the Genevan practice from Calvin's perspective. In November the measure was softened; the colloquies in the Lausanne classis were permitted again, probably because of the Academy and its students.[43] The frequency could be increased again, but the persons permitted to speak were restricted to one, plus the professors of Hebrew and Greek.[44] Once again Calvin warned Musculus of the danger of having no colloquies in the other classes of Bern: "Now, the less communication in doctrine, the greater will be the danger of destructive instruction."[45]

Sometime during this conflict Calvin addressed a memorandum on the "conferences of the pastors on Holy Scripture" to the Council of Bern.[46] He was invited to do so by Viret and the Lausanne ministers.[47] This document offers the most extensive description of the Genevan institution in Calvin's hand. We present it in the following translation, because it reflects the fullest and most coherent description of the *congrégation* in Geneva:

"Advice on the Conferences of the Pastors on Holy Scripture"

The response which pleased [you,] our renowned Sirs, to give us in writing regarding the conference on Scripture, which we are accustomed to hold weekly, does not correspond at all with what the Bernese preachers said to our brother, Master Pierre Viret.[48] And also because there are in the same response some passages dubious to us, we have thought it best—so as not to undertake anything that does not correspond with the intentions of our Sirs, but instead to follow what you have regarded as good and useful for the up-building of the Church—to put in writing point by point the form which we want to keep in our so called conferences, so that—when it is approved by you, our Sirs, as we hope—it will be observed without difficulty and that no one will be permitted to go against it.

[Material regulations]

First, that in the Lausanne *classis*, considering the distance between the places, there be three separate colloquies, so organized that the distance causes no trouble to anyone.

---

[43] Letter no. 1314 (CO 13: 463-468) and no. 1315 (CO 13: 468-472).

[44] The final verdict of the Council of Bern is given on 9 November 1549 (CO 13: 443f, no. 1301). The matter dies down in the correspondence during December.

[45] Calvin's next letter to Musculus, 7 December 1549 (no. 1325, CO 13: 490f).

[46] CO 13: 435-436 (no. 1295). The document is in Calvin's handwriting. It bears no date, but must be from September 1549. The wording suggests that it was written as a reaction to the verdict of the Bernese Council (CO 13: 374-376).

[47] CO 13: 428 (no. 1291).

[48] This response, dated 2 September 1549, is found in CO 13: 374-376 (no. 1254). See Viret's letter to Calvin with the request to write to the Council of Bern in CO 13: 427ff (no. 1291).

- That each colloquy choose a book of Scripture—one that will be the most useful— to expound.

- That the passage to be treated shall be defined by agreement a week earlier, so that they work on the text ably and no more or less than is deemed good, both for the instruction and the convenience of the brethren.

- That each of the ministers and professors [of the Academy of Lausanne] be bound to take his turn in expounding the passage assigned to him. The aim is to see how diligent each one is in his studies and in what way they explain the Holy Scripture for the edification of the people.

- That he who has put forth his exposition in that capacity shall be admonished personally among the brethren about the faults which have been noted in him, such as, if he has made a wrong argument on or exposition of Scripture, or that he does not have the gift of teaching, or that there is another vice that needs reproach.

[Formal Restrictions]

After the passage is expounded by the one whose turn it is, the matter as presented is not to be repeated in order to eliminate all redundancy, but only what has been omitted shall be added by those to whom God has given the grace to do so.

- No matter of discontent which causes debate or dissension shall be stirred up, but they must discuss peacefully what is relevant to the understanding of the passage and to the doctrine which can be deduced. When such a situation occurs, let the dean interfere by imposing silence on the dissenters.

- No topic shall be brought forward against the established reformation.[49] The one who tries to do so must be reprimanded by the authority of the dean.[50]

- If anyone raises a question on the [doctrinal] consequence of the passage, he shall speak modestly of what God has given him on the subject or wait for the statement on the matter by him who will be chosen by the *classis* as the most able one.

[General Observations]

However, no one shall be forced to attend every week under all circumstances.[51] Yet all shall be admonished to be present, except when they have

---

[49] Calvin reacts to a sentence in the verdict of the Council of Bern, sent to the ministers of Lausanne, limiting the colloquies to four times per year "*pourvu toutefois qu'aucun avis ne soit entendu contraire à la dispute de réformation tenue dans notre ville et au serment prêt*" (CO 13: 375 in the translation of Barnaud, *Pierre Viret.*, 352).

[50] Pierre Viret was *doyen* or *Decanus* of the *classis* of Lausanne. The dean was assisted in his work of supervision of the Churches by four *jurés*. The *decanus* and four *iurati* signed the letters written in the name of the Lausanne ministers (CO 13, no. 1314-1315).

[51] This could be an allusion to the clause in the last verdict of Bern of 9 November: the Lausanne colloquies can be held more frequently, *ea tamen conditione ut ne quis ad eos extraordinarios conventus cogatur* (CO 13: 444, sub 2).

a legitimate reason for their absence, both to profit personally and to censure the one expounding, if necessary.

Everything shall serve to attain a pure and simple understanding of Scripture and to draw maximum profit from it for the instruction of all, without sophisticated cleverness and without any dispute and even less controversy."

This document recalls the history of a conflict in the Bernese territories, but at the same time it reflects the practice and experience of the Genevan ministers. It is written from the perspective of their colleagues in the Lausanne area, but in case they chose to use this document, Calvin's name or person cannot be detected. It is not clear whether the Lausanne ministers submitted this "Advice" to the Council of Bern or not. It could have been incorporated in the extensive memorandum written by Viret in the name of all the Lausanne ministers.[52] This memorandum is important, because it was Pierre Viret who worked in Geneva during the early years of the reformation. The colloquies in Lausanne and the *congrégations* in Geneva were almost identical up to the crisis of 1549.

## D. Time and place

The time of day when the Bible studies begin is given in the historiography as 7.00 a.m.[53], or 9.00 a.m.,[54] without reference to a source. It must have been following the dawn service on weekdays (which took place at 6.00 a.m. in the summer and at 7.00 a.m. during the winter). Giving the ministers and the people time to assemble after the morning service, the starting time must have been 8 a.m. in summer and 9 a.m. in winter. On one occasion it is reported during the summer period that the Bible studies could last until around 10.00 a.m.[55] Sounding the church bell was the customary summons to assemble.

Following the Bible studies, the Company of Pastors held their closed meeting for business matters. Sometimes this meeting had to be adjourned *à midi aprez disner* (until midday after dinner).[56] Thus the whole Friday morning after the early service was reserved for the Bible studies and the deliberations of the Company of Pastors.

---

[52] CO 13: 415-417. An analysis is offered by Barnaud, *Pierre Viret*, 354ff.

[53] Charles Borgeaud, *Histoire de l'Université de Genève*, vol. 1 (Genève: Georg & Co, 1900), 53; Doumergue, *Jean Calvin*, vol. 3: 343, followed by R. Peter in Jean Calvin, *Deux congregations*, X.

[54] E. Doumergue, *Jean Calvin*, vol. 6, 17; cf. the reconstruction of J. Gaberel, *Histoire de l'Eglise de Genève depuis le commençement de la Réformation jusqu'à noz jours*, vol. 3 (Genève: Joël Cherbuliez, 1862), 490 (1e tableau); Heyer, *L'Église de Genève*, 65.

[55] An indicent, documented in the *Registres du Consistoire*, reports on a regular lay-member, Ayme du Nan, *comme il avoit ouy ung vendredi le presche à S. Gervays et après alla à la congregation où il demora assez longuement*. He is intimidated by someone who says *que c'estoit affaire de quelque riche homme d'aller aux congregations et y demorer jusques à dix heures* (CO 21: 432).

[56] RCP I: 76; II: 109.

Where did these meetings take place? In the early years a note in the records of the Council announced: "Regarding the *congrégation*, [it is decided] that it shall not take place in St. Pierre, but at Calvin's or at [the school of] Rive (whichever one wishes) and to ring the bell, as customary."[57] This regulation, half a year before Calvin's banishment in 1538, did not last long. After his return, the meeting place was St. Pierre again. Doumergue points to *le temple de l'Auditoire*, that is the small church Nôtre-Dame-la-Neuve; this could be the case for the years 1557 and following. In 1556, that chapel, which had been closed in 1536, was used as a church again, especially by the Italian and English-speaking refugees. Before that time, St. Pierre was used as a meeting place for the pastors' Bible studies.[58]

In the early 17th century the *congrégation* was reorganized and placed "at the time of the [early morning] service and in the pulpit of St. Pierre".[59] The Auditoire, used as a place of gathering since 1557, was replaced again by St. Pierre. Since the adjacent Chapel of the Maccabees [60] was used as a storeroom, we may assume that the Bible studies took place in the main Church building. The place of the Bible studies was thus easily accessible to the people who had attended the early morning service in the church.

## E. Structure or Liturgy?

Bible study meetings such as the *Prophezei* in Zurich and the *christliche Übung* in Strasbourg were instituted to replace the canonical hours. The study of Scripture was held at the traditional hour of the day, and therefore some form of liturgy was maintained. But in Geneva and the Swiss territories the Bible studies were held only once a week. Was it regarded as a form of Church service?

Every meeting was opened by this formulaic prayer:

We will invoke our good God and Father, asking him to pardon all our faults and sins and illumine us by his holy Spirit so that we have the true understanding of his holy Word, giving us grace so that we can study it purely and faithfully, to the glory of his name, to the edification of his Church, and to

---

[57] CO 21 : 223: *Touchant la congregation: qu'elle ne ce doyt plus tenyr en S. Pierre, mais chez Calvinus, out az Ryvaz laz où il leur playra, et de sonner laz cloche comment est de coutume* (taken from *Reg. du Conseil*, vol. 32, fol. 14). 'Ryvaz' is the Collège de Rive, the Latin school founded by the Genevans after the Reformation of 1536.

[58] Nicolas Colladon testified to the *congrégation* of 16 October 1551, in which Bolsec spoke out: *qui se feist en l'eglise de sainct Pierre en la maniere accoustumée* (CO 8: 192). J. Gaberel pointed to the *Auditoire*; Gaberel, *Histoire de l'Eglise de Genève*, 490.

[59] RCP IX: 218.

[60] The editors of RCP IX state that the ministers held their business meeting, following the *congrégation*, in a room above this chapel from the end of the 16th century (o.c., 181 n.234), and not, as has been assumed, in the cloister of St. Pierre (cf. *Saint Pierre, Ancienne Cathédrale de Genève* (Genève, 1891; reprint 1982), 89).

our salvation. This we ask him in the name of his only and beloved Son, our Lord Jesus Christ. Amen.[61]

The prayer at the beginning of the *Prophezei* in Zurich had the following wording:

Almighty, eternal, and merciful God, whose Word is a lamp to our feet and a light on our paths, open and enlighten our minds, so that we may understand your pure and holy Word, and in that which we have rightly understood may we be transformed so that we in no way displease your majesty, through Jesus Christ, our Lord. Amen.[62]

The Zurich and Genevan prayers both concentrate on the understanding of the Word in the Bible study meeting.

Next in the order of the *congrégation* was the reading of the chapter or passage of the Bible chosen for that morning. Surely it was read in French, but we do not know if the Hebrew or Greek text was read as well, as was the practice in Zurich. After the reading from Scripture, the designated minister explained the passage (*la proposition*). The text, written by the scribe, is always headed by the phrase: *Congrégation faicte par ...* (and followed by the date). The exposition was not regarded as a sermon. Often it is stated that this exposition resembled a lecture, as they knew it from the school and, later, the Academy.

The *proposant* always ended his exposition by inviting his colleagues to add their comments. For example, Calvin said at the end of his introductory exposition to his projected Harmony of Exodus – Deuteronomy: "I have not expounded the matter as it really deserves, but the brethren to whom God has given more gifts can add to it according to what they perceive to be for the edification of the whole Church."[63] Such a statement might sound obligatory, but it summarizes beautifully the purpose of the Bible study meetings: a collective study of Scripture and a recognition of the spiritual gifts distributed among the ministers. A similar statement is found in the only *congrégation*, surviving in manuscript, by a minister other than Calvin. Michel Cop said at the end of his exposition of Joshua 1:6-11: "This is what God has given me to say briefly on this passage. This passage is really rich and broad and contains grand teaching. Therefore, I beg the brethren to whom God has given much greater gifts than

[61] CO 8 : 93 (*Priere que les Ministres ont accoustumé de faire au commencement de la Congregation*, heading the publication of the text of the *Congrégation de l'election eternelle de Dieu* of 1551).

[62] ZIV : 365 : *Omnipotens, sempiterne et misericors deus, cuius verbum est lucerna pedibus nostris et lumen semitarum nostrarum, aperi et illumina mentes nostras, ut oracula tua pure et sancte intelligamus, et in illud, quod recte intellexerimus, transformeremur, quo maiestati tuae nulla ex parte displiceamus, per Jesum Christum, dominum nostrum. Amen.* Cf. Fritz Schmidt-Clausing, *Zwingli als Liturgiker. Eine liturgiegeschichtliche Untersuchung* (Göttingen: Vandenhoeck & Ruprecht, 1952), 67f, 142f; cf. Fritz Schmidt-Clausing, "Das Prophezeigebet. Ein Blick in Zwinglis liturgische Werkstatt," *Zwingliana*, vol. 12 (1964), 10-34.

[63] Ms.fr. 40b, f. 68b-69a : *Je n'ay pas deduit la chose comme elle meritoit bien, mais les freres ausquelz Dieu a fait plus de graces y pourront adjouster selon qu'ilz cognoistront estre d'edification pour toute l'Eglise,*

to me to supplement my deficiency, and I ask for assistance as it pleases Him to help me."[64]

Following the introductory exposition, the discussion began. One of the leading ministers gave the first critique. For example, in October 1551, Jean de St. André gave the exposition, and Farel, on a visit in Geneva, responded. After that, the other ministers and people present could take part in the discussion.

We know very little about these discussions. The few transcriptions reveal only a glimpse of the contributions. Only on the exposition of the book of Joshua is a collection of material preserved. The reactions of the other ministers to the introductory exposition are described in various ways. We find: *ce qui a esté adjousť* or *recite*. Since an *Addition* by Beza (probably because of Calvin's absence) has been taken down only twice, we cannot say if such descriptions only apply to the reactions by various ministers or also to the closing statements, which were followed by the final prayer. We have transcripts only of Calvin's closing statements. These are called *Resolution ou conclusion, Repetition, Sommaire,* or *Conclusion*. Even when the adjectives *briefve* or *sommaire* are used, the additional exposition is always approximately the same length. Therefore, it seems that the terms are synonymous.

The Bible study meeting was closed by a prayer, most often by Calvin. In all texts, printed and in manuscript, which contain *congrégations* or only *additions*, this final prayer is preserved. The prayer started in a customary way: "We thank our good God for the grace he has given us, when it pleased him to bring us to the knowledge of his Gospel, praying ..." The rest of the prayer reflects the contents of the biblical passage. Nearly all prayers end with a passage of intercession for the oppressed churches in France.

Although some form of liturgy was maintained, the Bible studies were not meant to be a church service. Exposition and discussion were essentially connected. Although these Bible studies were intended primarily for the ongoing training of the ministers, the presence and participation of lay people were valued.

## IV. One Purpose, Various Means

According to the *Ordonnances*, the Bible study meetings had a single purpose: "to preserve purity and concord in doctrine" among the ministers of the Word. However, this overall purpose was achieved by various methods and

---

[64] Ms.fr. 40a, f. 76b: *Voilà que Dieu m'a donné sur ce passage à dire briefvement. Le passage est bien riche et bien ample et contient grande doctrine. Et pourtant je prie les freres ausquelz le Seigneur a fait plus grand' grace qu'à moy, qu'ilz suppleent à mon defaut, et demande à l'assistance qu'il luy plaise me supporter.* This is not only the one single transcript of a *congrégation* by one of the other ministers, but also the only one with which to compare *"Ce qui a esté adjousté par M. Calvin"* (f. 76b-78b). Because some ministers seem to have exaggerated such humility, this formula was restricted in the 1570s to the following words: '*Voilà ce que Dieu m'a donné sur ce passage. Je prie les freres adjouster ce qu'ilz verront estre necessaire pour l'edification de l'Eglise (RCP III, 104).*

means: A) exegesis of biblical books in *lectio continua*; B) homiletical training; C) related disputations of propositions with a strong accent on doctrine; and D) brotherly censure of the exposition in the following session according to the standards of orthodoxy. These aspects must be treated here briefly, but deserve fuller attention.

## A. Exposition of Biblical Books

The method chosen to achieve the aim of the *congrégations*, that is, to preserve purity and unity of doctrine, was the study of the Bible—not primarily doctrinal topics. In this respect Geneva followed the lead of Zurich. As in the *Prophezei*, biblical books were studied in *lectio continua*. For the last fifteen years of Calvin's work in Geneva we know from Colladon's *Vie de Calvin* the order followed in Geneva: in 1549, Hebrews; from 1549 to 1550, the Catholic Letters; 1550-1553, the Gospel of John; 1553-1555, the synoptic Gospels; 1555-1559, the book of Psalms; 1559-1562, the Harmony of the last four books of Moses; 1562-1563 Galatians; 1563-1564, Joshua; 1564 and following years, Isaiah.[65]

Systematic exposition of entire books of the Bible was an effective method to keep the issue of doctrine close to its source, the Scriptures. It forced every minister to prepare himself for his turn at the exposition, to read Hebrew and Greek on a regular basis, and to explain the biblical text by consulting other exegetical works. In concentrating on one biblical book for a period of, in some cases, several years, they heard each other's exposition and had an opportunity to advance their knowledge of the texts. The fact that John Calvin was the Moderator did not reduce the input of the other participants. The fact that some of the colleagues, and especially Calvin, were considered more gifted expositors, gave the others a chance to learn from week to week.

The only complete *congrégation* by a minister other than Calvin, which has been both transcribed and preserved, is by Michel Cop (on Joshua 1:6-11), who came to Geneva in 1545. When he died in 1566, the secretary wrote a eulogy on Cop in the Register and mentioned that "among other things, he had helped to form Mr. Calvin in the Hebrew language."[66] There were other gifted colleagues from whom even Calvin could learn. In 1560 Nicolas des Gallars published the first of his biblical commentaries, *In Exodum, qui secundus est liber*

---

[65] Cf. Calvin, *Deux congrégations*, XVf ; Jean-François Gilmont, *Jean Calvin et le livre imprimé* (Genève : Librairie Droz, 1997), 375; T.H.L. Parker, *Calvin's Old Testament Commentaries* (Edinburgh: T. & T. Clark, 1986), 29-33.

[66] RCP III: 11 and note 5. See on Michel Cop: Emil Doumergue, *Jean Calvin. Les hommes et les choses de son temps* (Lausanne : Georges Bridel, 1905), vol. 3, 576-588. He published commentaries on Proverbs (1556) and Ecclesiastes (1558). See Paul Chaix, Alain Dufour, Gustave Moeckli, *Les livres imprimés à Genève de 1550 à 1600* (Travaux d'Humanisme et Renaissance, vol. 86) (Genève : Librairie Droz, 1966), 29, 31).

*Mosis, commentarii* (Genève: Jean Crespin, 1560)[67]. On 22 August 1559, a week before the Company of Pastors started their study of Exodus, permission to print had already been requested by Crespin [68]. Des Gallars was still working in Geneva when his book came out; in April 1560, he was assigned to a new task in London. He thus participated in the phase of the *congrégations* when they studied the historical part of Exodus. His expository insights, set down in his commentary, could have contributed both to the Bible studies and to Calvin's own Harmony. Des Gallars offered a complete and running commentary on Exodus. This may have influenced Calvin's suggestion to the Company to take the alternative approach of a Harmony.

It is a pity that hardly any expositions by the other ministers were recorded, for they all had equal obligations and opportunities to expound the Bible in the company of their colleagues. Whatever the personal relations between the colleagues were, their common undertaking of concentrating on the biblical text provided for a weekly chance to meet in spiritual unity. The *congrégations* as Bible studies must have been the core of the sessions held by the Company of Pastors of Geneva and its territories.

## B. Homiletical Training

It is clear that the Bible study meetings were closely connected to the task of preaching. The mere fact that the ministers assembled on Fridays following the early morning service suggests such a connection. Colleagues in Geneva regularly heard one another in the pulpit and could thus evaluate each other's sermons from an exegetical and homiletical viewpoint. When they came out of church, the memory of the morning's sermon was still fresh.

Other opportunities to hear and evaluate each other's sermons were provided by the visitations to the parishes in the country by colleagues from the city.[69] From the Registers it is clear that a position in the city required more talent. For example, when Claude Baudel was elected as minister in 1556, it was noted "that they are afraid that his voice is much too weak to preach in the city ...," and therefore the parishes of Russin and Dardagny are assigned to him.[70]

The distance of the villages to the city made it more difficult to be present in the *congrégations*, which put the village ministers at a disadvantage. Especially during the winter it could be hard for the ministers "from the country" (*les*

---

[67] Chaix et al., *Les livres imprimés*, 43; Jean-François Gilmont, *Bibliographie des éditions de Jean Crespin, 1550-1572*, vol. 1 (Verviers: Librairie P.M. Gasson, 1981), no. 60/6.

[68] Gilmont, *Bibliographie*, vol. 1, 131.

[69] The regulations for visitations state that the ministers should chose *deux de leur congregation* to visit the villages yearly. The first point concerns doctrine: *pour s'enquerir si le Ministre du lieu auroit mis en avant quelque doctrine nouvelle et repugnante à la pureté de l'Evanglie*. The second point concerns preaching: *que cela serve pour s'enquerir si le Ministre presche en edification ...* (OS II: 335).

[70] RCP II: 66f.

*freres de champs*) to travel to the city. On 23 December 1552, the Registers note that a session for censure is postponed until January 1553, "because brothers from the country cannot assemble, owing to the [Christmas] celebration of the [Lord's] Supper and to the glazed frost, which is very heavy."[71] Picture Geneva and the mountain roads covered in snow and ice! But since their preaching obligations did not involve as many weekday sermons, they could attend the Bible studies as often as required.

The exposition at the beginning of the *congrégation* was not a sermon. However, the fact that Theodore de Bèze noted the manuscripts of the Bible studies in the first catalogue of John Calvin's works as "sermons" proves that this was the category most similar to the Bible studies.[72] The studies were certainly meant to help the ministers prepare for their task of preaching. The exposition of biblical books in *lectio continua* may have resulted in series of sermons on the book which was being expounded in the Bible studies. Since no record of preaching by other ministers was kept, this suggestion remains a hypothesis. The texts, either in print or in manuscript, every now and then contain a reference to preaching. An early remark by Calvin may suffice for the moment to illustrate this. In a letter to the church in Lyon Calvin wrote of " our conference, in which a text of St. Paul was read, containing beautiful and rich material, which should be well-known to all those who preach on it, because it is the epistle for the first Sunday of Advent' (Rom. 13:11-14).[73]

The passage in the Church Order, stipulating the institution of the Bible study meetings, is introduced by the following line: "Further, just as it is necessary to examine the ministers carefully when they are to be elected, it is also necessary to have the right order to keep them in their duty."[74] That duty is first and foremost the exposition of Scripture in their main task of preaching. Following the paragraph on the Bible studies, the *Ordonnances ecclésiastiques* speak of necessary censure. In the category of tolerable, but reproachable sins we find: "Strange ways of treating Scripture which result in scandal; curiosity in

---

[71] RCP I: 147.

[72] De Bèze included in the first bibliography of Calvin's works the text on election in the category *Sermons imprimez et qu'on a recueillis quand il preschoit* and *Quelques sommaires des congregations faites sur Iosué, recueillis comme il traittoit les passages* in the category *Sermons sur le vieil Testament non imprimez* (CO 21: 47f). In 1575 he added to the first category: *concio in congregatione ad certum locum epistolae ad Galatas cum conciuncula vel exegesi particulae Catechismi ad extremum articulum dominicae orationis.*

[73] CO 11:402: *car en nostre congregation où on lisoit ung texte de S. Paul qui contient belle matiere et copieuse, et doibt estre fort commun à tous ceulx qui preschent par dela, pource que cest epistre du premier dimanche de l'advent …* (no. 397). This passage concerns the appearance of a Carmelite monk from Lyon in the Bible study meeting, who made a negative impression and was refused as a minister. The date of the *congrégation* is given by Herminjard as 12 May 1542 (*Correspondance des réformateurs*, vol. 8: 27). See also letter no. 395 (CO 11: 392ff). The text suggests that the ministers were expounding Paul's letter to the Romans in 1542.

[74] RCP I:3.

searching out empty questions; the propagation of some doctrine or custom not accepted in the Church; negligence in studying and especially in reading the Holy Scriptures." After the section on censure, the number, times and places of the sermons are fixed. This all indicates that the Bible study meetings were also intended as a stimulus for the ongoing task of preaching.[75]

## C. Brotherly Censure

When a minister finished his exposition, his colleagues could add their thoughts. Most often a senior minister from Geneva took the lead in this, while others could react in second and third place. The manuscripts of the *congréga-tions* do not disclose any critique, but only additional expository remarks. In the session following the Bible study meeting, the colleagues were expected to express their critique of the exposition which had been given by the leading minister. Not many cases of censure are noted in the Registers. It is possible that the dismissal of ministers in 1545 (Aimé Champereau, Pierre Delecluse, Simon Moreau) and again in 1546 (Henri de la Mare, Aimé Megret), all before the Company started the Register, was in some measure (apart from the ethical issues) the result of the testing of competence and soundness in doctrine. The case of Philippe d'Ecclesia is the only instance in which we see how the relation between the Bible studies, brotherly criticism, and steps of censure in the following session operated.[76] It is also the only documented case in which doctrinal deviation played a major role.

When d'Ecclesia became the subject of serious discussion, his colleagues must have been annoyed already for some time. A compilation of erroneous statements during the Bible study meetings had been made (but not noted in the Register): he "maintained various opinions which were not edifying, and he raised futile questions, often turning around or obscuring what had been well declared." The wording reflects the lines in the church order regarding correctible faults. These statements were read to him, apparently *in extenso*. The Register informs us that "he had frequently been warned in the past to desist from such statements and to speak in a more edifying manner."[77] The phase of brotherly criticism, on which we would like to have been informed is summarized in a few lines.

---

[75] In 1609 a new structure for the Bible studies was contemplated, because there were few lay members left. In the deliberations of the Company we read the following: *que l'usage de la congrega-tion est proprement pour voir quel profit font les pasteurs et la dexterité qu'ils ont à traiter l'Escriture saincte un chacun au troupeau qui luy est commis* (RCP X, 166). Testing the ability to preach is regarded as the main goal of the Bible studies. Further it is stated *que la congregation avoit jadis esté establie pour descouvrir les esprits, si en ceste Eglise il y avoit aucun qui ne fust orthodoxe en la doctrine.*

[76] On the various cases of censure against ministers, see J. Plomp, *De kerkelijke tucht bij Calvijn* (Kampen: J.H. Kok, 1969), 291-302 ; on D'Ecclesia, cf. Plomp, *De kerkelijke tucht*, 286, 289f, 302-309.

[77] RCP I: 47.

Then a course of corrective action was chosen: d'Ecclesia was forbidden both a turn in expounding Scripture in the *congrégation* and participating in the discussion. This sanction was to last until the next day of censure, that is for three months. If he did not comply, the matter would be brought before the Council. Philippe d'Ecclesia accepted this sanction, but asked his colleagues to keep it quiet (which they promised to do). All parties thus agreed to keep the matter within the bosom of the Company of Pastors.

In fact, this censure isolated d'Ecclesia from his circle of colleagues. It comes as no surprise when we read of his complaints. The ministers decided "that the Company should be purged of him" and to inform the Council.[78] But the Council did not give in to their wish, but urged reconciliation; however, the ministers set the stakes high by stating "that Master Philippe should not be accepted as a brother or minister in the *congrégation*." He was now also excluded from the sessions of brotherly censure. In response to his appeal, the decision was reaffirmed that he should not take his turn in presenting an exposition in the Bible study meetings. Still, on order of the Council, d'Ecclesia retained his post as minister of Vandoeuvre. This case of early 1549 died down until after the affair against the physician Jerome Bolsec.

It is in 1551 that a new procedure against d'Ecclesia starts. This time there were ethical charges against him: he did not live up to a promise of marriage, and, later, he was charged with usury.[79] But he was also accused of social contact with the condemned Bolsec. At the same time we observe that d'Ecclesia had been admitted as a full member of the Company again, because he spoke in public in the special *congrégation* of 18 December 1551 on the doctrine of pre-destination and co-signed the circular letter, written to the Swiss Churches in the Bolsec case. In 1552, the contact with Bolsec was held against him. D'Ecclesia admitted his social contact, but also stated that he did not agree with Bolsec in his stand on election. Then d'Ecclesia was confronted with the testi-mony of a witness to whom d'Ecclesia is to have said "that in the *congrégation*, when he stated his opinion on the issue of predestination, he had not said everything" (d'Ecclesia denied making the statement).[80] This is an important point: the ministers expected each other to be honest and to express their indi-vidual thoughts. That a heterodox view could not be held is, in the end, the consequence of the desire to achieve doctrinal unity.

In the second phase of charges against Philippe d'Ecclesia, the Council again tried to order a reconciliation. But this time the magistrates had to give in to the Company, and d'Ecclesia was deposed from the ministry in January 1553. One additional point should be noted. In connection with this case the Company

---

[78] RCP I: 56.

[79] RCP I: 76, 144ff.

[80] RCP I: 144-152.

decided "that henceforward any of the ministers who speaks after the one who gave the exposition shall himself also be censured if necessary, as it applies to him who expounded."[81] The critique should be both strict and mutual.

## D. Related Disputations

Following the public *congrégation*, the discussion was evaluated in closed session by the Company. This was the time and place for brotherly censure. From 1545 to 1552, however, the ministers also had theological disputations during these sessions.[82] Questions on doctrine, ethics and ecclesiastical policy were discussed on the basis of Latin propositions. In this method of working, the accent on "purity and concord of doctrine," the main goal of the Bible study meetings, was more central. Among the forty sets of propositions we find the names of sixteen of the twenty-two ministers for those years. John Calvin's name is not among those listed, but ten sets are anonymous. These propositions testify to the desire of the Genevan ministers to stand together and formulate their theological position on a wide range of subjects.

We do not know how the topics for discussion were chosen. Ethical questions arose in the course of day-to-day pastoral ministry. But it is also possible that doctrinal issues, which came up in the course of the *congrégations*, were noted for further discussion. In any case, the decision to hold such disputations was closely connected to the overall goal of the Bible studies, as noted in the *Ordonnances ecclésiastiques*. The study of Scripture is to lead to doctrinal unity.

## IV. Multiple Functions

The four means which we have just described, had side effects. These are nowhere formally laid down, but can be observed in the sources as accepted and maybe even envisaged functions of the Bible studies. The numbering and topics of the paragraphs in this fourth section correspond with those in the section above. The functions or side effects are: A) the sequence of biblical

---

[81] RCP I: 47.

[82] See my essay, "Calvin and Colleagues: Propositions and Disputations in the Context of the *Congrégations* in Geneva," to be published in the proceedings of the 8th International Congress on Calvin Research, held in 2002 at Princeton Theological Seminary. An annotated translation in English of the *propositiones*, found in RCP I (p.167-182), served as the basis of discussion in the Princeton seminar. It is not clear whether these sessions were open to the public, as Karin Maag suggests in relation to candidates for the ministry ("Calvin's Academic and Educational Legacy," in *The Legacy of John Calvin. Papers Presented at the 12th Colloquium of the Calvin Studies Society, April 22-24, 1999*, ed. David Foxgrover (Grand Rapids MI: Calvin Studies Society, 2000), 15f). The clause *propositiones inter nos disputatae* seems to point to the session of the Company, following the Bible studies and closed to the public. Maag's definition of "the *congrégations* or gatherings of ministers and interested lay-people, at which theological theses were presented and defended" confuses the Bible study meetings and the following session of propositions.

books expounded in the *congrégations* coincided with Calvin's program of writing commentaries on the Old Testament; B) a number of lay visitors frequented the meetings; C) candidates for the ministry were involved; and D) theological disputations may have served to advance doctrinal formulation.

## A. A Trial-run for Calvin's Written Commentaries

When we look at the order of biblical books studied in the *congrégations*, it is noteworthy that Calvin's commentaries on those books were published following their treatment in the circle of the Company. The only exception is Galatians, on which Calvin's commentary had already appeared in 1548. It appears that in 1562 the ministers wanted a New Testament book to interrupt a long series of years in which only Old Testament books had been studied. This interlude provided Calvin with time to finish his commentary on the Harmony, studied in the *congrégations* until 1562 (which appeared in 1563).

The following facts can be deduced from the few sources. The first is that Calvin provided the introduction to each biblical book chosen for study. Among the few transcripts are the introductions to the exposition of the Gospel of John (1550), to the Harmony of Exodus through Deuteronomy (September 1559), to Joshua (1562), and to Isaiah (January 1564). The very fact that Calvin introduced each series indicates that it was he who suggested which book to expound next in the *congrégations*.[83] Moreover, the introduction to the Harmony of the last four books of Moses shows that Calvin prepared the work plan that divided the sections of these four biblical books and presented the model of a Harmony. When the Harmony on the last four books of Moses was granted permission to be printed, the minutes of the Council record this work as "*la concordance des livres de Moïse laquelle a esté traictée en la congregation.*"[84] The relation between the Bible studies and the commentary was noted. The *conference des Escriptures* produced an important fruit in these commentaries. On 30 November 1563, Calvin wrote: "The brethren have urged me to expound the book of Joshua." He reported that he had only gotten as far as Chapter 3 (that is, in the process of writing),[85] while in the Bible studies Calvin and his colleagues had already reached Chapter 21 at that date.

These facts lead to the conclusion that Calvin's colleagues accommodated his program of writing commentaries, or, at least, that Calvin used the ongoing

---

[83] So much is stated for the choice of Isaiah in 1564: *Mesmes environs la mi-Janvier, il proposa le commencement du prophete Isaie en la Congregation, estant requis par les autres Ministres, qui par son conseil avoyent prins ce livre-là à exposer après Josué* (CO 21: 96). Cf. De Boer, 'Jean Calvin et Ésaïe 1 (1564)', 371-395.

[84] cf. Gilmont, *Jean Calvin et le livre imprimé*, 89.

[85] CO 20 : 199.

study of each biblical book in the *congrégation* to stimulate his own studies.[86] To be more accurate: the interaction was mutual. In the course of the Bible studies in which all colleagues participated, Calvin could on the one hand profit from their exegesis and, on the other, present his own thoughts on the text to his colleagues and confront himself with their critique. It is for this reason that we described the Company's program of exposition first, and only now Calvin's projected work on his commentaries as a secondary function. True, the commentaries are Calvin's work, but at the same time a fruit of the Company's work.

The following parallel suggests itself: Conrad Pellikan published his *Commentaria Bibliorum* in the 1530's on the basis of his expositions in the *Prophezei* in Zurich. John Calvin's work on a series of biblical commentaries resembles Pellikan's magnum opus in that it was also a study project of the *congrégations* of the Company of Pastors.

## B. Instruction of Lay People

The ministers of Geneva and, after 1559, the professors of the Academy [87] were obligated to attend the Bible studies. Also, students, such as Nicolas Colladon in 1551, may often have been regular participants.[88] However, a number of lay members also frequented these Friday morning meetings. It seems that in the early years (1536-1541) the *colloques* were intended for ministers only,[89] but it is clear that after 1541 a wider circle of people met in the *congrégations*. On two occasions the number of people present can be fixed at around fifty or sixty, including both ministers and lay-members; but the number may often have been larger. The number sixty is mentioned in a letter by Calvin. Writing about the *congrégation* of Friday 30 May 1544, Calvin reported to Farel on the demeanour of Sebastian Castellio and noted: "Yesterday there were around

---

[86] Cf. Parker, *Calvin's Old Testament Commentaries*, 14f: "The most probable explanation is, not that the commentaries arose out of the *Congrégations*, but that the *Congrégations* were organized to fit in with a commentary that Calvin had begun to write, that he pushed ahead of the *Congrégation's* exposition, and that the *Congrégation* had the first benefit of Calvin's interpretation, no doubt delivered as a summary rather than read verbatim." Cf. Gilmont, *Jean Calvin et le livre imprimé*, 74-77, 89f, 375.

[87] *Ordonannces ecclésiastiques* on « Les Professeurs Publiques » : « Le Vendredi, qu'ilz se trouvent, tant qu'il sera possible, à la congregation et au Colloque des Ministres » (CO 10b: 85; OS II: 373).

[88] Maag, "Calvin's Academic and Educational Legacy," 15f.

[89] In 1608-1609 members of the city Council proposed a change of time so that they could be present in the *congrégations,* but did not have to spend half their morning. They suggested that the dawn service on Fridays and the Bible studies be conflated—as it was eventually decided (*RCP* X, 167). But in 1608, the ministers still resisted any change, with this argument, for example: *Que s'il falloit venir à quelque changement, seroit beaucoup mieux seant de venir à la premiere institution où les congregations se faisoyent en particulier, comme aussi cela se practique ailleurs et ès Classes voisines* (*RCP* X, 88). *En particulier* means: "ministers only," without the public, as it was decided in the *classes* of Lausanne under pressure from Bern in 1549.

sixty people present when the Scripture was studied in the meeting."[90] The number fifty or more can be established by studying the list of witnesses of Jerome Bolsec's critique during the *congrégation* of 16 October 1551. The names of thirty-one lay-members are listed.[91] In that year there were eight ministers in the city and ten in the country-side,[92] which gives a total of almost fifty participants.

The ministers tried to accommodate the many lay participants. When the study of the last four books of Moses was organized "in the form of a Harmony" in 1559, Calvin defended his own composition and laid down a working plan for his colleagues:

> Because the topics are so intertwined, it seemed right to our Company to follow a clear order. It is not that we tried to change anything in what Moses said by the Holy Spirit, but it is in order that they who in the following may frequent the Bible studies may have a clear ease and learn better how they should read both the histories and the doctrine, which are so intertwined.[93]

The fact that twice in the preceding years the lay members had asked for their own forum of Bible studies, in which they could take a more active part, may have prompted the Company of Pastors to accommodate the regular visitors.[94]

Calvin knew that lay members valued the weekly Bible studies. In relation to the trouble in the Bernese territories on the colloquies he wrote in one of his letters to Musculus:

> And not only for the ministers is such training useful, but a number of the people who are lead by an outstanding zeal to understand the Scripture experience part of its usefulness. Maybe there are only a few of those in

---

[90] CO 11: 721 (no. 554). See on Calvin and Castellio: Hans R. Guggisberg, *Sebastian Castellio 1515-1563. Humanist und Verteidiger der religiösen Toleranz* (Göttingen: Vandenhoeck & Ruprecht, 1997), 40f; William G. Naphy, "Calvin's Letters: Reflections on their Usefulmess in Studying Genevan History," *ARG* 86 (1995), 78-86 (67-89).

[91] CO 8: 185f.

[92] William G. Naphy, *Calvin and the Consolidation of the Genevan Reformation* (Manchester – New York: Manchester University Press, 1994), 58 (Table 7).

[93] Ms.fr. 40a: f. 133a-b: *Or les loix sont esparses (comme d<esja> nous avons dit). Elles ne sont pas toutes escrites d'un fil c<ontinuel n>i par certain ordre. Autant en est-il des autres livres. On verra là des sentences qui appartiennent à la doctrine, et puis il y avoit des histoires meslées. D'autant donc que les choses sont ainsi entrelacées, il a semblé bon à nostre compagnie de suivre un ordre cert<ain>. Non pas que nous attentions de rien changer en ce qui a esté di<ct>é à Moyse par le Saint Esprit, mais c'est à fin que d'orenavant ceu<x> qui peuvent hanter les congregations, puissent avoir une certaine addresse et qu'ils cognoissent mieux [133b] comme ils doivent lire tant les histoires que la doctrine qui sont ainsi entremeslées. Tant c'en faut donc que ceci soit pour empescher qu'on ne lise ce qui a esté escrit par un prophete tant excellent et principal entre tous ceux qui ont vescu souz la Loy, que plustost c'est à fin qu'on se puisse bien guider et que les choses soyent cognues plus familierement. Car beaucoup ne font que vaguer en lisant Exode, d'autant qu'ilz sont preoccupez seulement de ce qui est là dit. Mais quand nous le lirons, il nous faut mettre la doctrine à part et nous faut aussi lire l'histoire à part.*

[94] *RCP* II:59 (in late January 1555), 70 (on 1 January 1557). Karin Maag takes this special form, chosen in 1557, as "monthly disputations"; cf. Maag, "Calvin's Academic and Educational Legacy," 16.

Lausanne, but because the decree [to suppress the colloquies] is general, I speak of the whole region. I know there are here pious men, who have no reason to be humble about their learning, who would rather miss two sermons than one exposition of Scripture like those heard here.[95]

A rather stunning statement from Calvin who always hammered home the idea that no one should miss a sermon!

Among the lay members of the Bible studies we find a variety of citizens: some born in Geneva and many refugees, doctors and lawyers, schoolmasters (such as Sebastian Castellio) and printers (Conrad Badius, Jean Crespin, Robert I. Estienne), but also artisans.[96] The *congrégations* seem to have provided for meeting and social contacts for all who wanted to advance their learning and express their dedication to the Reformed faith. Visitors, like the former bishop Pier Paolo Vergerio, found their way to the Bible studies.

The fact that the Bible studies were open to the public also accounts for conflicts in doctrine, which in turn resulted in the writing of reports which pull the *congrégation* from its historical obscurity. The cases of the teacher Sebastian Castellio, who also wanted to become a minister (1544), and the physician Jerome Bolsec (1551) exploded in the context of the Bible studies. Especially in the early years, men with a mission seem to have regarded the *congrégation* as a platform to advance their religious ideas. In his *Contre le secte phantastique* of 1545, Calvin gives an example of sectarians who presented themselves as ministers of the Word and tried to influence the people. He recalls an Antoine Pocquet who

about two years ago [in 1543], having lived in this city for a while and spread his wicked thinking, so acted from the start and sought by subtle means to gain my endorsement in order to advance himself among those who defer in some authority to me, as if I approved of his diabolical errors. Now he did not act his part so well that I was unable to recognize him for a dreamer and madman, as I proved him to be in our *congrégation* …[97]

When brotherly censure among the ministers was in order, the Bible studies, as places of public discussion, were also the platforms to refute erroneous doctrine in the presence of the people.

## C. Examination of Candidates

The election and examination of candidates for the ministry provides the context of the passage on the *congrégation* in the Genevan church order. The

---

[95] CO 13: 433f (no. 1294 of 22 October 1549).

[96] See my forthcoming essay "The Presence and Participation of Lay People in the *Congrégations* of the Company of Pastors in Geneva."

[97] CO 7: 163. Calvin used Chapters 23-24 to quote and refute some writings of Pocquet.

selection and nomination was made by the Company of Pastors. After the Council approved their choice, the candidates were examined. Therefore, we can expect to find a connection between the Bible studies and the theological training and examination of candidates for the ministry.

Candidates were instructed to make two presentations before the Company of Pastors. Close reading of the *Registers* informs us that the first presentation was always an *exposition*, the second a *predication*. For example, Jean Fabri (although he had already been a minister in Lyon) was instructed to prepare an exposition of 1 John 5:7 for the next day, "*à l'heure du midi*," that is, in the session of the Company.[98] At the end of 1549, the ministers studied the Catholic Epistles in the *congrégations*.[99] The first text, from 1 John, that Fabri was to expound could fit into the series of epistles studied in the *congregations*. Fabri's second presentation was a sermon on John 5:24, to be preached before the brethren one week later. During that week Fabri was also examined on doctrine. Finally he was presented to the people in St. Pierre as "minister of the Word."

It seems that the distinction between exposition and sermon was deliberate. It shows how the Bible studies as such differed from the task of preaching. That distinction also explains why the text chosen for the candidate's exposition could be chosen from the biblical book which they were discussing in the course of the Bible studies.

Other examples corroborate these conclusions. In 1552, Jean Macar was ordered to expound Psalm 110 and to deliver a sermon on Ephesians 4.[100] In 1557, Matthieu Grandjean's text for his exposition was Acts 15, for his sermon 1 Peter 2. Claude du Pont was ordered to deliver an exposition of Psalm 82 (the text of his sermon is not noted), while François Morel, Sieur de Coulogne, expounded Psalm 125 and preached on Ephesians 6 [101]. The ministers studied the book of Psalms from 1555 to 1559.[102]

This procedure of examination is constant throughout the years. In January 1564, the pastors started the exposition of Isaiah, for which Calvin delivered the introductory exposition during the last months of his life. On 10 November 1564, the ministers had probably reached Chapter 29 in their regular exposition of Isaiah. Two candidates for the ministry, Charles Perrot and Jean-François Salvart, were instructed to prepare an exposition (*pour exposer en*

---

[98] RCP I : 62: *Et apres qu'il l'eut exposé, les freres luy remonstrerent ce qu'ilz y trouvoient à redire, comme on a acoustumé de fere.* Because the Council initially opposed the election of yet another minister, Fabri could deliver only his exposition on Friday 18 October.

[99] CO 21: 71.

[100] RCP I: 149.

[101] RCP II: 75f.

[102] CO 21: 79.

*maniere de leçon* and *proposer*) of the first verses of Isaiah 29.[103] Apparently the first text was chosen from the Old Testament book they were studying, while the text for the sermon was from the New Testament.

The public in the Bible studies also consisted of a number of possible candidates for the ministry. The principal of the Collège de Rive, Louis Enoch, was elected as minister in 1554 (St. Gervais).[104] The tutor of the children of Germain Colladon, Mathieu Grandjean, was promoted to the ministry in 1557.[105] In 1563, Jacques des Bordes, "who held the position of lecturer in philosophy, was ordered to preach in the absence of Monsieur d'Anduze."[106] In his position as professor of the Academy, des Bordes was obliged to partake in the Bible studies. Now he became assistant preacher. One of the manuscripts from the Joshua series has the heading "Summary of the *congrégation*, presented by Monsieur [des] Bordes on Chapter 23, by Mr. Calvin." Alas, only Calvin's closing statements in the *congrégation*, and not des Bordes' presentation from December 1563 were noted.[107] It seems that it was only in 1564 that des Bordes became minister (at St. Gervais).

The Registers contain a number of testimonies of good Christian conduct, asked of and given by the Company. One such letter concerns Antoine Herault; it provided him with a positive recommendation at the request of the ministers of Neuchâtel (November 1551). The testimony was unanimous: "Heraldus has lived among us in a manner befitting a Christian man. He has been a frequent attender at the sermons and lectures (*in concionibus et lectionibus*), and has devoted himself to the other exercises of piety."[108] Does this include regular attendance at the Bible studies? Having received this letter of recommendation from the Company, Antoine Herault was installed as minister of Valengin, a village in the Neuchâtel area, four months later.

## D. Confessional Formulations

We saw that theological discussion of doctrinal propositions was an important part of the *congrégations*. Connected to this function of doctrinal formulation were the various efforts to formulate consensus on the most debated issues between the churches. The fact that such articles on doctrine were written *in*

---

[103] RCP II: 110f. Perrot had to deliver a sermon on Romans 6. Perrot and Salvart were further examined *par forme de dispute* on various points of doctrine by Theodore de Bèze.

[104] RCP II: 67.

[105] RCP II: 70f.

[106] RCP II: 101. Des Bordes had studied in Geneva since 1562 (cf. Viret's letter of recommendation to Calvin on the young Jacques des Bordes, CO 19: 379). In 1566 he returned to his native town, Bordeaux. Pierre d'Airebaudouze had been sent to Montpellier.

[107] Ms.fr. 40b, f. 141a.

[108] RCP I: 77.

*extenso* in the Register testify to the importance of these discussions on doctrine in the bosom of the Company of Pastors in Geneva.

In 1549 a set of twenty articles on the sacraments was sent to Bern. There should be doctrinal unity between the churches because, as the Genevan ministers wrote, "some men from our Company are actually serving in churches on Bernese territory, just as on the other hand several of your men are in charge of churches within the dominion of Geneva." Ministers in remote villages especially suffered from the tensions between Bern and Geneva, as the Registers regularly testify. The articles on the sacraments were signed by all the ministers of Geneva.[109]

The most well-known example of doctrinal unity is the *Consensus Tigurinus*, created by Calvin and Bullinger. The Consensus is written in the Register and thereby incorporated in the doctrinal standard of Geneva.[110] A final, but lesser known example of doctrinal consensus arose out of the doctrinal dealings with Jerome Bolsec. The full theological dossier is incorporated in the Registers, but not a text of the consensus. This was formulated in a special *congrégation* on 18 December 1551 at the end of the trial against Bolsec. This time the topic was not a passage from the Gospel of John, which was discussed from 1550 to 1553, but a public presentation of the doctrine of predestination by Calvin with additional statements from twelve ministers and one of the lay members, Claude Baduel. The ministers regarded the contents of this *congrégation* as their *Consensus Genevensis*. To their regret, they were unable to persuade the other Swiss Churches to condemn Bolsec's teachings as clearly as they had expected in the wake of the Consensus Tigurinus.[111] These three examples of doctrinal formulations are connected to the Company of Pastors and the doctrinal aims of the Bible studies.

---

[109] RCP I: 51-55. Only the name of Philippe d'Ecclesia is missing, probably because he was excluded from the Company and stayed home in the village of Vandoeuvres.

[110] RCP I:64-70.

[111] The text of this *congrégation* is printed in CO 8:89-140. The manuscript of these presentations, probably written by the scribe Denis Raguenier, has not been preserved. The text was published only in 1562 (*Bibliotheca Calviniana*, vol. 2: 62/6). Often Calvin's book of January 1552, *De aeterna Dei praedestinatione*, is regarded as the "Consensus Genevensis." This is due to a faulty translation of the sub-title of that work: *Consensus Pastorum Genevensis Ecclesiae à Io. Calvino expositus* (translated for example by Wilhelm H. Neuser as "entworfen von Johann Calvin," in: *Johannes Calvin: Von der ewigen Vorherbestimmung Gottes*, ed. Wilhelm H. Neuser (Düsseldorf, 1998), 1). A better translation of the sub-title is: "The Consensus of the Pastors of the Church of Geneva [that is: as expressed on 18 December 1551], Explained by John Calvin." I am preparing a fuller chapter on the Bolsec case in the context of the Bible studies and on the *congrégation* of 18 December 1551 as the "Consensus Genevensis."

## VI. Conclusion

The weekly meeting for Bible study must have had a profound influence in making the Company of Pastors into a coherent and competent body. As in Zurich, the ministers of the Word in Geneva took and kept the lead in the Bible studies. However, compared to Zwingli's institution, the character of the *congrégations* in Geneva was less academic. The primacy of the biblical languages, the Septuagint, and the Latin translation of the Bible were left to the ministers' personal preparations. The biblical text was read and the studies were conducted in French so that the public could profit from the discussions. The role of regular visitors was more active than in Zurich, but still restricted to the discussion time. The character of the *congrégations* can be described as ministerial, compared to the academic stature of the *Prophezei* in Zurich and the more democratic form as advanced by John à Lasco in London, Jean Morély in France, and in the later *prophesyings* of the Puritan movement.[112]

We end this essay with a practical question: was the *congrégation* a place where the ministers or visitors felt safe to express their opinions or raise questions? Or was the role of reformed doctrine and the Company of Pastors as a body too oppressive? The answer to this question depended on one's own stand on the role of doctrine. The standard for orthodoxy was the Catechism of Geneva. Yes, there could be censure at the end of the line. But first there was always ongoing confrontation with the books of the Bible, opportunity for discussion of doctrine and the stimulus of every colleague presenting on an equal basis both exegesis and propositions. Even the brotherly critique in its regular form must not be seen as "censure," but as part of the process of ongoing education. Thus the *congrégation*, seen in its primary function, was an in-service theological training center for the members of the Company of Pastors. Observed in the light of secondary effects, these Bible study meetings were a stimulus for the Reformed movement as a whole. They played a role in the writing of biblical commentaries, educating the laity, shaping the development of young ministers and furthering the confessional development of the Reformed church.

---

[112] See Denis, "La prophétie dans les Églises de la Réforme," 289-316. See on Jean Morély his *Traicté de la discipline & police chrestienne* (Lyon : Ian de Tournes,, 1562 ; reprint Genève : Slatkine Reprints, 1968), Chapter 4, and Philippe Denis – Jean Rott, *Jean Morély (ca 1524 – ca 1594) et l'utopie d'une démocratie dans l'Église* (Travaux d'Humanisme et Renaissance, vol. 278) (Genève : Librairie Droz, 1993), 78-83. On the Netherlands : F.A. van Lieburg, *De reformatorische profetie in de Nederlandse traditie* (Apeldoorn: Willem de Zwijgerstichting, 2001).

# A Response to "The *Congrégation:* An In-Service Training Center for Preachers to the People of Geneva"

*G. Sujin Pak*

Erik de Boer has richly contextualized and clarified the definition, character, and functions of the *congrégation* of Geneva by defining it as a "Bible study meeting" and highlighting its direct ties to biblical exegesis, ministerial training, preaching, and the preservation of doctrinal unity. He has also underscored the correspondence of Calvin's own commentaries from 1549 forward to these Friday biblical study meetings and demonstrated the significant lay interest and attendance in these meetings. Finally, de Boer has provided clear examples of the functions of the *congrégation* in the education of candidates for ministry, the instruction of lay people, and the establishment of a kind of forum for confessional formulation and the refutation of false doctrines.

My comments contain very little direct critique, as this is a new area of study for me. Instead, I will highlight and suggest various avenues this essay raises for further discussion. Furthermore, since Professor de Boer has indicated the important and perhaps central role of Calvin in the *congrégation*, I would also like to supplement this discussion with a few insights from Calvin's *Institutes* and prefaces to some of his commentaries that I think pertain to the theoretical and practical institution of the *congrégation*. Finally, I want to suggest continuing fruitful projects to which I see this essay pointing Calvin scholars.

As the available sources for these Bible study meetings demonstrate the predominance of John Calvin, so do the content and purposes of these meetings loudly resound the concerns of Calvin in their emphases on pedagogy, usefulness, edification, and clarity in order to gain—as Calvin says—"a pure and simple understanding of Scripture and to employ it in the best way for the instruction of all."[1] We find echoed in the practices of these Bible study meetings the pedagogical imagery in Calvin's *Institutes* when he describes Scripture as a tutor and the church as a school.[2] Furthermore, Calvin's firm conviction that proper biblical exposition must be useful for the edification of the church

---

[1] CO 13:376.

[2] *Institutes* 4.1.4.

is a principle clearly at work here in the *congrégation*.[3] Indeed, one of my own fascinations with the Genevan *congrégation* is its possibilities as an embodiment of some of Calvin's key exegetical principles.

I find here another important connection between Calvin's own expressed exegetical principles and the practices of the *congrégation* of Geneva. In his dedication of his commentary on Romans and, even more clearly, in his words to the reader of the 1559 edition of the *Institutes* Calvin describes the importance of communal exegesis (or a community of exegetes), the need for accountability amongst fellow disciples of Christ in the practice of interpreting Scripture, and the necessity for others less qualified or experienced in biblical exposition to be taught by those more skilled. We find the following portrayal from Calvin's 1559 edition of the *Institutes* come to life in the practices of the *congrégation*:

> Although Holy Scripture contains a perfect doctrine, to which one can add nothing ... yet a person who has not much practice in it has good reason for some guidance and direction, to know what [one] ought to look for in it ... Perhaps the duty of those who have received from God fuller light than others is to help simple folk at this point, and as it were to lend them a hand, in order to guide them and help them to find the sum of what God meant to teach us in his Word.[4]

The *congrégation* appears to be a school of exegesis operating on several levels: the opportunity for ministers to be occupied in regular biblical interpretation with constructive and critical feedback, the education of future ministers in the art of scriptural exposition, and the instruction of the laity in the proper understanding of Scripture. In addition to the importance of being trained in the interpretation of Scripture, Calvin also emphasizes the importance of accountability in the *Institutes* and in these commentary prefaces—an emphasis found in the biblical study meetings as well, as one of its functions involved the establishment of a system of accountability for the regular study of Scripture among the Genevan pastors through the encouragement toward diligence and the likely accompanying pressure to use the biblical languages to interpret the text.

---

[3] For example, he begins the preface to the 1560 French edition of his *Institutes*, "In order that my readers may better profit from this present work, I should like to indicate briefly the benefit they may derive from it" (6, see also p. 8). For other examples, see *Institutes* 4.6.3; 1.17.1; 2.2.16; 3.21.3; 4.1.10. In his comments on 2 Tim. 3:16, Calvin sees in Paul's words a commendation of Scripture on account of its authority and on account of its utility (*Commentaries on the Epistles to Timothy, Titus, and Philemon*, trans. Rev. William Pringle [Grand Rapids, Mich.: William B. Eerdmans, 1948], 248-50). Calvin also names the overriding purpose of his labors in several of his commentaries as an ecclesial purpose. For example, in his dedication of his commentary on Romans to Simon Gryneus, Calvin conveys, "I do not dare to say anything of myself, except that I thought that the present work would be of some profit, and that I have been led to undertake it for no other reason than the common good of the church" (CO 10:403-405). Likewise in his preface to the Psalms Calvin proclaims, "I have held nothing to be of more importance than the edification of the church" (CR 59:35, 36).

[4] *Institutes*, 6.

Furthermore, this emphasis on accountability manifested itself in the possibility of brotherly censure.

ÉFrom Professor de Boer's presentation of the correspondence of Calvin's commentaries from 1549 forward to these Friday Bible study meetings, there is an important and useful challenge to the scholars and students of Calvin's commentaries. What does it mean to consider the *congrégation* as a social or exegetical context for Calvin's commentaries after 1549? Can one note any kind of alteration in style, tone, or method in the later commentaries as opposed to his earlier ones? Are there evidences of a kind of communal exegesis at work in these commentaries? How much is Calvin himself a student and man among his peers, or does the prominent mark of Calvin on the Bible study meetings indicate that Calvin was its primary teacher?

The correspondence between Calvin's commentaries and the order of study in the Bible studies meetings also points us to the project of comparing the texts of Calvin's commentaries to the records of the *congrégations* of Calvin's exposition on the same biblical books. Perhaps this project could begin to answer some of the questions raised in the previous paragraph. If I had one criticism of de Boer's essay, it would be that it would have been very interesting if he had taken a small passage as a test case for the comparison and contrast of Calvin's commentaries and his work in the Bible studies meetings. However, I understand that this essay is part of a larger work, and I look forward to Professor de Boer's further work in this field.

Professor De Boer has described a case in which the *congrégation* acted as a testing ground for current ministers in the instance of Philippe de Ecclesia, and cases (Bolsec and Castellio) in which the Bible study meeting also acted as a testing ground for certain laymen who sought a calling to the ministry and desired a platform in which they may express religious ideas and gain recognition. Both Castellio (in 1544) and Bolsec (in 1551) used the forum of the *congrégation* to express their contrary theological ideas and to challenge and criticize John Calvin.[5] This leads to another important aspect that merits further discussion. The cases of Castellio and Bolsec reveal the risk of doctrinal disturbance in these Friday Bible study meetings. We might ask why the Company of Pastors and Calvin in particular would take this risk.[6] Another question is why

---

[5] Castellio began a doctrinal disturbance at one of the biblical study meetings on Friday, 30 May 1544. The Register of the Company of the Pastors of Geneva gives the account of Jerome Bolsec and shows that he instigated a doctrinal disturbance at a Friday biblical study meeting. See Philip Edgcumbe Hughes, trans. and ed., *The Register of the Company of Pastors of Geneva in the Time of Calvin* (Grand Rapids, MI: William B. Eerdmans, 1966), 137. This event is dated Friday, 16 October 1551. See the discussions in James Mackinnon, *Calvin and the Reformation* (New York: Russell & Russell, 1962), 113-114, 117-119) and Bernard Cottret, *Calvin: A Biography*, 296-297.

[6] For example, Calvin writes in his commentary on Romans that uppermost in his mind was what would best assist "humbler minds" and "simple-minded readers." He clearly states that a commentary that provides various interpretations of a passage "creates much difficulty for simple-minded readers, who are hesitant as to which opinion they ought to accept." Instead, Calvin

allow lay involvement at all at the *congrégation*. Perhaps one answer is found in Calvin's letter to Wolfgang Musculus already mentioned by de Boer in which Calvin warned Musculus of the danger of *not* having these *congrégations*—that the less communication on matters of doctrine, the more dangerous the possibilities that destructive doctrines will spread.[7] Thus, not only did these meetings act to ensure that the Genevan pastors were regularly involved in the practice of interpreting Scripture, they also acted to ensure the proper formulation and preservation of doctrine not only among the pastors, but also among candidates for ministry and lay persons. To de Boer's list of the tasks of the *congrégation* I might add, then, that it functioned to *root out* heresy by the very space it allowed for disputation.

Finally, I find in Erik de Boer's essay an intriguing suggestion on the role of biblical exposition in the process of confessional formation. While the role of sermons has long been recognized as a primary source for the process of confessional formation and the social regulation of doctrine, biblical exegesis and commentaries in particular have often been considered by some to have had much less of a role in this process. The understanding of the *congrégation* as a Bible study meeting open to the public and the practices of these meetings indicate that the role of biblical exegesis in the social regulation of doctrine may need to be reevaluated. An issue also raised is the role of these Bible study meetings in actually regulating the doctrinal purity of sermons themselves—another concern often expressed by John Calvin.[8] Questions we might consider include the following: How much were the Bible study meetings about *controlling* doctrine, especially since the understanding of the purpose of these meetings as retaining consensus in doctrine in the end meant that a heterodox view could not be endured (i.e., the dissenter must either acquiesce or be silenced)? How much did these meetings operate from the top down, whether explicitly by the authority of the dean as described in the *Ecclesiastical Ordinances* of 1541[9] or implicitly by virtue of the influential power Calvin possessed? Or to reiterate the question with which de Boer concluded his essay, "Was participation in the *congrégation* attractive to pastors and lay people, or was the Company of Pastors and these Bible study meetings too oppressive?" As Professor de Boer points out, the opportunity for open study of biblical books and discussion of

---

undertakes the task himself to point to the best interpretation and "relieves them of the trouble of forming a judgment" (CO 10:403-405). For one who would rather make the judgment for his readers, it is interesting that he would condone a forum that potentially invites different interpretations.

[7] CO 13:490.

[8] The connections De Boer has drawn between the *congrégation* and preaching also resonate with Calvin's own concerns for the strengthening and preservation of proper and pure preaching. For Calvin, the church is the "faithful keeper of God's truth," for, he writes, "by its ministry and labor God willed to have the preaching of the Word kept pure." (*Institutes*, 4.1.10).

[9] CO 13:375f.

doctrine in which everyone is able to participate at some level must have been attractive, especially given the number of lay people who attended according to the records of these meetings. And while brotherly critique was just a part of the process of theological training, the consequences for some such as D'Ecclesia, Castellio, and Bolsec were severe.

These comments and questions are just an attempt to begin a larger conversation; so without further ado, I open the floor to discussion in hopes that others far more knowledgeable than I in the history of Calvin and Geneva will shed more insight. Thank you, Dr. Erik de Boer, for your stimulating essay and my thanks to the Calvin Studies Society for this opportunity for the pursuit of further knowledge.

# A Tale of Three Churches: Parishes and Pastors in Basel, Strasbourg, and Geneva

*Amy Nelson Burnett*

## I. Introduction and Terminology

In Charles Dickens' classic novel, *A Tale of Two Cities*, Lucie Manette and her father flee the political persecution of pre-revolutionary Paris to lead a quiet life in London. Some two hundred and fifty years before the French Revolution, a very real Frenchman named Jean Calvin fled growing religious persecution in Paris to pursue a quiet life of scholarship—though he settled in Basel, not London. After leaving Basel for Geneva in 1536, Calvin was forced into exile again, living in Strasbourg for three years before returning to Geneva in 1541.

Scholars have long recognized the importance of Calvin's years in Basel and Strasbourg for his development as the reformer of Geneva. Calvin formed close friendships with Simon Grynaeus in Basel and especially with Martin Bucer in Strasbourg. In Basel he observed the establishment and development of a reformed ministry, while in Strasbourg he participated in that ministry as pastor of the French church. Calvin's experiences in the first two cities helped shape his practical understanding of the ministry he helped establish in the third. But Calvin was not totally free to shape Geneva's church as he wished. Like his counterparts in the two German-speaking cities, he had to work within existing structures and constraints. Comparisons across time and between the three cities thus combine to provide a broader context for understanding the reformed ministry established in Geneva.

An examination of the pastoral ministry in Basel, Strasbourg and Geneva before and in the three decades after the Reformation yields some surprising results. There were significant differences in the structure of the ministry and the provision of pastoral care between the German-speaking cities on the one hand and Geneva on the other. Those differences are most striking in four areas: the quality and quantity of preaching and pastoral care before the Reformation; the significance of the parish after the Reformation; the number of pastors and the turnover rate among them; and the overall composition of the pastoral corps.

A comparison of pastoral care that begins with the late medieval parish clergy must first clarify the terminology used. The priests directly responsible for pastoral care in the late medieval church were given a variety of titles in Latin, German and French, and the word used in one language did not necessarily mean the same as its cognate in another language. This situation is complicated by the fact that the English words used to translate the French, German or Latin terms reflect developments in England, which differed from those on the Continent. Terminological precision is important, though, because there were very important legal, economic and social distinctions among those priests responsible for the cure of souls.[1]

Generally speaking, the late medieval parish clergy could be divided into three groups, distinguished by social status, pastoral responsibilities, income level, and job security. At the top of the parish hierarchy were the *rectors,* who were the legal holders of a parish benefice. They were appointed for life and entrusted with the responsibility for and the legal monopoly over the cure of souls. In return, they received the income from the parish benefice. A rector could be an individual, but it could also be an ecclesiastical corporation such as a monastery or collegiate church. For the purpose of this paper, where the rectors were non-resident or otherwise not personally involved with pastoral care, they are not counted among the parish clergy.

The *curates* were the priests who actually exercised the cure of souls. This group could include a resident rector, a vicar who carried out the pastoral duties of a non-resident rector, or the *Leutpriester* who was appointed to incorporated parishes, where the incumbent of the benefice was an ecclesiastical institution. Both vicars and *Leutpriester* were paid by the rector out of the revenues of the parish benefice. They also had the right to fees paid for the performance of their sacramental and liturgical duties. Their appointment could be permanent and irrevocable, especially for curates serving incorporated parishes, or for a fixed term and contractual.[2]

Lastly, there were *coadjutors* or *assistants,* priests hired by the rector or the curate to assist in the cure of souls. Assistants were often newly-ordained priests who served a type of apprenticeship under older and more experienced curates. The assistants were also supported out of the rector's benefice or by the ecclesiastical corporation into which the parish had been incorporated. The

---

[1] To give one example of the difficulties, *rector ecclesiae* was used in Alsace for the legal holder of a parish benefice with cure of souls, but in French, a *recteur* was only a chantry priest. For a good overview of the German and Latin terms for the parish clergy, from which my usage is derived, see L. Pfleger, "Untersuchungen zur Geschichte des Pfarrei-Instituts im Elsass. II. Der Pfarrklerus," *Archiv für Elsässische Kirchengeschichte* 7 (1932): 1-100, especially 3-14.

[2] There is no single term to describe the individual who bore the chief pastoral responsibilities for, as opposed to collecting the income of, the parish benefice. Such a term is needed, however, to distinguish these men from their assistants or coadjutors, often also called vicars. While there were differences in status between resident rectors, vicars hired by non-resident rectors, and *Leutpriester* hired by ecclesiastical institutions, these three were closer to each other than they were to the coadjutors sometimes hired to assist them.

assistant's position was contractual and of fixed term. He was entirely depen-dent on the rector or ecclesiastical corporation that had hired him.[3] Although chaplains or altar-priests might be obliged to assist in pastoral care where nec-essary, particularly in rural parishes, for the most part they had no pastoral responsibilities.

This hierarchy within the parochial clergy had implications for the quality of pastoral care in the late medieval church. For instance, the hiring of an assistant could ease the workload of the curate, but it also diminished the revenues of the benefice's incumbent. Where the curate and the rector were not identical, the position of assistant could bring about a conflict of interest, for the help he brought to the former came at the expense of the latter. The traces of this parish hierarchy continued to varying degrees in each city after the Reforma-tion. This is most true for Basel.

## II. Basel

Although it was not the earliest of the cities to adopt the Reformation, Basel was the first to create institutional structures for its new church, and the prac-tices it established would influence those of the other two cities. Perhaps because it was the first, Basel was also the most conservative of the three churches in its retention of the parish as the basic unit of pastoral care.

At the time of the Reformation, Basel had eight parish churches for its roughly 10,000 inhabitants. In addition to its curate or acting parish priest, each of the larger parishes also had one or two assistants who aided the curate in his liturgical and pastoral duties. Among those duties, according to the statutes of Basel's episcopal synod of 1503, was explaining the day's Gospel text in a brief sermon during the parish mass on Sundays. Priests were also enjoined to speak the Lord's Prayer, the Ave Maria, and the Apostles' Creed or the Ten Commandments in German every Sunday.[4] In addition to the parish pastors, the city hospital had a priest responsible for the pastoral care of its residents. Last but certainly not least, the city had two endowed preacherships affiliated with the cathedral and a third at the collegiate church of St. Peter. The preacher of St. Peter was also required to assist with pastoral care. The city thus had about sixteen secular clergy who provided regular preaching and pastoral

---

[3] Pfleger, "Untersuchungen," 37-48. Such assistants, or "vicaires coopérateurs," were common in the diocese of Geneva as well; see Louis Binz, *Vie Réligieuse et Réforme Ecclésiastique dans le Diocèse de Genève pendant le grand schisme et la crise conciliaire (1378-1450)*, Mémoires et Documents Publiés par la Société d'Histoire et d'Archéologie de Genève 41 (Geneva: Julien, 1973), 437-40.

[4] Hermann Scholl, ed., *Concilia Germaniae*. Vol. 6: *Concilia 1500-1564* (Aalen: Scientia, 1982), 8. On the renewed emphasis on parish preaching during the fifteenth century, see Michael Menzel, "Predigt und Predigtorganisation im Mittelalter," *Historisches Jahrbuch* 111 (1991): 337-384.

care, although they had both assistance and competition from the mendicant houses—both Franciscans and Dominicans—in the city.[5]

Basel's pre-Reformation church was dominated by ecclesiastical institutions. All of the city's parish churches were incorporated into one of the city's religious foundations, making these institutions ultimately responsible for pastoral care. Although such incorporation was open to abuse, it could also prevent abuse, for it meant that the city's parish clergy were all under the supervision of the corporation that appointed them. A series of reforms within the city's collegiate churches and monasteries in the later fifteenth century had done much to improve both the quantity and the quality of Basel's parish clergy. An investigation instigated by the Council of Basel, for instance, led to the hiring of a second assistant for the parish of St. Theodor. Several of Basel's curates, as well as its three preachers, were hired under contractual agreements specifying that the incumbents be learned men who would reside in the city, live appropriately, and perform their duties satisfactorily. Priests who did not meet these requirements could be removed from office.

The presence of a university in the city also contributed to the relatively high educational level of Basel's parish clergy. It not only created the expectation that curates would be well-educated, but it also provided a pool of educated candidates who could serve as parish clergy. Twelve of the seventeen curates whom I have identified as serving Basel's parish churches during the 1520s had some university education, and most had earned at least a bachelor's degree. Several had studied in Basel and retained some affiliation with the university even after appointment to a parish post.

As Luther's ideas began to spread through Basel, they found enthusiastic support among many of the city's inhabitants, but not among the majority of the parish clergy.[6] The curates and preachers of the cathedral parish and of St. Peter proved to be steadfast opponents of the evangelical movement. Two of the city's eight parish priests supported the growing evangelical movement in the early 1520s, but one of them lost his post in 1522. The same fate threatened the other, but Marx Bertschi became curate of St. Leonhard before he could be deposed from St. Theodor, which became the most staunchly Catholic parish in the city. Under Bertschi's leadership, St. Leonhard became one of the focal

---

[5] On the development and staffing of Basel's medieval parishes, see Johannes Bernoulli, "Die Kirchgemeinden Basels vor der Reformation," *Basler Jahrbuch* (1894): 220-243; (1895): 99-162. Eduard Lengwiler discusses Basel's preacherships in a broader context, *Die vorreformatorischen Prädikaturen der deutschen Schweiz von ihrer Entstehung bis 1530* (Fribourg: Kanisius, 1955), passim.

[6] The most detailed treatment of the decade of the 1520s is Rudolf Wackernagel, *Geschichte der Stadt Basel* (Basel: Helbing & Lichtenhahn, 1907-1925), 3: 317-524; there is a brief presentation in English in Hans R. Guggisberg, *Basel in the Sixteenth Century. Aspects of the City Republic Before, During and After the Reformation* (St. Louis: Center for Reformation Research, 1982), 19-35; see also Paul Roth, *Die Reformation in Basel, I. Teil: Die Vorbereitungsjahre (1525-1528)*, Basler Neujahrsblatt 114 (Basel: Helbing & Lichtenhahn, 1936), 5-14.

points for the evangelical movement. Another parish church joined the evangelical movement in 1523, when Johann Oecolampadius was appointed as the vicar for the ailing curate of St. Martin, and then became the official curate two years later. The assistant priests of both churches followed the lead of their curates in supporting the Reformation, as did the priest of the hospital and a few of the city's mendicants; but in 1525, two more evangelically-inclined curates were deposed and replaced with loyal Catholic priests.[7]

Basel's Council had supported Oecolampadius' appointment to St. Martin, but it did not assume patronage rights for the other parish positions until after the final victory of the evangelical party in 1529. With the adoption of the Reformation, the magistrate took the opportunity to consolidate the city's parish structure. The smallest parish was eliminated, and three other parish churches lost their independent status to become subordinate to the cathedral parish. The changes left Basel with four parish churches, each of whose pastors had at least one assistant, the three filial churches, each with one pastor, and a preacher for the hospital.[8]

The Reformation also brought a general shuffling of parish posts, as evangelical pastors were recruited to replace the curates who had left the city rather than accept the Reformation. The vacant posts proved fairly easy to fill: they went to the assistant priests and former mendicants who had led the evangelical movement through the 1520s. Only two pastors had to be recruited from outside the city. At the end of 1529, the city had a dozen pastors, and another pastor was added in 1533. The number of city pastors would remain constant at thirteen for the rest of the century. This was a drastic reduction in the total number of clergy within the city, but it was not much less than the number associated with the parish ministry before the Reformation.[9]

Basel's ministry was thus almost fully staffed from the official foundation of its reformed church. There was, however, a great deal of instability in the composition of the city's clergy during its early years (Table 1). Although three of the city's evangelical pastors were still at their posts at mid-century, five of the twelve men in office in 1529 had either died or left the city by 1539, and some of the pastors appointed to replace them did not remain very long. In the decade fol-

---

[7] The parish church of St. Ulrich had an evangelical curate in 1523, but the priest was suspended after he married in 1524 and deposed early the following year. The priest of St. Alban, appointed after his predecessor was deposed in 1522, also had evangelical leanings, but he was dismissed and expelled from the city in 1525; Wackernagel, *Geschichte*, 467-8.

[8] The new parish structure was outlined in the Reformation ordinance of 1529; see Emil Durr and Paul Roth, eds. *Aktensammlung zur Geschichte des Basler Reformation in den Jahren 1519 bis Anfang 1534* (Basel: Historische und antiquarische Gesellschaft, 1921-1950), 3: 388-89. Hereafter, ABR.

[9] The names of the city clergy are listed at each synod. The first synod, held in May, 1529, listed eleven city pastors (ABR 3: 483-84). The synod of May 1533 listed twelve pastors (ABR 6: 270), while the spring 1534 synod participant list has thirteen city pastors plus the theology professor Simon Grynaeus; see Basel Staatsarchiv, Kirchen Akten C3, 26r-27r. Hereafter, BstA.

lowing the Reformation, ten men were appointed as city pastors. Turnover among the city clergy continued to be fairly high through the next two decades, with nine new pastors appointed during the 1540s and six more during the 1550s. Taken altogether, 37 men served the Basel church in the thirty years after the Reformation. Twenty-four of these served only city parishes, and another nine held posts first in rural parishes and then moved into the city. Only four men began as city pastors and then moved to rural parishes.[10]

Most of Basel's pastors were outsiders who came to Basel from surrounding regions. Only seven of the 37 came from Basel itself, and only two of these were appointed before 1540. The largest group—seventeen pastors—came from the neighboring territories of Alsace and southwestern Germany. Eight more came from other parts of Switzerland. Only two pastors came from further away.

Recent studies of the late medieval clergy in south Germany and Switzerland have suggested that between 33-40% of the parish clergy had some university education.[11] The percentage of Basel's earliest Protestant pastors with a university education was well above that level—as it had been before the Reformation (Table 4). Over three-quarters of them (29 out of the 37) had at least some university education, and eleven had studied theology after receiving a master's degree. This high level of education was not the result of a gradual improvement after the Reformation but was present from the beginning: five of the thirteen pastors who served the Basel church in 1529 had doctorates in theology; another three had a university degree.

Nineteen of the 33 pastors whose background is known were former Catholic priests (Table 7). Twelve of these had held positions in Basel before the Reformation and were appointed to posts in the reformed church either at the time of the Reformation or over the course of the next decade. All of these men belonged to the generation that had reached adulthood at the time of the Reformation. The few former priests appointed to Basel posts after 1540 were also older men who had broken with the Catholic church in the 1520s. The remainder of the appointments from the 1540s on went to a new group: young

---

[10] Biographical information on Basel's pastors drawn from Karl Gauss, *Basilea Reformata. Die Gemeinden der Kirche Basel. Stadt und Land und Ihre Pfarrer seit der Reformation bis zur Gegenwart* (Basel: Historische und antiquarische Gesellschaft, 1930); and Hans Georg Wackernagel, ed., *Die Matrikel der Universität Basel* (Basel: Verlag der Universitätsbibliothek, 1951ff), vol. 1-2.

[11] According to Francis Rapp, about one-third of the secular clergy in the diocese of Strasbourg had some university education, *Réformes et Réformation à Strasbourg: Église et Société dans le diocese de Strasbourg (1450-1525)* (Paris: Ophrys, 1974), 430-32; see also his "Communautés rurales et paroisses en Basse-Alsace jusqu'à la fin du XVIe siècle," in *Les Communautés rurales. Rural Communities.* Vol. IV. *Europe occidentale (Italie-Espagne-France).* 20e Congrès de la Société Jean Bodin, Varsovie, mai 1976 (Paris: Dessain & Tobra, 1984), 459-470. Oskar Vasalla says the percentage of clergy with some university education was about 40% in the diocese of Chur, and even higher among urban clergy; see Oskar Vasalla, "Über das Problem der Klerusbildung im 16. Jahrhundert," *Mitteilungen des Instituts für Österreichische Geschichtsforschung* 58 (1950): 441-456.

men who had been trained specifically for the Protestant ministry and had served either as teachers or as Protestant pastors in a rural parish before being promoted to a city parish.

Basel's Reformation ordinance of 1529 firmly anchored the new church within the older parish structure.[12] The ordinance largely retained the division of labor between pastors and their assistants that had existed in the pre-Reformation church. The parish pastors preached for the main worship service on Sunday, administered the sacraments, visited the sick, and were responsible for doctrinal and moral oversight of their parishioners. The assistant pastors preached the weekday morning sermons and assisted the senior pastor in his other duties. The assistants were referred to as deacons, but their responsibilities were in fact the same as the pre-reformation coadjutors or assistant priests.[13] The Reformation brought about a distinct improvement in the position of these assistant pastors, since they now had permanent posts and established stipends paid by the magistrate.

The ordinance also retained a modified form of the medieval *Pfarrzwang,* the requirement that parishioners attend their parish mass on Sundays and seek pastoral care, particularly confession and yearly communion, from their parish priest. Although Baslers were free to hear weekday sermons wherever they wished, they were required to attend the main worship service on Sunday and to receive the Lord's Supper only in their parish church. This requirement was justified on two grounds: it hindered the spread of Anabaptist views, and it made the exercise of church discipline more effective.

The system of ecclesiastical discipline introduced in Basel at the end of 1530 also functioned within the existing parish structure, although this was not part of the original plan proposed by Oecolampadius. The Basel reformer envisioned a twelve-man commission charged with disciplinary oversight for the entire city, in the same way, for instance, that the marriage court had responsibility for all marriage cases in the city. Oecolampadius recommended that this disciplinary commission be comprised of the four parish pastors, four Council members, and a layman from each parish. The Council apparently feared the public attention that such a committee might receive and shied away from creating a city-wide commission. After going through some revision, the final ban ordinance created instead a disciplinary body of *Bannherren* within each parish, comprised of two Council members and a layman, with the senior pastor acting in an advisory capacity. There was no expectation that the *Bannherren* from

---

[12] ABR 3: 389-90.

[13] The assistant priests were also called deacons in France. Glenn Sunshine discusses their function in the early French Reformed churches, but he draws a comparison with the Catholic order of deacon rather than with the ordained priests who functioned as assistants; see Glenn S. Sunshine, "Geneva Meets Rome: The Development of the French Reformed Diaconate," *Sixteenth Century Journal* 26 (1995): 329-346.

each parish would meet together, and the procedure created by the ordinance remained entirely at the parish level.[14]

Although the Council assumed all patronage rights over the city's churches, the procedure for choosing new clergy was not formally defined. In most cases the Council confirmed a nominee rather than making the selection itself. The procedure developed for appointment to positions in the city was yet another means of strengthening parish identity, for the election process involved some participation by the congregation concerned. Candidates for a parish post were expected to give a trial sermon to the congregation before an election for the position could be held. Those with the right to vote on a new pastor included Council members, guild leaders, government officials, university faculty, and teachers who resided in the parish, parish officials such as the *Bannherren,* and a few "honorable men" chosen from the parish.[15]

By the later sixteenth century, the voters chose among three nominees for parish pastor, but given the high level of turnover within Basel's ministry, it is doubtful that there was more than one candidate for any position in the decades immediately following the Reformation. In those cases where the congregation's choice of a pastor was limited to endorsing a single candidate, the actual selection of the city's ministers rested in the hands of the individual or group who had the right to nominate candidates. This right apparently belonged to the city's pastors, and particularly to the cathedral pastor who functioned as their leader. Basel's clergy may have met together on in informal basis even before the official adoption of the Reformation, but the first concrete evidence of such meetings in the sources dates from the early 1530s.[16]

---

[14] For Oecolampadius' original proposal, see Ernst Staehelin, ed., *Briefe und Akten zum Leben Oekolampads, zum vierhundertjährigen Jubiläum der Basler Reformation,* Quellen und Forschungen zur Reformationsgeschichte 10, 19 (Leipzig: Heinsius, 1927-34), 2: 448-61, no. 750; summary in Ernst Staehelin, *Das theologische Lebenswerk Johannes Oekolampads,* Quellen und Forschungen zur Reformationsgeschichte (Leipzig: Heinsius, 1939), 506-12. For the broader context of Oecolampadius' views on church discipline, see Olaf Kuhr, *"Die Macht des Bannes und der Buße". Kirchenzucht und Erneuerung der Kirche bei Johannes Oekolampad (1482 - 1531),* Basler und Berner Studien zur historischen und systematischen Theologie 68 (Bern: Peter Lang, 1999). The ban ordinance is printed in ABR 5: 60-62; also in Staehelin, *Briefe und Akten,* 2: 536-38, no. 809.

[15] When Oswald Myconius came to Basel in 1531 in the hope of being appointed pastor of St. Alban, he was required to give a trial sermon before that congregation; see Thomas Platter's account of Myconius' trial sermon in Heinrich Boos, ed., *Thomas und Felix Platter, Zur Sittengeschichte des XVI. Jahrhunderts* (Leipzig: Hirzel, 1878), 82-83. Simon Sulzer had served as vicar for pastor Wolfgang Wissenberg for a year before being elected as parish pastor of St. Peter in 1550, so there was no need for him to give a trial sermon; but his successor, Johann Jung, was invited from Aarau to give a trial sermon before he was elected in 1553. Cf. the lists of names of men entitled to elect the pastor of St. Peter in 1542, 1549, and 1553 (BStA Kirchen Archiv JJJ, St. Peter: Pfarrherr, nos. 5-10).

[16] The earliest mention of the meetings occurs in the diary of pastor Johannes Gast from May 1531; see Paul Burckhardt, ed., *Das Tagebuch des Johannes Gast. Ein Beitrag zur schweizerischen Reformationsgeschichte,* Basler Chroniken 8 (Basel: Schwabe, 1945), 149.

In fact, through the decade of the 1530s Basel's pastors showed themselves unable to function as a united body. In the months immediately following Oecolampadius' death in 1531, they were divided over the use of the ban, and only a visit by the Strasbourg reformer Wolfgang Capito was able to resolve the crisis. More serious divisions broke out in 1535, after the appointment of Andreas Karlstadt as pastor of St. Peter and theology professor at the university. In 1538 a proposed revision to the university statutes divided the city's pastors yet again, eventually developing into a power struggle between Karlstadt and Myconius.[17] There is no telling how this conflict would have ended if left to run its course, but it was cut short by Karlstadt's death in the plague epidemic of 1541.

The factionalism dividing Basel's clergy during the 1530s did immeasurable damage to the city's church. Perhaps its most significant long-term consequence was the way it changed the relationship between the church and the magistrate. In the early years of the Reformation, the pastors had met regularly in synods to present their grievances to the Council and to seek their help in improving church attendance, strengthening the authority of the pastors, and punishing all forms of irreligious or immoral behavior. The Council was initially willing to endorse the recommendations made at these synods. By the later 1530s, however, the previously cooperative relationship between clergy and magistrate had gone sour, and at the end of 1539 the Council issued a new ordinance that placed the church more tightly under the magistrate's control.[18] If Basel's church had become subservient to the city's magistrate, it was only because, at least from the magistrate's point of view, the pastors had proven incapable of solving their own problems and were instead disrupting the church.

This lesson was not lost on Jean Calvin, who observed the situation in Basel from his new home in Strasbourg. As he wrote to Guillaume Farel at the end of 1539, although Myconius and his supporters believed they were fighting for the liberty of the church, they were causing more harm than good.[19] If nothing else, the bitter divisions in Basel's church showed Calvin the importance of having a united ministry that presented a solid front to magistrate and laity. This lesson would have been driven home by the contrast between Basel's factionalized ministry and the relatively smooth functioning of Strasbourg's pastors as a collective body.

---

[17] Friedrich Rudolf, "Oswald Myconius, der Nachfolger Oekolampads," *Basler Jahrbuch* (1945): 14-30; Burckhardt, *Tagebuch*, 32-47.

[18] Amy Nelson Burnett, "Controlling the Clergy: The Oversight of Basel's Rural Pastors in the Sixteenth Century," *Zwingliana* 25 (1998): 129-142.

[19] 31 Dec. 1539, CO 10: 439. Myconius himself lamented the harmful effect of dissension among the city's clergy in a letter to Calvin, 10 Feb. 1542; CO 11: 367-369.

## III. Strasbourg

There are some striking similarities between the churches of Basel and Strasbourg on the eve of the Reformation. Despite its larger population—with close to 20,000 inhabitants, it was twice the size of Basel—Strasbourg had about the same number of parish clergy as did Basel. Fifteen or sixteen secular priests served as curates and assistants. Eight of the city's nine parishes were incorporated into collegiate chapters that appointed the curate; most of the churches had one or two assistants as well.[20] Strasbourg's ecclesiastical corporations had not been touched by the wave of reforms that Basel experienced, and there were complaints at the end of the fifteenth century about the rapid turnover among the city's curates. There were, however, a few exceptions to this gloomy picture. The curate of the cathedral parish, for instance, was traditionally an educated priest, and the cathedral preacher at the turn of the century, Geiler von Kaysersberg, was one of the city's best-known inhabitants. The parish pastors were expected to preach regularly—even if the laity preferred the sermons of the mendicants.[21]

As evangelical doctrines began to circulate in Strasbourg, the city's curates did not present a united front. Three parish priests supported the evangelical movement from its inception. It was perhaps the loyalty of the remaining curates to the old church that prompted the inhabitants of several parishes to assert the right to choose their own pastors. By August, 1524, the Council gave in to popular demand and assumed responsibility for all clerical appointments.[22]

As part of the process of assuming control of the city's church, the Council eliminated two of the city's parishes and re-assigned their inhabitants to one of the remaining seven parish churches. A few prominent newcomers who had become leaders of the evangelical movement had already been given parish posts by this time—Martin Bucer and Wolfgang Capito became pastors of St. Aurelien and New St. Peter respectively; Caspar Hedio, appointed cathedral preacher in 1523, had openly joined the evangelical side soon after arriving in the city. Within a relatively short time, the remaining parish posts were filled with regular clergy or with several of the assistant priests who had embraced the reform.

Nevertheless, it took several years before the city had a full complement of evangelical clergy. In 1525, Strasbourg had only twelve pastors: eight parish pas-

---

[20] Mirium U. Chrisman, *Strasbourg and the Reform: A Study in the Process of Change* (New Haven: Yale University Press, 1967), 32-33; Luzian Pfleger, *Kirchengeschichte der Stadt Strassburg im Mittelalter*, Forschungen zur Kirchengeschichte des Elsass 6 (Colmar: Alsatia Verlag, 1941), 45-54.

[21] Francis Rapp describes the economic situations that made rapid turnover among the vicars almost inevitable, *Réformes et Réformation*, 306-18; cf. Pfleger's description of late medieval pastoral care, *Kirchengeschichte*, 163-164.

[22] Chrisman, *Strasbourg*, 113-16; William S. Stafford, *Domesticating the Clergy. The Inception of the Reformation in Strassburg 1522-1524*, American Academy of Religion Dissertation Series 17 (Missoula: Scholars Press, 1976), 166-175.

tors, three of them with assistants, plus the cathedral preacher (Table 2).[23] This core of parish pastors proved remarkably long-lived. Six of the twelve were still in office twenty years later, although some of them were in failing health. The challenge facing Strasbourg's newly reformed ministry was not so much one of turnover among the existing clergy, as in Basel, but rather a shortage of qualified pastors, particularly assistants who would work with the parish pastors. This staffing problem was gradually remedied over the course of the next decade, as a dozen more men were appointed to the ministry, all as assistant pastors. By the mid-1530s, the city had eighteen ministers; after the Interim the number stabilized at a little over twenty posts.[24] Turnover among these pastors was fairly low. Only five new pastors were hired between 1536-1545, and even with the disruptions to Strasbourg's church caused by the imposition of the Interim, only eight more men were hired in the decade 1546-1555.

The men who served Strasbourg's evangelical church were very similar to their Basel counterparts in background and training. Between 1525-1555, at least 38 men held pastoral positions in Strasbourg. Strasbourg had a somewhat larger number of local pastors at the beginning of the Reformation than did Basel, but outsiders still predominated. Seven of the city's pastors were native Strasbourgers. Four of these were among the first evangelical clergy; over the next thirty years only three more Strasbourgers entered the city's ministry. Twelve more pastors came from the surrounding areas of Alsace or just across the Rhine in southwestern Germany. Ten pastors came from the Palatinate or Württemberg, a reflection of the city's diplomatic, political and economic ties with those areas that extended back to the fifteenth century. Their presence in Strasbourg is analogous to that of the pastors from other parts of Switzerland who served in Basel.[25] The remaining six pastors came from other parts of Germany.

Strasbourg's ministers were well educated, though they lagged somewhat behind their Basel counterparts in this regard (Table 5). Over half had some university education. Eleven had received their masters' degrees, and several of

---

[23] The eighth parish, St. Wilhelm, was suppressed the following year.

[24] Lorna Jane Abray lists only thirteen members of the church assembly in 1536 and sixteen in 1552; see Lorna Jane Abray, *The People's Reformation: Magistrates, Clergy, and Commons in Strasbourg, 1500-1598* (Ithaca: Cornell University Press, 1985), 242-243. There were, however, eighteen city pastors who submitted to censure at the 1533 synod; see Hans Georg Rott et al., ed., *Quellen zur Geschichte der Taufer. Elsass I.-IV. Teil* (Gutersloh, 1959-1988), 2:49-54. Hereafter listed as TAE. Bornert's estimate of 25 or 26 pastors generalizes for the entire century and includes two suburban churches, the French church and a short-term preachership at one of the city's convents; see Bornert, *La Réforme protestante du culte à Strasbourg au XVI. siècle,* Studies in Medieval and Reformation Thought 28 (Leiden: E.J. Brill, 1981), 54. Biographical information for these pastors from Marie-Joseph Bopp, *Die evangelischen Geistlichen und Theologen in Elsass und Lothringen von der Reformation bis zur Gegenwart* (Neustadt a.d. Aisch: Degener, 1959).

[25] K. Stenzel, "Straßburg, Basel und das Reich am Ende des Mittelalters," *Zeitschrift für die Geschichte des Oberrheins* 104 (1956): 455-488.

them had formal training in theology. As in Basel, the men who assumed posts at the beginning of the Reformation were among the best educated: nine of them had earned master's degrees, and seven of these had gone on to study theology. Four of these nine men were parish clergy in the early 1520s, which implies that in Strasbourg, as in Basel, even before the Reformation there was an expectation that the parish clergy have a university degree.

It may have been difficult for the Reformers to maintain those high standards in the wake of the Reformation, however. There is no information about the educational level of seven out of the twelve men who entered Strasbourg's ministry between 1526-1535. Four had at least matriculated at a university but seem not to have received degrees; a fifth (Wolfgang Musculus, the later Reformed theologian) was a former monk who received his education within his order. In recruiting its clergy, Strasbourg did not have the advantages of Basel, whose university made a significant difference in raising the educational level of the new Protestant clergy. Nevertheless, both Basel and Strasbourg provide specific evidence to support Robert Scribner's conclusion that the preachers of the Reformation were much better educated than the population as a whole, and that as a group they demonstrated considerable geographic mobility.[26]

Like their Basel counterparts, Strasbourg's earliest pastors came largely from the Catholic priesthood: at least eighteen and perhaps as many as 23 were either secular or regular clergy before the Reformation (Table 8). As in Basel, almost all of these priests were appointed within a decade of the Reformation: only four former priests entered the Strasbourg ministry after 1535. The pastors appointed in the 1540s were young men specifically educated for the ministry in Strasbourg, Basel and/or Wittenberg; a few of them had been Protestant pastors elsewhere before coming to Strasbourg.

Strasbourg's parishes remained the basic level of ecclesiastical organization after the Reformation. As in Basel, the parishes were most important for the exercise of church discipline and the detection of Anabaptists. In October 1531, the Council created the office of *Kirchspilpfleger*, or parish warden, modeled on Basel's *Bannherren*.[27] Each of Strasbourg's parishes had three wardens: one from the ruling Council, one from the larger council of guildsmen, and a third chosen as representative of the parish. As a group, the parish wardens were responsible for oversight of the city's pastors and for assisting the pastors

---

[26] Robert W. Scribner, "Practice and Principle in the German Towns: Preachers and People," in *Reformation Principle and Practice. Essays in Honour of A.G. Dickens*, ed. Philip N. Brooks (London: Scolar Press, 1980), 95-117.

[27] Mandate printed in Timotheus Wilhelm Röhrich, *Mittheilungen aus der Geschichte der evangelische Kirche des Elsaß* ( Strasbourg: Treuttel & Würz, 1855), 1: 257ff; summarized in Johann Adam, *Evangelische Kirchengeschichte der Stadt Strassburg bis zur französischen Revolution* (Strasbourg: Heitz, 1922), 177-78; also see Walther Köhler, *Zürcher Ehegericht und Genfer Consistorium*, Quellen und Abhandlungen zur Schweizerischen Reformationsgeschichte 9-10 (Leipzig: M. Heinsius, 1932-42), 2: 408-409.

in administering church affairs. Three years later, the city's first church ordinance charged the parish wardens, together with their pastor, with the exercise of church discipline within each parish. The ordinance also required that babies were to be baptized in the parishes where they were born.

As already mentioned, popular pressure to choose the parish pastors had caused the Council to assume patronage rights for the parish churches. Over time, the congregation's role in the selection of their pastors was minimized, but it was never completely eliminated. In 1531, the parish wardens were given the right, together with the parish pastors, to appoint the assistant pastors and sacristans for the city's churches. The church ordinance of 1534 defined more precisely the procedure to be followed in choosing a new parish pastor and expanded the procedure for selecting assistant pastors. The ordinance placed the chief responsibility for selecting a new parish pastor in the hands of a newly-created commission, the Examiners, comprised of two Council members and three of the 21 parish wardens. The Examiners were to select one or more candidates for the position, each of whom preached a trial sermon to the congregation. After the trial sermons had been given, one of the city pastors preached on the office of the ministry, urging the congregation to pray for God's governance of the selection process. Then the Examiners, the wardens from that parish, and twelve "God-fearing men" also from the parish met to elect the new pastor, who was presented to the Council for confirmation. At the end of the procedure, the newly-confirmed pastor was presented to the congregation by one of the other city clergy, who would also give a sermon on the congregation's duties towards its new pastor.

The selection of an assistant pastor was less structured. In this case, one or more candidates were selected by the Examiners, the parish's three wardens, and the parish pastor. The candidates were then to give several sermons, and the parishioners' feedback was sought before the final election was held. The examiners and parish wardens also had the right to remove unsatisfactory assistants from their posts, but complaints about parish pastors were to be brought before the Council.[28] In practice, the pastors seem to have had considerable latitude particularly in choosing their assistants. In 1540 it was brought to the attention of Strasbourg's Council that the new assistant pastor at New St. Peter, Georg Schmidt, was a former monk turned Anabaptist who had been reconciled with Strasbourg's church. The Council was apparently satisfied with Schmidt's credentials and his orthodoxy, for he remained at New St. Peter throughout the 1540s.[29]

From the early years of the Reformation, Strasbourg's pastors worked together to encourage the evangelical movement among the populace, to publicize and defend changes to doctrine and liturgy, to petition the magistrate to

---

[28] *Martin Bucers Deutsche Schriften* (Gutersloh: Gerd Mohn, 1960 -), 5:29-30. Hereafter, BDS.

[29] TAE 3: 404, no. 1015; cf. Bopp, *Die evangelischen Geistlichen*, 481.

act more vigorously to establish the new church, and to deal with the day-to-day tasks of ministry. Eventually this cooperation was formalized in the *Kirchenconvent*, the weekly meeting of all pastors in the city, plus the pastors from two parishes on the outskirts of Strasbourg. We do not know precisely when the pastors began to meet regularly, but it was probably sometime during the second half of the 1520s. The relative informality of these early years is indicated by the fact that the meetings were held in the home of Matthäus Zell, the cathedral pastor.[30]

Through the 1530s and into the 1540s, Strasbourg's *Kirchenconvent* proved to be much more effective than was that of Basel. The strong sense of cooperation that existed among the leaders of Strasbourg's church contributed to the *Kirchenconvent's* effectiveness. Rather than being divided into rival factions, the ministers were united under Bucer's leadership. Those pastors who had challenged the drive towards more precise definition of doctrine and a stricter institutional framework at the 1533 synod were removed from office. Four of the five pastors who entered Strasbourg's ministry in the decade after 1535 had close ties to Bucer.[31] Only at the end of the 1540s, as Bucer and his allies tried to establish a more stringent form of church discipline on a voluntary basis, was the unity of Strasbourg's *Kirchenconvent* broken. The split developed largely along generational lines. The pastors unwilling to introduce the new system of discipline into their parishes were those who had led the church from the 1520s; Bucer's staunchest supporters had joined the Strasbourg ministry in the 1540s.[32]

By this time, of course, Calvin was no longer a part of the Strasbourg ministry. He had spent the 1540s shaping the pastoral corps of Geneva into a remarkably united Company of Pastors.

---

[30] Henri Strohl notes that by the beginning of 1525, the pastors were beginning to act as a body; see Henri Strohl, "Théorie et pratique des quatre ministères," *Bulletin de la Société de l'Histoire du Protestantisme Française* (1935), 125. Chrisman interpreted this to mean that the weekly meetings began in 1524, but this is hardly persuasive; see Chrisman, *Strasbourg*, 204. Wendel, whom Chrisman cites, is a bit more cautious, saying only that by 1531 the pastors had already been meeting for several years; see Wendel, *L'Eglise*, 46-47. On the location of the meetings, see Adam, *Evangelische Kirchengeschichte*, 12. Adam also mentions that the pastors lay behind the issuing of a mandate against the Anabaptists in June, 1527. For a later example, see the petition to the Council from January 1529, signed by Capito, Hedio, Zell and Bucer, "together with their [fellow] workers for the Gospel of Christ," TAE 1:194-196.

[31] Bucer recruited two of them for the city's ministry: one was his assistant at St. Thomas, and the fourth was his amanuensis who eventually married his stepdaughter, Alithea Oecolampadius.

[32] Amy Nelson Burnett, *The Yoke of Christ: Martin Bucer and Christian Discipline*, Sixteenth Century Essays and Studies 27 (Kirksville, Mo: Sixteenth Century Publishers, 1994), 180-207, with references there to older literature.

## IV. Geneva

Before looking at Geneva's Company of Pastors, I want to make a general observation about the pastors included in this comparison. To someone familiar with the churches of Basel and Strasbourg, it is striking that neither the published sources nor subsequent studies of Geneva's clergy make a clear distinction between the pastors who served in the city and those in Geneva's rural parishes. In both German-speaking cities, the practical circumstances of size and distance dictated a clear separation between urban and rural clergy. Strasbourg had some twenty rural parishes, most of them small enclaves some distance from the city and surrounded by lands subject to other lords.[33] Basel's territory was both larger and more cohesive geographically than Strasbourg's. Most of its 27 parishes were scattered among the valleys and foothills of the Jura to the southeast of Basel, and they were not within easy traveling distance of the city.

Because of the distances involved, the rural parishes of both cities fell into two categories. Each city had a handful of parishes in the immediate vicinity whose pastors held an intermediate status between their rural and urban colleagues. These pastors were not fully integrated into the city's ministry, but they were close enough that they could participate somewhat in the business of the city church, and perhaps even live in the city. By the second half of the sixteenth century, these "suburban" churches were often used as training grounds where young pastors could gain some experience before being transferred to larger churches, especially those in the city. Most of Basel and Strasbourg's rural parishes, however, were quite distinct from the city parishes. Their pastors had a broader range of pastoral duties, and their parishioners had quite different concerns and priorities. Because the income of a rural pastor was tied to the cycle of agricultural production, even the rhythms of daily life were different.

Geneva had a smaller hinterland than the two other cities, both numerically and geographically. It controlled only ten rural parishes, and most of these were within a few miles of the city. Hence communication and cooperation between city pastors and their rural counterparts was much easier—a fact demonstrated by the inclusion of the rural pastors in the Genevan Company of

---

[33] None of the studies of the Strasbourg Reformation pay much attention to the rural parishes. Study of the rural parishes is made more difficult by the fact that the number and the confessional allegiance of these parishes varied over the course of the sixteenth century. According to James Kittelson, Strasbourg had fourteen parishes that were visited regularly over the course of the sixteenth century; see James Kittelson, "Successes and Failures in the German Reformation: The Report from Strasbourg," *Archiv für Reformationsgeschichte* 73 (1982): 153-174. Jean Rott points out that there were another half dozen parishes subject to Strasbourg's (Protestant) ecclesiastical institutions; see Jean Rott, "Les visites pastorales Strasbourgeoises aux XVIe et XVIIe siècles," in *Sensibilité religieuse et discipline ecclésiastique. Les visites pastorales in territoires protestants (Pays rhénans, comté de Montbéliard, pays de Vaud) XVIe-XVIIIe siècles* (Strasbourg: Istra, 1975), 5-17, especially pp. 12-13. See also Bernard Vogler, "Recrutement et carrière des pasteurs strasbourgeois au XVI siècle," *Revue d'histoire et philosophie religieuses* 48 (1968): 151-174; for the list of parishes whose pastors attended the 1533 synod, see TAE 2:70-75.

Pastors. Geneva's rural churches were thus closer to the "suburban" churches of Basel and Strasbourg than they were to the genuinely rural parishes of the two cities. Although a comparison between Geneva's rural parishes and the suburban parishes of the other two cities might be fruitful, this paper will consider only those pastors who served churches in the city of Geneva, because they are the most directly comparable to the pastors of Basel and Strasbourg already discussed.

Geneva's late medieval church was similar in many ways to those of Basel and Strasbourg. The city's 10,000 inhabitants were divided among seven parishes. Two of these parishes were located primarily outside the city's walls, and their churches were pulled down along with the rest of the suburbs in the years immediately preceding the Reformation.[34] Only two of the seven parishes were incorporated into ecclesiastical foundations. Of the remaining five parishes, the papacy controlled patronage rights to St. Germain and St. Gervais, while the Charansonnex family seems to have made the benefice of Madeleine its personal possession. As a consequence, the city's largest parishes, those which had the greatest need for competent curates, were ripe for the abuse of non-residence. Indeed, from the late fourteenth century these benefices were held by rectors who enjoyed the lion's share of the income and employed a series of vicars to provide pastoral care. The remaining four parishes generally had resident rectors, but non-residency could be a problem there as well. All told, the city had at least nine, and perhaps as many as twenty parish clergy.[35]

Although the latter estimate suggests a higher number of parish clergy in Geneva than in either Basel or Strasbourg, it is hard to escape the impression that the level of preaching and pastoral care in pre-Reformation Geneva was much lower than that in the other two cities. The heart of Geneva's problem was control of appointment to a parish benefice. In the case of Strasbourg and particularly of Basel, incorporation resulted in the hiring of fairly well educated priests and provided measures to ensure the satisfactory performance of their duties. In Geneva, the non-resident rectors evidently showed little interest in the performance of the men they hired as vicars. The same differences can be

---

[34] Louis Blondel includes a map showing Geneva's parish boundaries and discusses the impact of the destruction of the city's *faubourgs*; see Louis Blondel, *Les faubourgs de Genève au XVme siècle*, Mémoires et documents publiés par la Société d'Histoire et d'Archéologie de Genève 5 (Geneva: Jullien, 1919), 18-19, 28, 110.

[35] On Geneva's pre-Reformation parishes generally, see Henri Naef, *Les origines de la Réforme à Genève*, 2 vols. (Geneva, 1936-68), 1: 9-25; Binz, *Vie Réligieuse*, 318-22. Jean-Etienne Genequand describes the parish and clergy of St. Gervais in his "La visite pastorale de Saint-Gervais en 1446," *Bulletin de la Société d'histoire et d'archéologie de Genève* 14 (1968), 3-76, esp. 11-15. Binz estimates that there were twenty parish clergy in the city in the mid-fifteenth century, p. 443; but judging from his earlier discussion of the vicars in the city, this number seems rather high. It is probable that he included the non-resident rectors (whom I have excluded from the active parish clergy) within this number. Both the churches of St. Germain and St. Gervais had one assistant in addition to the curate. I have not been able to determine which, if any, of the other parish churches had assistants.

seen with regard to the amount of preaching in the city. The parish clergy were expected to preach in both German-speaking cities. In addition, both cities had at least one learned preacher who gave sermons on Sundays, feast days, and daily during Advent and Lent. In Geneva, by contrast, the mendicant houses provided sermons during Advent and Lent, but there were no endowed preacherships, and the quantity of preaching in the city on the Rhone lagged far behind that available in its German and Swiss counterparts.[36]

Although the Reformation brought a consolidation of parishes in both Basel and Strasbourg, the general parish structure remained intact in those cities. This was not the case in Geneva, where the Reformation led to a breakdown of the traditional parish structure. Evangelical preaching began in Geneva in private homes and in the open air, and it did not gain a foothold in any of the city's parish churches. None of the parish clergy embraced the reform. Instead, the Franciscan convent church of Rive became a center of evangelical preaching.[37] After the abolition of the mass, reformed preaching continued at Rive and was introduced in both the cathedral and the church of St. Gervais, the parish church on the right bank of the Rhone; the remaining parish churches were simply closed down.

St. Gervais was a distinct enough part of the city to retain its parish identity, but the closing of the parish churches in the heart of Geneva left its inhabitants free to attend any service they chose. The Reformers themselves recognized the importance of parish identification for providing pastoral care, particularly for the exercise of church discipline. In early 1537 Calvin and his associates asked the Council to define the parish boundaries between the city's three churches, but a year later the Council still had not done so. One of the consequences, Calvin lamented in a letter to Bullinger, was that the people regarded the ministers as preachers rather than as pastors.[38] Calvin's distinction is important as a reminder of how closely pastoral care was tied to the parish in the medieval church.

The church ordinance adopted after Calvin's return to the city in 1541 finally dealt with the issue of parish boundaries. It distributed the city's inhabitants into three parishes, with Madeleine replacing the Franciscan church as the third parish, and it specified that the suppressed parishes were subsumed within the cathedral parish. The ordinance also required children to attend catechism instruction, and all inhabitants to receive the sacrament, at their own

---

[36] Thomas A. Lambert, "Preaching, Praying and Policing the Reform in Sixteenth-Century Geneva," Ph.D. dissertation (University of Wisconsin-Madison, 1998) 283-284; Naef describes preaching by the mendicants as one of the conflicts that arose in Geneva over the right to preach, in his *Origines*, 155-171.

[37] E. William Monter, *Calvin's Geneva* (New York: Wiley, 1967), 49-53.

[38] Suggestions for a church ordinance, 16 Jan., 1537; CO 10: 8. Cf. Calvin to Bullinger, 21 Feb. 1538, CO 10:154.

parish church. After five years of disarray at the parish level, such provisions were only a weak attempt to re-establish parish discipline. [39]

The ordinance undermined parish identity in a subtler way by its creation of a consistory whose lay members were chosen on a city-wide, rather than a parish-wide basis. Like Basel's *Bannherren* and Strasbourg's parish wardens, Geneva's elders were a mixed group taken from the small council, the large council, and the city at large; but unlike their counterparts in the other two cities, they were not in any way linked to the newly-reintroduced parishes, nor was there any attempt to distribute the elders evenly throughout the city. To the extent that moral surveillance was linked to geographical boundaries, it was to the neighborhoods or *dizaines* of the city, for the *dizeniers* who were responsible for preventing "disorder and insolence" in each of these neighborhoods had the duty to report infractions to the proper authorities. [40] In essence, the establishment of a city-wide consistory and the previously-existing office of *dizenier* meant that the parish was superfluous for the purpose of church discipline.

Rather ironically for a church reputed to foster ideals of democracy, the parish's loss of significance resulted in the virtual exclusion of the laity from the selection of Geneva's pastors. The 1541 church ordinance described a three-stage process for appointing new ministers. Candidates were first examined in doctrine and conduct by the Company of Pastors, which in practice included the delivery of a trial sermon before the pastors and representatives of the Council. Successful candidates were presented to the Council, which appointed them to the ministry and then presented them to be received "by the common consent of the company of the faithful." This was far less input in the election process than was granted the laity in either Basel or Strasbourg. [41]

The city's weak parish structure also changed each pastor's relationship with his colleagues. In both Basel and Strasbourg, ministers were appointed to a specific parish post, whether pastor or assistant. They became members of the *Kirchenconvent* by virtue of their appointment to a parish post, and there continued to be a clear demarcation of duties, privileges and pay between senior and assistant pastors through the sixteenth century. The position of assistant was the entry-level post for young pastors hoping for a job in the city. Synod

[39] RCP 1: 5

[40] Church ordinance provisions establishing the Consistory, RCP 1: 6-7; on the pre-Reformation office of *dizeniers* and their authority after the Reformation, see Lambert, "Preaching," 43-45; 240-241.

[41] Provisions of ordinance, RCP 1: 2-3; cf. the description of the appointment of Jean Fabri, RCP 1: 61-63. On the occasion when more than one position was available, the selection of new pastors was part of a single process, with candidates assigned on the basis of their performance in the examination, RCP 2: 75-77. Geneva's church ordinance of 1561 acknowledged that even the limited voice of the laity in the selection process had been ignored in practice, and it made more clear that laity could raise objections to the newly-elected minister before he was presented; see Wilhelm Niesel, ed., *Bekenntnisschriften und Kirchenordnungen der nach Gottes Wort reformierten Kirche*, 2nd ed. (Zollikon-Zurich: Evangelischer Varlag, 1938), 43-44.

documents always identified pastors by their position: pastor of St. Leonhard, assistant at St. Peter, and so forth. In Strasbourg, the protocol of the 1533 synod often does not give the names of the pastors but identifies them only by their positions.[42] In Geneva, however, entrance into Geneva's ministry was closer to matriculation in a corporation such as university faculty or guild than it was to the reception of the legal rights and responsibilities of an ecclesiastical benefice. Pastors were first admitted to the ministry, and only then given a specific assignment. The official records of Geneva's church, both those kept by the Company of Pastors and by the Consistory, seldom mention which church each pastor served.

The smaller size of Geneva's reformed ministry in the first decade of its existence contributed significantly to the breakdown of the parish structure. For five years after the adoption of the Reformation, the Genevan church had at most five, and at its lowest point in 1540 only two pastors. This contrasts sharply with the thirteen men who served in Basel, a city of the same size. Strasbourg, which was about twice as large as Geneva, also suffered from an understaffed ministry in the very early years after the Reformation. As we have seen, though, the number of Strasbourg's ministers roughly doubled over the second half of the 1520s. That city's prompt actions to increase the size of the ministry are a striking contrast to Geneva, which proved incapable of retaining even those ministers it already had. The situation of the Genevan church was made even worse by the fact that several of its rural parishes were vacant, and pastoral services had to be provided by ministers from the city. The city's pastors certainly felt the heavy workload. In March 1539 they asked the Council to appoint two deacons who would assist with baptisms, marriages, visiting the sick and administering the Lord's Supper. The Council refused their request, claiming a lack of funds; it was a higher priority to repair the city's walls than to hire additional clergy.[43]

After Calvin's return to Geneva, the pastoral situation improved somewhat, but change came only gradually. The church ordinance increased the number of city clergy to five pastors and three assistants. At least in theory, this provision reintroduced into the Genevan church the hierarchy of function that existed in both Basel and Strasbourg. In Geneva's case, however, there were more "senior pastors" than there were parishes, and so the hierarchy meant something different from the medieval system in which a single parish pastor had one or more assistants. Moreover, Geneva's clergy, whether hired as "ministers" or "assistants," were all admitted to the Company of Pastors on an equal basis, which tended to blur the distinction between them.

---

[42] Participant lists from Basel's synods from the 1530s and early 1540s can be found in BStA Kirchen Akten C3; the Strasbourg synod in TAE 2: 35-55.

[43] Amédée Roget, *Histoire du peuple de Genève depuis la Réforme jusqu'à l'Escalade*, 7 vols. (Geneva, 1870-1883), 1: 152-153. Roget presumably uses the word *diacres* to mean coadjutors or assistants who would, as the pastors asked, help with baptisms, weddings, visiting the sick, and administering the Lord's Supper.

Despite the provisions of the church ordinance, it took several years for Geneva's ministry to reach full strength, in part because the vacant rural parishes still needed to be filled. Several pastors initially appointed to city parishes were transferred into the country within a short time. Making the situation even more difficult was a severe outbreak of the plague that began in 1542 and did not end until 1546, claiming the lives of two pastors and disrupting the normal functioning of the church.[44] Not until 1547 did the city reach the statutory level of eight ministers, and the pastors had to fight the Council to maintain that number. In 1549, after one of the city's pastors was deposed for misconduct, the Council initially refused to appoint a replacement, arguing that "the church could be well served with six [men], and that this number sufficed."[45]

Even with its full complement of eight pastors, Geneva's church continued to be understaffed in comparison with other cities. In fact, the ratio of pastors to total population worsened as the city absorbed several thousand religious refugees during the 1540s and 1550s.[46] The influx of foreigners increased the burden of pastoral care significantly. Although the English-, Spanish- and Italian-speakers were able to establish their own churches, French-speakers—by far the largest proportion—were absorbed within the city's church. To meet the spiritual needs of these refugees, the Genevan Council reopened the church of St. Germain in 1557 and hired two more pastors. The additional pastors did not make much of a difference to the workload of their colleagues, however, for by the end of the 1550s at least one and sometimes two of Geneva's pastors was away from the city at any given time on extended loan to another church.[47]

A comparison between the church ordinance for Basel and that for Geneva gives us some understanding of the practical implications of Geneva's understaffed ministry.[48] There were few differences in the preaching schedule prescribed for both cities. Both ordinances maintained the rhythm of Sunday services from the medieval church, although the masses and canonical hours were both transformed into preaching services. On Sundays, there were ser-

---

[44] RCon 2: XVII; it is perhaps not coincidental that the Registers of the Company of Pastors do not begin until 1546.

[45] RCP 1: 62.

[46] Monter, *Calvin's Geneva*, 165-170.

[47] Three different pastors were sent to Paris: Nicolas des Gallars went to Paris in the summer of 1557; Jean Macard was sent to replace him in early 1558, and was in turn replaced in early 1559 by François Morel (or de Colonges); RCP 2: 78, 80, 82, 84. Theodore Beza was away from the city for over a year attending the Colloquy of Poissy in 1561-62; RCP 2: 97. A new influx of refugees in the wake of the St. Bartholomew's Day massacres prompted Beza to suggest that those refugees who were themselves ministers be allowed to conduct supplementary worship services. The Council refused the request, fearing perhaps that this would increase the tensions between native Genevans and the French refugees; see Eugene Choisy, *L'Etat chrétien calviniste à Genève au temps de Théodore de Bèze* (Geneva: Eggimann, 1902), 86.

[48] ABR 3: 383-409; RCP 1: 1-13.

mons at daybreak, intended specifically for servants and travelers, the main morning preaching service in each of the parish churches, a noon sermon or catechism, and an afternoon or vespers service. However, Basel's supply of ministers meant that more sermons could be preached at the same time—there were thirteen sermons over the course of the day, as opposed to the eight in Geneva. The services were also better distributed throughout Basel: each of the city's seven parish and filial churches had at least one service, and there were sermons as well in two former conventual churches, one on each side of the Rhine.

There was also more preaching in Basel during the week. The ordinance prescribed daily sermons at daybreak in three of the churches, a daily sermon in the cathedral before the Council met, and another preaching service in the cathedral at 9 a.m. Every afternoon there was an hour long exegetical lecture on Scripture which ended with a short German sermon. Geneva, in contrast, could not institute daily sermons in 1541. Its ordinance prescribed that preaching services be held on Monday and Friday mornings in all three churches. In addition, there was a morning sermon in the cathedral on Wednesdays and in the other two churches on Tuesdays. The shortage of pastors in the 1540s made it difficult to implement even this more limited preaching schedule. The hiring of additional pastors allowed a gradual increase in the number of services, however, and by 1551 there were apparently daily sermons in Geneva—but never as many as five a day, as in Basel.[49]

Since Genevans were required under penalty of fine to attend at least one sermon on Sunday, the smaller number of sermons preached would mean that the city's churches were considerably more crowded than those of Basel.[50] That in turn leads to another consequence of Geneva's small ministry: its important ramifications for relations between pastors and their parishioners. Both Basel's Reformation Ordinance of 1529 and Strasbourg's church ordinance of 1534 refer to the bond between pastor and parishioners as that of a shepherd and his flock that required a certain familiarity between them.[51] This kind of bond was scarcely possible in Geneva, given the small size of its pastoral corps in proportion to the number of inhabitants.

In addition to the problem of chronic understaffing, the Genevan ministry also suffered from a high rate of turnover in the decade following the city's Reformation. William Naphy counted 31 pastors who served Geneva between 1538-1546, with over half of them serving rural parishes.[52] If we look only at the

---

[49] Lambert, "Preaching," 285-291. Lambert points out that the preaching schedule in the ordinances—as, indeed, the prescription concerning the number of pastors in the city—was purely theoretical and reflected what Calvin wanted, not what he had actually achieved in 1541.

[50] Lambert, "Preaching," 303, 317-320.

[51] ABR 3: 390; BDS 5: 35; cf. Bucer's treatise *Von der Waren Seelsorge,* which is built around the metaphor of shepherd and flock; BDS 7: 90-241.

[52] William G. Naphy, *Calvin and the Consolidation of the Genevan Reformation* (Manchester: Manchester University Press, 1994), 57-59.

pastors who served the city churches at some point in their career, the situation is a bit more nuanced. In the years 1536-1566, Geneva's urban churches were served by 37 men. This is the same number as served the churches of either Basel or Strasbourg during a comparable period. With roughly half as many posts per inhabitant, the turnover rate in Geneva was thus about twice as high as in the other two cities. As Naphy's figure implies, much of the turnover came in the decade after the Reformation: fourteen city pastors were hired between 1537-1546. In the following decade, the number of new pastors dropped dramatically: only four new pastors assumed city posts between 1547-1556. Turnover rose again to fourteen in the years between 1557-1566, as new men were hired to replace those city pastors sent to France as missionaries.

Naphy's figure highlights an important fact: much of the turnover in Geneva's ministry immediately after the Reformation involved the city's rural parishes. To understand the situation more fully, we must go back to the relationship between urban and rural parishes in the three cities. Compared to the two German-speaking cities, the situation of Geneva's rural parishes was desperate. Five of the ten parishes did not have a resident pastor until 1543, and the other rural parishes seemed unable to keep a pastor for more than a few years. To meet the needs of the rural churches, a surprisingly high proportion of city pastors—seven out of the 37—were transferred to rural posts, most of them during the first half of the 1540s.[53] In both Basel and Strasbourg, the flow moved in the other direction, from rural to urban parish.

A comparison with Basel's rural church helps put this observation in a broader perspective. Although there was some turnover of personnel in Basel's rural church in the decade after the Reformation, the proportion was nowhere near as high as it was in Geneva. However, in the decade leading up to Basel's adoption of the Reformation in 1529, there seems to have been significant turnover among the rural clergy. Many of the rural priests who left were replaced by pastors who favored the evangelical movement. Thus by 1529 most of Basel's rural pastors were already committed to evangelical beliefs.[54] It seems likely that the high number of vacancies among Geneva's rural parishes was a consequence of the relatively rapid adoption of evangelical beliefs within the city, which allowed little time for the rural clergy to adapt themselves more gradually to the new ecclesiastical regime.

The need for rural pastors provided both a challenge and an opportunity for Calvin. On the one hand, the city was desperate for evangelical ministers

---

[53] Bernard, Bourgoing, Des Gallars, De La Mare, Ninaud, Champereau, and de Ecclesia. De la Mare had served the Genevan church from 1536.

[54] In the fall of 1528 Oecolampadius sent a pastoral letter to thirteen rural pastors in the fall of 1528; cf. Staehelin, *Lebenswerk*, 463-465. The addressees were referred to as "those who preach the Gospel of Christ in Basel's territory"; it is unlikely that Oecolampadius would have included Catholic priests among this group. At Basel's first Protestant synod held in May 1529, nine more pastors were listed as "to be presented" to their new parishes. Thus 22 of Basel's 27 parishes had pastors who were evangelical by conviction in 1529.

and could not afford to be too picky about whom it hired. On the other hand, there were so many vacancies in the rural church that Calvin could transfer less capable pastors to rural parishes if more qualified candidates for a city post came along. Church leaders in Basel and Strasbourg did not have the same possibility: once a pastor was hired for the city church, he could expect to stay there until he died or chose to leave.

As already mentioned, in Geneva the movement from urban to rural post was made easier in the 1540s by the fact that rural and urban pastors alike were members of the Company of Pastors. In theory, at least, the pastors shared the same status—although even in the 1540s there are indications that this equality was more theoretical than real.[55] By the later 1550s, however, this theoretical equality had been replaced by a very real sense of hierarchy and a growing perception that rural posts were inferior to urban ones, functioning as stepping stones on the career path. There was a near mutiny among some of the rural pastors in 1562, when Jean Le Gaigneux was chosen as a city minister without first serving a rural parish where he could demonstrate and develop his pastoral abilities. A few of the disgruntled pastors who had hoped to be promoted to a city post complained that "they would never have entered the ministry if they had thought they'd be left in the country, when they could have had another means of living"—a statement which the other pastors found "very strange" and which left Calvin "greatly astonished."[56] Their near revolt apparently paid off, for, with only one exception, the pastors appointed to city posts over the next few years had first served in one of the city's rural parishes.

How do Geneva's city pastors compare with those in Basel and Strasbourg? When we look only at city pastors, we see a number of similarities. As in the other two cities, Geneva's first-generation pastors were outsiders; only one Genevan (possibly two) served as a pastor after the Reformation (Table 3).[57] As is well known, almost all of Geneva's pastors came from France. In Basel and Strasbourg the number of pastors from a given area decreased proportionally to distance from the city, but in Geneva distance did not make much difference. Roughly the same proportion of pastors came from the eastern edge of France (from Burgundy south along the Rhone valley to Provence), from central France, and from the southwest. In comparison, the north was under-represented, with only four pastors, although this included Calvin himself.

---

[55] At least two city pastors, Henri de la Mare and Aimé Champereau, protested at being transferred to rural posts in the 1540s; Naphy, *Calvin*, 61, 70-71.

[56] RCP 2: 98-99.

[57] In comparison with the biographical data available on the clergy of the two German-speaking cities, that available for Geneva is surprisingly meager, particularly regarding education. Hence I cannot draw direct comparisons between the cities' pastors, but I have approximated with what information there is on Geneva's clergy from Naphy, *Calvin*, 58, and Henri Heyer, *L'Église de Genève, 1555-1909. Esquisse historique de son organisation, suivie de ses diverses constitutions, de la liste de ses pasteurs et professeurs et d'un table biographique* (Nieuwkoop: B. De Graaf, 1974).

There is only sketchy information on the education and background of Geneva's pastors before they came to the city (Table 6). Nine of the 37 attended a university, most for several years, and four more are referred to in the Register of the Company of Pastors as "Maistre," a title that presumably was given only to those who had earned an M.A. Another six were teachers in either Lausanne or Geneva before entering the ministry. Thus it is safe to say that at least half of Geneva's pastors had an education well beyond the norm.

All in all, these statistics are not so very different from those of Strasbourg and Basel. The dramatic expulsion of Calvin and Farel in 1538 tends to obscure some underlying similarities between Geneva's first generation of Protestant pastors and those of the other cities. We have already seen the very minor role played by native-born clergy in the newly-reformed churches of Strasbourg and Basel. Because they are so closely associated with the cities they reformed, we tend to forget that—like Farel and Calvin in Geneva—both the Basel reformers Oecolampadius and Myconius, and the Strasbourg reformers Bucer, Capito, and Hedio, were outsiders who arrived in their respective cities in the early years of the Reformation movement.

What distinguishes Geneva from Strasbourg and Basel is the presence, among the earliest of the city's reformers, of men who held benefices in the Catholic church, but were not ordained as priests. This indicates a slightly higher social standing among the city's earliest reformers than in either of the German-speaking cities, where the reformers came from the urban artisanate. This difference would continue through the first generation of reformers, as a number of men from France's lesser aristocracy entered the Company of Pastors.[58]

It is equally significant that none of the priests already in Geneva at the time of the Reformation, regardless of their geographic origin, became pastors after 1536 (Table 9). This anomaly may be related to the small number of pastoral positions in Geneva's reformed church. This is speculation of course, but it seems probable that if the magistrate had hired as many pastors as either Basel or Strasbourg at the outset of the Reformation, it would have recruited priests already in the city who were willing to serve the new church. It is also likely that the pool of well-educated former priests in Geneva was not as large as that in Basel or Strasbourg. William Bouwsma has argued that in comparison to the other two cities, Geneva was a cultural backwater in the years before the Reformation. Its Latin school was weak, and it did not have a printing industry

---

[58] In addition to Calvin himself, François Bourgoing (Sieur d'Aignon), and Michel Cop, the son of François I's personal physician, held canonicates before their conversions to Protestantism. Theodore de Bèze, Pierre D'Ayrebaudouze, François de Morel (de Collonges), and Nicolas Des Gallars came from the lesser nobility; cf. also Robert M. Kingdon's analysis of the backgrounds of the Genevan pastors sent to France as missionaries in his *Geneva and the Coming of the Wars of Religion in France, 1555-1563,* Travaux d'Humanisme et Renaissance 22 (Geneva: Droz, 1956), 138-143.

to attract a circle of humanists as occurred in both Basel and Strasbourg.[59] Hence the number of former priests in Geneva with enough education to be considered suitable for the Protestant ministry in the aftermath of the Reformation may have been smaller than in the other two cities.

In the years immediately following the Reformation, there seems to have been a preference for hiring educated clergy where they could be found. None of Geneva's three reformers, Calvin, Farel, and Viret, were ordained priests, but their colleagues included two former Franciscans and a secular priest who had studied in Paris. The clerical status of the other two is uncertain, but one had also studied in Paris and the other was one of those called "Maistre." Whatever Calvin's feelings about the competence and commitment of these men, they were not uneducated.[60]

Not enough is known about the pastors recruited after Calvin's return to Geneva to draw any conclusions regarding their education or background. Naphy has demonstrated that there was a decisive change beginning in 1544, with the appointment of men who were well educated and of higher social and economic standing than their predecessors.[61] To hazard a guess based on developments in Basel and Strasbourg, it may be that the men appointed to Geneva's ministry before 1544 were former priests who were not as well educated as either the priests appointed immediately after the Reformation or the laymen appointed after 1544. In both of the German-speaking churches there was a natural assumption, through the first decade after the Reformation, that pastors would be former priests. Only in the early 1540s did the proportion of former priests to laymen shift, and by the later 1540s neither church was recruiting former priests for the ministry. That pattern may be equally true for Geneva, although the data is lacking to provide definitive proof.

There remained an important difference between the laymen recruited for the ministry in the German-speaking cities and those in Geneva that would become apparent only during the second half of the sixteenth century. By the 1550s, Basel and Strasbourg's new ministers were young men who had grown up and been educated within the Protestant church and its newly-established schools. An increasing percentage of them were native sons who had been supported by civic stipends as they prepared for the pastorate. As a group, they had very little direct contact with Catholicism.[62] The background of Geneva's pastors was dramatically different. Many of them came to the city as religious

---

[59] William J. Bouwsma, "The Peculiarity of the Reformation in Geneva," in Steven E. Ozment, ed., *Religion and Culture in the Renaissance and Reformation* (Kirksville: Sixteenth Century Journal, 1989), 65-77.

[60] On Calvin's attitude towards his fellow pastors in the early 1540s, see Naphy, *Calvin*, 53-7.

[61] Naphy, *Calvin*, 73-75.

[62] Amy Nelson Burnett, "Generational Conflict in the Late Reformation: The Basel Paroxysm," *Journal of Interdisciplinary History* 32 (2001): 219-244; Vogler, "Recrutement et carrière."

refugees. Their personal experiences with the Catholic church was therefore much different from that of their German-speaking counterparts. This raises the question why Genevans did not send their sons to be trained as pastors in the way parents in Strasbourg and Basel did. The answer may have something to do with the relative lack of funding to support native Genevans preparing for the ministry, but to answer this more fully would go beyond the chronological limits of this paper.[63]

# V. Conclusion

How does this comparison with the ministries and ministers in Basel and Strasbourg deepen our understanding of Geneva's Company of Pastors? First, the greater number of pastors in Basel and Strasbourg not only provided greater stability to the ministry, but also allowed the continuation of the parish ministry much as it had been before the Reformation. In contrast, Geneva's parish structure was weakened as a result of the Reformation, and it never regained the importance that it had in the medieval church. On a more speculative note, there may be a link between the lower quality of the parish clergy and the relative infrequency of preaching in late medieval Geneva, and the smaller number of reformed pastors in that city after the Reformation. Because they initially had lower expectations from the ministers—to quote Calvin again, they were seen as preachers, not pastors—the city's inhabitants may not have expected the same number of pastors and level of pastoral care as their counterparts in Basel and Strasbourg.

The weakening of Geneva's parish structures would have important consequences both theologically and practically. Geneva's ministry more closely resembled the city-wide churches of the apostolic and patristic period than it did the parish-based churches of the later middle ages. Calvin had no prior experience as a parish pastor and was perhaps less influenced by implicit expectations about how the pastoral ministry functioned than were his counterparts in Basel and Strasbourg. This freed him to develop a city-wide pastoral ministry following the example of the early church. The corporate ministry developed in Geneva in turn helped the spread of the reformed church into France. A church that did not bind its pastors' activities to a specific geographical space but saw them as responsible for all believers in the city could more easily be

---

[63] Karin Maag notes that the Genevan magistrate rarely supported Genevans who studied outside of Geneva, in contrast to Zurich's practice; she says nothing about Genevan support for poor students studying at the city's own Academy; see Karin Maag, *Seminary or University? The Genevan Academy and Reformed Higher Education, 1560-1620*, St. Andrews Studies in Reformation History (Aldershot, Hants.: Scolar Press, 1995), 142-143.

introduced as a minority church into cities where the older parish structures remained in the hands of the Catholic hierarchy.[64]

Second, the high turnover rate among Geneva's clergy in the generation after the Reformation worked against the assimilation of the clergy into the local populace. The pastors of Basel and Strasbourg may have been outsiders, but over the course of their long careers, they adapted and became part of their city's culture. Geneva's clergy differed not because they were foreigners, but because they were more transient. The high turnover contributed to the distance between Genevans and pastors that Naphy has described in some detail.[65] The small number of city pastors was another contributing factor to the distance between pastors and parishioners, since Geneva's ministers simply could not establish closer ties with the large number of people entrusted to their pastoral care.

Last but not least, a comparison of the pastors of each city demonstrates the importance of sensitivity to chronology and local circumstances. The Protestant ministry in these three churches was not static but assumed different characteristics with each passing decade. Complicating the picture is the fact that the introduction of evangelical ideas came a decade later to Geneva than it did to either of the German-speaking cities. As a consequence, the political and religious developments of the 1530s through the 1550s influenced the three churches at different points in their evolution and institutional development. Comparisons that do not take account of these changes mask similarities and exaggerate apparent differences.

Ultimately, Dickens' *Tale of Two Cities* was a story of contrasts. This "Tale of Three Churches" is one of some surprising similarities, but also of more important and fundamental differences between the ministers and the ministries of the churches with which Jean Calvin was involved. It is also a necessary reminder that sometimes we appreciate best what is most familiar when it is placed in a broader context.

---

[64] Natlie Zemon Davis develops the contrast between the Catholics' geographically-bounded sense of the sacred with the Protestants' view of urban space as both more open and more uniform in her "The Sacred and the Body Social in Sixteenth-Century Lyon," *Past and Present* 90 (1981): 40-70.

[65] Naphy, *Calvin*, 144-166.

## Comparison of Clergy Entering the Ministry

### Table 1: Origin of Basel Pastors, 1529-1559

|  | No Info | Basel | Alsace/ SW Germany | Swabia | Switzerland | Elsewhere | Total |
|---|---|---|---|---|---|---|---|
| 1529 | 1 | 1 | 4 | 2 | 3 | 1 | 12 |
| 1530-39 | 0 | 1 | 3 | 3 | 2 | 1 | 10 |
| 1540-49 | 1 | 4 | 3 | 0 | 1 | 0 | 9 |
| 1550-59 | 1 | 1 | 0 | 2 | 2 | 0 | 6 |
| Total | 3 | 7 | 10 | 7 | 8 | 2 | 37 |

### Table 2: Origin of Strasbourg Pastors, 1525-1555

|  | No Info | Strasbourg | Alsace/ SW Germany | Palatinate/ Württemberg | Elsewhere | Total |
|---|---|---|---|---|---|---|
| 1525 | 0 | 4 | 7 | 0 | 1 | 12 |
| 1526-35 | 3 | 1 | 3 | 5 | 0 | 12 |
| 1536-45 | 0 | 1 | 1 | 2 | 2 | 6 |
| 1546-55 | 0 | 1 | 1 | 3 | 3 | 8 |
| Total | 3 | 7 | 12 | 10 | 6 | 38 |

### Table 3: Origin of Geneva Pastors, 1536-1564

|  | No Info | Geneva/ Vaud | E Central/ SE France | Central France | Southwest France | Northern France | Total |
|---|---|---|---|---|---|---|---|
| 1536 | 0 | 2 | 1 | 0 | 0 | 2 | 5 |
| 1537-46 | 3 | 1 | 1 | 3 | 4 | 2 | 14 |
| 1547-56 | 0 | 0 | 3 | 1 | 0 | 0 | 4 |
| 1557-66 | 3 | 0 | 2 | 4 | 5 | 0 | 14 |
| Total | 6 | 3 | 7 | 8 | 9 | 4 | 37 |

### Table 4: Education of Basel Pastors

|  | No Info | Matriculated | BA | MA | Theology | Total |
|---|---|---|---|---|---|---|
| 1529 | 4 | 0 | 1 | 2 | 5 | 12 |
| 1530-39 | 1 | 3 | 3 | 2 | 1 | 10 |
| 1540-49 | 2 | 1 | 0 | 3 | 3 | 9 |
| 1550-59 | 1 | 1 | 0 | 2 | 2 | 6 |
| Total | 8 | 5 | 4 | 9 | 11 | 37 |

## Table 5: Education of Strasbourg Pastors

|  | No Info | Matriculated | BA | MA | Theology | Total |
|---|---|---|---|---|---|---|
| 1525 | 3 | 0 | 0 | 2 | 7 | 12 |
| 1526-35 | 8 | 4 | 0 | 0 | 0 | 12 |
| 1536-45 | 3 | 1 | 1 | 0 | 1 | 6 |
| 1546-55 | 4 | 3 | 0 | 1 | 0 | 8 |
| **Total** | **18** | **8** | **1** | **3** | **8** | **38** |

## Table 6: Education of Geneva Pastors

|  | No Info | Matriculated | Degree | "Maistre" | Teacher | Total |
|---|---|---|---|---|---|---|
| 1536 | 2 | 0 | 2 | 1 | 0 | 5 |
| 1537-46 | 7 | 2 | 2 | 3 | 0 | 14 |
| 1547-56 | 3 | 0 | 0 | 0 | 1 | 4 |
| 1557-66 | 6 | 0 | 3 | 0 | 5 | 14 |
| **Total** | **18** | **2** | **7** | **4** | **6** | **37** |

## Table 7: Background of Basel Pastors

|  | No Info | Basel Priest | Non-Basel Pastor | Teacher | Student | Artisan | Total |
|---|---|---|---|---|---|---|---|
| 1529 | 1 | 7 | 3* | 0 | 0 | 1 | 12 |
| 1530-39 | 1 | 5 | 3* | 1 | 0 | 0 | 10 |
| 1540-49 | 2 | 0 | 3† | 3 | 1 | 0 | 9 |
| 1550-59 | 0 | 0 | 3** | 2 | 1 | 0 | 6 |
| **Total** | **4** | **12** | **12** | **6** | **2** | **1** | **37** |

*All were former Catholic clergy
†none were former Catholic clergy
**One was a former Catholic priest

## Table 8: Background of Strasbourg Pastors

|  | No Info | Strasbourg Priest | Non-Strasbourg Pastor | Teacher | Student | Other | Total |
|---|---|---|---|---|---|---|---|
| 1525 | 0 | 11 | 1* | 0 | 0 | 0 | 12 |
| 1526-35 | 3 | 2 | 5** | 0 | 1 | 1 | 12 |
| 1536-45 | 0 | 1 | 3† | 1 | 0 | 1 | 6 |
| 1546-55 | 1 | 1 | 1 | 1 | 4 | 0 | 8 |
| **Total** | **4** | **15** | **10** | **2** | **5** | **2** | **38** |

*Was a former Franciscan
**Some or all of these may have been Catholic clergy
†Two were former Catholic clergy

## Table 9: Background of Geneva Pastors

|         | No Info | Priest | Canon/ Minor orders | Prot. pastor | Teacher | Student | Total |
|---------|---------|--------|---------------------|--------------|---------|---------|-------|
| 1536    | 1       | 2      | 1                   | 1            | 0       | 0       | 5     |
| 1537-46 | 6       | 3      | 2                   | 2            | 0       | 1       | 14    |
| 1547-56 | 2       | 0      | 0                   | 1            | 1       | 0       | 4     |
| 1557-66 | 2       | 1      | 0                   | 8            | 2       | 1       | 14    |
| **Total** | **11** | **6** | **3**               | **12**       | **3**   | **2**   | **37** |

# A Response to "A Tale of Three Churches: Parishes and Pastors in Basel, Strasbourg, and Geneva"

*Gary Neal Hansen*

Let me begin by saying that I enjoyed Dr. Burnett's paper a great deal, and I am honored to respond to it. Dr. Burnett is quite correct in her initial assertion: context does deepen understanding in historical questions. She has done us a great service in doing the careful digging required to see the context of the Company of Pastors clearly. She draws the context out in two dimensions. On the one hand, we have the geographic dimension: she compares Geneva with two other prominent centers of the Reformed movement. On the other hand, we have the chronological dimension: she traces the religious, and specifically pastoral, staffing of the churches in these cities before the Reformation and in its early decades. In this she provides us with a careful statistical picture of ministry in these three cities, a picture fascinating both for the similarities among them and the differences between them.

My comments will be primarily in the form of summaries of some issues she traces and questions growing from this research for our discussion together. I want to discuss four issues under the headings of chronology, geography, statistics, and turnover. Laying some of the comparisons side by side may make it easier to draw conclusions as well as pointing to questions.

First, let us look at the chronological dimension. Dr. Burnett's research shows us church and ministry changing statistically over time. These changes reflect and embody changes in the understanding of church and ministry, as well as a general hunkering down for hard work.

Regarding the church, with the onset of the Reformation we see some reduction of parishes in each city, even while in Basel and Strasbourg the general parish structure was maintained. Basel moved from eight parish churches to seven churches. Strasbourg went from nine parish churches to seven. Geneva shrank from seven parishes to three churches including, for a time, the transformed Franciscan convent church. In Dr. Burnett's paper this count of parish churches for each city omits other religious institutions such as monastic houses and chapels. When one thinks about the wholesale elimination of these latter institutions, the consolidation of church life into a few Protestant churches seems a much more radical change.

Regarding the overall shape of the clergy, Dr. Burnett shows us a similar pattern of reduction over time. Each city started with a large number of religious, a small number of whom did the kinds of work Protestants continued to affirm (preaching and pastoral care), and ended with a similar small number of Protestant ministers. Basel went from four hundred religious, sixteen of whom did pastoral work, to thirteen Protestant ministers. Strasbourg went from over one thousand religious, with fifteen or sixteen priests doing pastoral work, to an eventual number of Protestant pastors in the low twenties. Geneva went from some four hundred religious, with from nine to twenty of the priests exercising pastoral responsibility, to five Reformed ministers, then two, then eight including three assistants, and eventually ten.

This is a remarkable shrinkage in the numbers of people whose profession and livelihood depended on the Church, but if one counts only those with pastoral responsibility there is hardly any change. Both comparisons are important. It is too easy to look at the total number of Reformed ministers in each of these cities and conclude that they were in a state of shortage, until one sees that the totals are not much different from the number of priests doing similar work prior to the Reformation.

However, though it was not the primary focus of the paper, the sheer numerical reduction of the religious institutions and personnel is striking. In the high numbers of religious prior to the Reformation one sees a clear context for the anti-clerical and anti-monastic polemics one finds so frequently in Calvin's commentaries. To Calvin, even apart from any specific corruptions, the sheer number of people on the late medieval church's payroll who were not involved in the crucial work of preaching and teaching would indicate laziness and waste. The reduction of churches and clergy speaks volumes about the nature of the religious changes brought about by the Reformation. The ministry was to be centered on preaching and teaching, and the clergy were to be removed from their pervasive place in society.

From another perspective, though, the Reformed emphasis on the preaching ministry as very nearly the only ministry could appear to be a radical abbreviation of the kinds of vocational service one could offer to God, as well as a limiting of the kind of help one could receive from the church's servants. If the ministry one received was primarily preaching (and of course discipline, which often led to the injunction to hear more sermons), surely some of the laity felt they lost something in the form of ritual, confession, and a variety of forms of prayer. I would enjoy hearing Dr. Burnett's thoughts on the implications of these numerical changes for the understanding of church, ministry, and Christian life in these early Reformed cities.

Second, let us turn to the geographic dimension. A striking feature of the research in comparing these three Reformed cities is the sheer variety of organizational patterns. While in Basel and Strasbourg a church would typically have a pastor, and perhaps an assistant, Dr. Burnett shows that in Geneva there were more pastors than there were churches, and these pastors were distinct from the assistants. She shows the use of the term "deacon" for assistant pastors in Basel in 1529, and in Geneva in 1539 for a proposed office for assisting in sacramental and pastoral tasks. Geneva also continued its distinctive office of *dizeniers* in bringing city-wide discipline to the neighborhood level. One sees much variation in the different patterns and procedures that developed for the selection of pastors in these cities, the still different patterns for the selection of assistant pastors, and the varying degrees of involvement of lay people in these processes both geographically and over time. Again we see variety in the systems that were developed for the exercise of discipline in these churches. All this variety—this lively evolution—came sometimes at the instigation of the pastors, and sometimes at the behest of the Council. That order varied according to changing circumstances, is a lesson in itself about the early Reformed movement. It is also a wise word to those of us whose commitments in the Reformed tradition are ecclesiastical as well as academic, since there is sometimes a tendency to claim Reformation continuity and divine prescription for our own structures.

In these various attempts to organize Reformed cities we may see hints of somewhat different concepts of the relation of church, ministry, and civic life. Dr. Burnett seems to show that in Basel and Strasbourg the dominant locus of the Church was the parish, and that it was therefore the parish that needed to be reformed by the civic authorities. In these two cities, the civic authorities increasingly shaped and guided the reforms even if the work of reform had begun through the parish clergy. This is seen in the magistrate consolidating the churches, the magistrate retaining some patronage rights over pastoral appointments, and the magistrate instituting a system of discipline organized at the parish level.

Dr. Burnett seems to show Geneva having a somewhat different pattern: the reforms were not as focused on the parish and not so driven by the Council. The Council hesitated to define parish bounds, and rather than a parish-based system of discipline they came to have a city-wide Consistory responsible for discipline. Even appointments to pastoral office were less focused on the parishes, since approval was to the ministry first, and then the parish; moreover, as Dr. Burnett notes, in the records ministers were rarely cited with reference to the church they served. The picture seems to be not a set of parishes needing to be reformed by the Council, but a city which needed to be reformed by the church. Or one might say it is a picture of a church which essentially is the city rather than the parishes. The church sought to reform its city, instituting a system of city-wide discipline, and in Geneva church leaders could influence the Council, while in Basel and Strasbourg the magistrate influenced the church.

Third, I would raise a question for Dr. Burnett on some mysteries lying within the statistics. In each table there is a column representing pastors for whom no information is available on a given topic. In the case of geographic origin this is only a small number. On the vocational background of the ministers the number of unknowns ranges from four in Basel and Strasbourg to eleven in Geneva. Since in the case of Geneva this amounts to about thirty percent, the lack of information is significant. Regarding educational background, however, the number of unknowns is still larger: a low of eight with unknown education in Basel (about one fifth) and a high of eighteen unknown for both Strasbourg and Geneva (quite nearly half). I do not criticize the research because information is not available on these people. I am much more eager to applaud what has been discovered regarding the one-half to four-fifths we do know about. However, I wonder whether this makes any of the particular conclusions of the paper at all tentative. I suspect that Dr. Burnett may have some theories about the background of these individuals which could not be documented sufficiently to be stated in the paper, and I would like to hear her thoughts about them.

Fourth, and last, the question that I found myself asking repeatedly had to do with the levels of pastoral turnover of in each city. Dr. Burnett cites high levels of turnover in both Basel and Geneva in the early decades of the Reformation. The two questions this raises in my mind are, first, what the reasons for the turnover were and, second, whether it was a problem. The paper only gives a tantalizingly partial picture of the reasons. For Basel, death and moving away are mentioned as reasons, but the proportion of the two reasons is not stated. Some moved from city to country parishes, or in the other direction. How many moved out of Basel entirely, and why?

Turnover in Geneva was high as well, but while Dr. Burnett seems to see this as a problem it looks to me to be a sign of strength. The paper cites two instances when the Council resisted making appointments, once arguing that more than six pastors were not needed—and this for a city of ten thousand. This may be a sign of Council resistance to Calvin's reforms, or perhaps it is a sign that the church in Geneva was run very efficiently. Most of the turnover cited in Geneva was due to plague deaths or service outside Geneva as missionary pastors. If Geneva could regularly send its pastors away to places of greater need, it looks more like a very efficient training center than a set of troubled churches. In this I wonder if there is an analogy to be drawn between Geneva and a seminary with a very active field education program. Turnover in seminaries is very rapid and also highly desirable for the sake of the churches.

# Calvin and Erasmus on Pastoral Formation

*Laurel Carrington*

In June of 1535, an ailing and dispirited Erasmus arrived in Basel to oversee the printing of his final masterpiece, the *Ecclesiastes sive de Ratione Concionandi Libri*, from Froben's press. It is doubtful that he had the least awareness of another recent arrival in that city, a young exile from religious persecution in France, who was hard at work on the edition of the work that would define his thinking, the *Institutes of the Christian Religion*. Neither man remained long in Basel: in March of 1536, Calvin left for Ferrara, while on July 12th of that year Erasmus's life came to an end. Their paths had merged for less than a year.

Erasmus's final year in Basel was certainly nothing like his earlier periods of residence in that city, the most recent beginning in 1521 when he had left Louvain because of the increasing stridency of the theologians at the university there. During those years, Erasmus was at the center of the intellectual life of the city, surrounded by admiring younger scholars and the constant stream of visitors who came to gain an introduction to the great man. Yet the 1520's were not a happy time for him, for it was during that time in particular that he was increasingly embroiled in controversies with the evangelical reformers, most significantly with Luther, but also including Hutten, Oecolampadius, Capito, and Leo Jud. He also quarreled with the circle of humanist reformers in France and with the Ciceronians in Italy. In the aftermath of the February 1529 iconoclasm in Basel, Erasmus retreated to Freibourg, from whence he produced two bitter manifestos against the evangelical reform in the form of an exchange with Gerard Geldenhouwer and Martin Bucer. However, his residency in Freibourg also marked the publication of his call for peace and unity, the *De Sarcienda Ecclesiae Concordia*.

At the same time the aging Erasmus was calling for an end to religious strife, the young Calvin was articulating those convictions that would most sharply differentiate his beliefs from those of the earlier generation of humanist reformers who had contributed in no small measure to his development as an interpreter of Scripture. The path that brought him to Basel was even more tortuous than that of Erasmus. As a young student, first of theology in Paris and then of law at Orleans, Calvin was well aware of the work of the humanist reformer and of the leaders of the French reform at Meaux. According to

Quirinus Breen, "had Calvin not been converted to radical Protestantism he would doubtless have been for life a Roman Catholic of the type of Bude, as LeFebre, or Erasmus, only less so."[1] Such a counter-factual statement may strike some of us as well-nigh meaningless, and yet there is truth in its implication that Calvin identified for a period in his youth with the humanist reform. The theological perspective of the 1536 *Institutes* leave no doubt, however, that the Calvin who appeared in Basel in 1535 was no Erasmian.

It is with this fundamental fact in mind that we must approach any comparison of Calvin and Erasmus in regards to their views concerning the spiritual formation of pastors. Because there are a number of similar points of comparison and contrast in the life's work of these two that bear remembering, I would like to begin with a preliminary sketch to lay the groundwork for our main theme.

## I. Background

The first observation one might make is that, unlike Calvin, Erasmus never served in a pastoral capacity, nor did he become involved in the work of administration. He was a reformer, but he did not lead a process of reform. His interests were, first, in articulating a vision of an authentic spiritual life that was Christ-centered and grounded in scripture, and second, in devoting himself to a textual critique of scripture based on a knowledge of the "three tongues," Latin, Greek, and Hebrew. He also wrote educational treatises, the last of which, the very *Ecclesiastes* that he completed while he and Calvin were in Basel, was a program of education and preparation for pastors. However, unlike Calvin, Erasmus did not establish a school, although his educational treatises were widely influential.

There is no body of work in Calvin's vast output that corresponds directly to these works of Erasmus, although it is true that he wrote the *Institutes* primarily in his capacity as educator, as an interpretive guide to Scripture for his students.[2] In the same way, other than Book IV of the *Ecclesiastes*, which is a compendium of *loci* upon which the preacher can draw, there is no equivalent to the *Institutes* in Erasmus's background; yet this does not suggest that Erasmus was not in any sense a theologian. Erika Rummel's account of Erasmus's *Annotations on the New Testament*, subtitled "from philologist to theologian," claims that as Erasmus's dialogue with readers expanded, the nature of his role shifted from textual critic to expounder of doctrine.[3] Certainly Erasmus's defense of his readings of the scriptural manuscripts as well as his rendering of

---

[1] Quirinus Breen, *John Calvin: A Study in French Humanism*, 2nd ed. (Hamden, Connecticut: Archon Books, 1968), 8.

[2] See Barbara Pitkin, *What Pure Eyes Could See: Calvin's Doctrine of Faith in Its Exegetical Context* (New York, Oxford: Oxford University Press, 1999), 11.

[3] Erika Rummel, *Erasmus' Annotations on the new Testament: From Philologist to Theologian* (Toronto, Buffalo: University of Toronto Press, 1986).

the New Testament into Latin had theological implications, and Erasmus himself held fast to the view that no discussion of doctrine was meaningful without a sensitivity to the texts in their original languages. Manfred Hoffmann's study of Erasmus's hermeneutic describes him as a "rhetorical theologian," by which Hoffmann means that the path Erasmus took to theological insight was through the application of rhetorical principles to the study of scripture, particularly in the reading of figurative language.[4] Finally, although Erasmus, once more unlike Calvin, wrote little by way of direct commentary, he did take on the task of paraphrasing the New Testament, a work which he himself suggested could be regarded as a commentary by those who were fearful of regarding it as a restatement.[5]

Thus we can say so far that Erasmus and Calvin were educators, each in his own way, just as each in his own way was a theologian. We can likewise judge them both to be humanists, although the extent of Calvin's humanism and its role in his thought is a matter for dispute. William Bouwsma's sixteenth-century portrait attributes a significant strain in Calvin's thinking to humanism, not only as a young man but throughout his life.[6] Alexander Ganoczy is more guarded in identifying Calvin with the humanist reformers, although he will acknowledge their influence. His conclusion is that Calvin would use the tools they bequeathed to him, but to his own purpose.[7] We thus acknowledge critical divergences in the two men's convictions and life's work, but not an absolute dichotomy. For Erasmus's humanistic reform was Christ- and Word-centered, and Calvin had an understanding of ministry that attached tremendous importance to what Serene Jones has called the rhetoric of piety.[8] In addition, both Calvin and Erasmus were sharply critical of the state of the church during their time, believing that pastors must express the love of God by living morally upright lives and ministering to the spiritual needs of their flocks. Ever the loyal Catholic, Erasmus still recognized, as much as the evangelical reformers, the extent to which this was not the case.

Parallels and points of contrast appear in Erasmus's and Calvin's biographies as well as in their respective approaches to reform. In his early life Erasmus was influenced by the simple piety of the *devotio moderna*, as was Calvin

[4] Manfred Hoffmann, *Rhetoric and Theology: The Hermeneutic of Erasmus* (Toronto: University of Toronto Press, 1994).

[5] *Collected Works of Erasmus* (Toronto: University of Toronto Press, 1974- ), 5: 197, 45-53; hereafter, CWE.

[6] William J. Bouwsma, *John Calvin: A Sixteenth Century Portrait* (New York: Oxford University Press, 1988).

[7] Alexandre Ganoczy, *The Young Calvin*, trans. David Foxgrover and Wade Provo (Philadelphia: The Westminster Press, 1987), 178-181.

[8] Serene Jones, *Calvin and the Rhetoric of Piety* (Louisville, KY: Westminster/John Knox Press, 1995).

through his studies with Mathurin Cordier.[9] Orphaned as an adolescent, Erasmus was by his own account pressured by his guardians into entering a monastic order, the Augustinian canons at Steyn, where he spent five formative years which were not necessarily happy but nonetheless not unfruitful. The monastery had a good library, and Erasmus was able to gain a wide acquaintance with the classics. Like Calvin, however, Erasmus did not end up following the path that had been marked for him by his elders when he was young. He obtained release from the monastery to study theology at Paris, where he continued with his humanistic studies, living at the same college Calvin would attend, the famous (or infamous) College de Montaigu. The experiences of the two were dramatically different, however, for Erasmus would complain bitterly about the unsanitary conditions at Montaigue, while Calvin was apparently content with his residency there.

Like the young Calvin, the young Erasmus early on identified his enemies: they were the very scholastic theologians with whom he was expected to study in Paris, and the conservative critics of the pagan classics who warned about their corrupting influence on those whose sole pursuit should be Christian faith. In his *Antibarbari* Erasmus rebuked such critics without mercy, and developed the argument that would characterize his lifelong position, that study of the classics was an aid to piety, first for the excellence of the moral philosophy that these pagans were able to achieve, but second and more importantly, for the demonstration they offered of language that was clear, beautiful, and persuasive. By point of contrast, Erasmus claimed, the scholastics wrote in a style that was sordid and crabbed, to conform to the trifling emptiness of their teaching.[10]

Thus Erasmus embraced the humanist equation of good speaking with good thinking and, correspondingly, with good character. When on a trip to England in 1499 he made the acquaintance of Thomas More, John Colet, and their circle, he found a new focus for his energies in the study of the New Testament. Following the lead of Lorenzo Valla, whose *Elegantiae* he had first encountered in the library at Steyn, he determined to turn his interest and skill in language to the study of the one text that was supreme over all others. His goal was twofold: to cleanse the text as much as possible of the accumulated errors of centuries of scribes, and to present to the public a translation from Greek into Latin that would function as an alternative to the Vulgate. For this work he would require a knowledge of Greek, and thus he set to work in earnest, studying every hour he could snatch out of the day.

In following the path of Erasmus' education, we see a pattern of self-education under circumstances that were not of his choosing, a description that could easily apply to Calvin as well. The shape of their respective departures

---

[9] Ganoczy, 57.

[10] The *Antibarbari* can be found in English Translation in CWE 23.

from pre-ordained roles would reflect at least partly the choices available to them in their respective generations. In Calvin's case, the departure would take the form of a conversion, although the exact point of conversion and the question of how sudden or gradual it may have been are subject to dispute. In Erasmus's case, the departure would express itself in a severe sense of alienation from the surroundings and approach that seemed to suit his peers, first in the monastery and later in the university. He would find his true home in the intellectual fraternity of the humanists.

Like Calvin, and unlike the guild of theologians, the mature Erasmus deeply believed that Scripture should be made available to the people. Indeed, we can profit from a direct comparison between passages each of them wrote on the subject. In his preface to Olivetan's French translation of the Bible, Calvin writes of the vital importance of scriptural teaching for God's faithful:

> But I desire only this, that the faithful people be permitted to hear their God speaking and to learn from Him teaching. Seeing that He wills to be known by the least to the greatest; since all are promised to be God-taught [Is. 29:9]; since He confesses as yet always to be working among His own, whom he calls "weaned from milk, torn from the breasts" [Is. 28:9]; since He gives wisdom to children [Matt. 11:25], and directs that the gospel be preached to the poor [Matt. 11:5]. When, therefore, we see that there are people from all classes who are making progress in God's school, we acknowledge His truth which promised a pouring forth of His spirit on all flesh [Joel 2:28; Acts 2:17].[11]

Erasmus himself expresses a similar *sententia* in the *Paraclesis*, the introduction to his first edition of the New Testament:

> Indeed, I disagree very much with those who are unwilling that Holy Scripture, translated into the vulgar tongue, be read by the uneducated, as if Christ taught such intricate doctrines that they could scarcely be understood by very few theologians, or as if the strength of the Christian religion consisted in men's ignorance of it. The mysteries of kings, perhaps, are better concealed, but Christ wishes his mysteries published as openly as possible. I would that even the lowliest women read the Gospels and the Pauline Epistles. . . Would that . . . the farmer sing some portion of them at the plow, the weaver hum some parts of them to the movement of his shuttle, the traveler lighten the weariness of the journey with stories of this kind![12]

Along with a piety that was shaped by Scripture, Erasmus' reform de-emphasized ceremony in favor of cultivating an inward disposition favorable to receiv-

---

[11] Quoted from John Calvin, *The Institutes of the Christian Religion*, 1536 ed, trans. Ford Lewis Battles (Grand Rapids, MI: William B. Eerdmanns Publishing Company, 1975), 374.

[12] *Christian Humanists and the Reformation: Selected Writings of Erasmus*, revised ed.; ed. and trans. John C. Olin (New York: Fordham University Press, 1975), 96-97.

ing and doing God's will. Through the *Praise of Folly*, the *Colloquies*, the *Enchiridion*, and other works, Erasmus used a combination of satire and persuasion to turn his readers away from superstitious reliance on relics, pilgrimages, special vows, and the mindless repetition of formulas and, instead, to turn them towards a sincere and childlike faith. It was because of such early writings that reformers such as Leo Jud, Conrad Pelican, and Wolfgang Capito believed that Erasmus held to a spiritual interpretation of the Eucharist.[13] Erasmus was to spend the last decade of his life in a struggle to distinguish his position from that of the reformers, whom he denounced with a shrillness born of frustration. The frustration was returned by those who regarded Erasmus as a powerful shaper of public opinion who chose to back away from the full consequences of his own teaching.

Yet both Calvin and Erasmus were united in their recognition that the laity could not depend on their uninformed opinion in their encounter with scripture; as Calvin writes, "Many are led either by pride, dislike, or rivalry to the conviction that they can profit enough from private reading and meditation; hence they despise public assemblies and deem preaching superfluous." Speaking of the church as the external means of grace, he continues, "In order, then, that pure simplicity of faith may flourish among us, let us not be reluctant to use this exercise of religion which God, by ordaining it, has shown us to be necessary and highly approved."[14]

Erasmus would not quarrel with these conclusions, but his emphasis in defining the role of scholarship in particular is different. Part of the goal for his own work was to counteract the effects of time, language, and historical circumstances, which might render the original meaning obscure to contemporary readers. The fragility of the manuscripts themselves, and the carelessness of scribes, necessitated a scholarly effort at recovery of the original text. Most important, however, Erasmus believed that God had deliberately arranged the verbal tapestry of Scripture in such a way that the deepest mysteries lay hidden, like gems. The 1515 adage Sileni Alcibiadis *makes this point clearly:*

> If you remain on the surface [of Scripture], a thing may sometimes appear absurd; if you pierce through to the spiritual meaning, you will adore the divine wisdom . . . in both the domains of nature and faith, you will find the most excellent things are the deepest hidden, and the furthest removed from profane eyes. In the same way, when it is a matter of knowledge, the real truth always lies deeply hidden, not to be understood easily or by many people.[15]

---

[13] The writings detailing Erasmus' participation in this controversy can be found in *Opera Omnia Desiderii Erasmi Roterodami* (Amsterdam: North-Holland, 1969- ), IX-1. Hereafter, ASD.

[14] *Institutes*, 4.1.5.

[15] Margaret Mann Phillips, *Erasmus on His Times: A Shortened Version of the "Adages" of Erasmus* (Cambridge: Cambridge University Press, 1967; reissued, 1980), 82.

There is in Erasmus's approach in particular a tension between his belief in the clarity and accessibility of scripture and his respect for the mysterious wisdom that these writings offer only to the trained eye. In the case of Calvin, it seems as well that his desire for the most humble layman to know the word of God is tempered by his belief in the special teaching mission of the clergy. We will have more to say later on this point; for the time being, we simply note that neither Calvin nor Erasmus wanted to turn that function over to the obscurantist, self-important scholastic theologians; nor did Calvin wish his ministers and presbyters to replicate the Roman hierarchy. But for Calvin and for Erasmus, the primary concern of pastors was to impart the Word of God. We thus turn now to a consideration of how both men represent the functions and qualifications of the clergy.

## II. The Clergy

Calvin's primary discussion of the ministry occurs in Book IV of the *Institutes*, where he states concisely that "in the office of the pastors also there are these two particular functions: to proclaim the gospel and to administer the sacraments."[16] Calvin's understanding of the pastoral function is derived from scriptural passages describing the mission of the apostles, as for example Christ's sending them out to "preach the gospel and to baptize those who believe unto forgiveness of sins" (Matt. 28:19). Teaching includes public proclamation and private admonition; thus, pastors have an obligation to see to it that their people are receiving correct doctrine, and that they are not through neglect living in ways contrary to the demands of that doctrine. In Calvin's words, "[pastors] have been set over the church not to have a sinecure but, by the doctrine of Christ, to instruct the people to true godliness, to administer the sacred mysteries and to keep and exercise upright discipline." This last demand includes the directive that pastors reflect godly teaching in their own lives and conduct.

Erasmus in Book I of the *Ecclesiastes* lists what he considers to be the functions of bishops and priests: they are to administer the sacraments, to pray for the people, to judge, to ordain, and to teach.[17] In cases of necessity, baptism may be performed by someone other than a priest, but for all of the other sacraments an ordained priest is required. Intercessory prayer has the same function under the new law that was served by sacrifice under the old. In matters where conflicts arise, from questions pertaining to marriage to the decisions of princes to go to war, the best course would be to allow those who understand God's law to deliver judgment. (Erasmus, realizing that this is perhaps a vain hope, lapses into the subjunctive.) Even more sublime than the dignity of judging is the power of ordination, "especially since the power of conferring the gifts of the Spirit is imparted through the sacrament."[18] But highest of all the

---

[16] *Institutes*, 4.3.6.

[17] ASD V-4, 198:232-234.

[18] ASD V-4, 200:267-268.

priest's functions, greater than the power of administering the sacraments, is the charge of teaching the Lord's flock.[19] As for Calvin, teaching for Erasmus involved, in addition to imparting true doctrine, admonishment, chastising, and consoling one's people, as well as refuting anyone who would undermine the truth of the gospel.

The most obvious conclusion we can draw so far is that Calvin has eliminated from his description of the pastor's functions three items that Erasmus includes: intercession, ordaining, and judging. But more striking than this is the fact that Erasmus assigns the greatest value and dignity to the pastor's function of teaching, *docere*, even over the celebration of the Eucharist. Calvin gives a tart critique of the Roman priesthood in his commentary on Isaiah: speaking of the mass, he writes, "Priests are set up by the pope and his followers to sacrifice Christ, not to teach the people."[20] While Erasmus professed clearly his loyalty to the interpretation of the sacrament taught by the Roman church, he shared with Calvin a supreme valuation of the word of God in the spiritual life.

Both Calvin and Erasmus maintain that in the execution of such sublime functions, the pastor must not become arrogant, but must ever be mindful that the dignity of his office is entirely a gift from God.[21] Calvin will likewise emphasize that the pastor "must bring to his work nothing of his own."[22] Calvin continues, "We can be sure that whatever comes from man's own cleverness may be ignored. God demands for himself alone the honor of being heard in his church . . . Hence it follows that none should be recognized as servants of God, none should be counted just and faithful prophets or teachers, unless God is speaking through them, unless they invent nothing by their own will, but preach only what God commands." What God wants preached is his pure, undiluted Word.

In order to do this properly, Calvin and Erasmus agree that a pastor must have the requisite training. For an understanding of Erasmus's ideal program of training for pastors there is no better source than the *Ecclesiastes* itself. It is lengthy, written in four books as a summation of his thinking about how pastors should prepare for their work. The first book addresses the office of the priesthood, while the next two describe the rhetorical training required of the preacher: invention in Book II; memory, action, elocution, amplification, figures, and tropes in Book III; and a compendium of *topoi* for sermons in Book IV. Erasmus gives in the first book a brief description of the qualifications the pastor should bring to his work, couched in terms that balance the individual's gifts of nature, his application of himself to study, and the activity of the Holy Spirit:

---

[19] ASD V-4, 200:270-274.

[20] Commentary on Isaiah 61:6 in *Calvin: Commentaries,* Joseph Hartounian and Louise Pettibone Smith, ed. and trans., Library of Christian Classics XXIII (Philadelphia: The Westminster Press, 1958), 373.

[21] ASD V-4, 78:938-939.

[22] Commentary on Jeremiah 1:9, in *Calvin: Commentaries,* 377.

Our industry does not diminish the energy of the Spirit, so much should we avoid faith in ourselves, but we should attribute all our successes to the Spirit, who alone causes the deeds of men to prosper. But rather if the coming of heavenly grace discovers in us either certain gifts of nature, for example a healthy body, a good voice, an articulate tongue, a quick mind, a faithful memory; or some faculty brought about through human industry, such as that of ordering an argument which dialectic provides, strength in speaking which rhetoric confers, or the knowledge of natural things which physics presents, grace does not take these away, but perfects them, turning them to the use of piety and the glory of Christ.[23]

First and foremost, however, Erasmus specifies that "a clean heart and a faultless life demonstrate the faith and authority of the preacher."[24] An outer show of such things as fasting, self-denial, vigils, masses, prayers, almsgiving, special clothing, and the like amounts to a lie if the heart is full of the love of money and fame, self-love, hatred and envy, and similar vices. Emphasizing the inner disposition over outer signs, Erasmus writes, "It is not water administered to the body that reveals this purity, but he who baptizes only the minds of men by the spirit and by fire."[25]

For Calvin, the function of proclaiming the gospel is split into two emphases: teaching and preaching. In terms of teaching, pastors must be trained in true doctrine. Yet how are they to learn what is true in order to be certain of what is expounded? Robert Kingdon's *Geneva and the Coming of the Wars of Religion in France* describes the approach Calvin would develop:

A program of intense study was required of all candidates for the Calvinist ministry in France. One of the sources of the Reformation had been scholarly, critical study of the Bible, and each Calvinist minister was expected to be well equipped for the continuing task of Biblical study and Exegesis. Not only must he be able to read, write, and speak classical Latin with a skill approaching perfection; he must also master the Hebrew and Greek of the original Bible texts and learn thoroughly Calvin's own painstaking technique of line-by-line exegesis. Only a man with a high degree of linguistic and philological ability could be entrusted with the task of interpreting to less learned or otherwise preoccupied people the very words of Almighty God.[26]

The focus on the three tongues is the hallmark of the humanist approach embraced by Erasmus, as well as the demand for a mastery of Latin according to the standards of the classics. Kingdon describes Calvin as instructing clergy

---

[23] ASD V-4, 110:588-596.

[24] ASD V-4, 84:65-66.

[25] ASD V-4, 84:78-79.

[26] Robert M. Kingdon, *Geneva and the Coming of the Wars of Religion in France, 1555-1563* (Geneva: Librairie E. Droz, 1956), 14.

personally, in lectures and in informal discussion, prior to the more formalized setting of the Geneva Academy, which was established in 1559. One might say that there was almost never an occasion in which Calvin was not teaching, from his sermons to the *Institutes* themselves.

Students developed a close rapport with their teachers, in many cases living with them and in all cases in a position to engage in lively conversation. The care they received from their instructors extended to their personal lives, a phenomenon that Calvin himself experienced in his relationship with Martin Bucer during his time in Strasbourg. In Geneva and other cities influenced by the Calvinist reform, the Company of Pastors kept a careful eye on the moral character of the clergy as well as their doctrinal purity.

In looking at the training of Calvin's pastors we find one particular point of contrast with Erasmus, lying in the two men's varying sense of mission. Erasmus would feel beleaguered and increasingly under attack as he developed his New Testament, but he always maintained the support of the papacy, which he enlisted in his efforts to silence his most vociferous critics. If in his declining years he felt the climate had become more dangerous for him than it had been hitherto, his position as a potential martyr was one that he had not sought and that he strongly resented, blaming the evangelical reform for poisoning the atmosphere. Calvin's students, on the other hand, saw themselves, as they undertook their vocation, in the role of missionaries spreading the true faith in hostile territory. This belief comes through most clearly in Calvin's own dedicatory letter to Francis I. The enforcing of theological rigor and stringent personal discipline was a requirement for these conditions.

Erasmus's criticism of the evangelicals scornfully dismissed the comparisons they would draw between themselves and the apostles. He also found distasteful the insistence on doctrinal conformity, both in his own relations with the Roman church and the evangelicals' relations with one another. The most famous instance of this was his statement in the *Diatribe on Free Will* to the effect that this matter should be one on which Christians should feel free to disagree:

> I have always had a deep-seated inner revulsion from conflict, and so have always preferred sporting in the spacious plains of the Muses to engaging in swordplay at close quarters. And I take so little pleasure in assertions that I will gladly seek refuge in Skepticism whenever this is allowed by the inviolable authority of Holy Scripture and the church's decrees; to these decrees I willingly submit my judgment in all things, whether I fully understand what the church commands or not. . . And so, as far as my own position is concerned, I would say that many and various views on free will have been handed down by the ancient writers, and that as yet I have no settled opinion regarding them beyond a belief that a certain power of free will does exist.[27]

---

[27] CWE 76: 7-8.

A passage from Calvin's commentary on Micah 3:8 could well have been written in response to Erasmus's position:

> [W]e conclude that when we deal with wicked and criminal men, we need the support of heaven's own constancy. And this is the almost universal and perpetual situation of all the servants of God. For those who are sent to teach the world are sent into warfare . . . [D]octrine should be taught to all the faithful so that they may distinguish wisely between the faithful servants of God and imposters who falsely claim his name . . . For God will always give a spirit of judgment and discretion. But today unhappy souls are dragged to perpetual ruin, because in fact they shut their eyes, or blink voluntarily, or willingly involve themselves in obscurities, saying: "I cannot judge; I see on both sides learned or famous men, or at least men of some reputation and importance. Some call me to the right, others to the left. Where should I go? I prefer to shut my mouth and my ears." Thus many make ignorance a pretext for inaction.[28]

Calvin's emphasis on doctrinal certitude, contrasted with Erasmus's distaste for assertions, finds a parallel in Calvin's assigning priority to faith over love, a priority that Erasmus reverses. In describing the first quality an aspirant to the priesthood must bring, Erasmus declares that it is love for the message one desires to impart to others: "Most important to the goal of persuasion is to love that of which you are persuading; the very heart of the one who loves provides passion to speech."[29] Citing John 5:35 describing John the Baptist, "He was a burning and shining lamp," Erasmus notes that "The burning is first, the light after";[30] and he goes on to specify that ardor is in the mind, while light comes through from the doctrine. For Erasmus, this ordering leads to the admonition to the preacher to practice what he preaches: "And works have their own light, says the Lord: 'Let your light so shine before men, that they always see your good works' [Matt. 5:16]. And truly just as the light of good works without love is hypocrisy, so is doctrine weakened and ineffective unless it springs from a spirit burning with love."[31] Later, in Book III of the *Ecclesiastes,* Erasmus concludes a section devoted to the rules of interpretation by echoing St. Augustine's admonition in the *De Doctrina Christiana* "that we love Holy Scripture even before we learn."[32]

By way of contrast, Calvin makes clear that for him faith is first, even before love: "For the teaching of the Schoolmen, that love is prior to faith and hope, is mere madness; for it is faith alone that first engenders love in us."[33] Further, Calvin holds

---

[28] Commentary on Micah 3:8 in *Calvin: Commentaries,* 383.

[29] ASD V-4, 84:51-52.

[30] ASD V-4, 84:55-56.

[31] ASD V-4, 84:56-59.

[32] ASD V-5, 288:951.

[33] *Institutes,* 3.2.41.

that faith must rest on knowledge. He rejects the decision of those like Erasmus who submitted to the church's authority: "We do not obtain salvation either because we are prepared to embrace as true whatever the church has prescribed, or because we turn over to it the task of inquiring and knowing."[34] Knowledge of the truth and faith in the promises of the gospel lead to certainty, a conviction that can come only through the action of the Holy Spirit. Furthermore, without the support of this absolute certitude, the pastor will not be able to do his work, which is to reflect in his teaching what is only of the Holy Spirit.

I would like now to return to a question raised earlier, having to do with the tension in both Erasmus's thinking and Calvin's between their belief in Scripture's accessibility on the one hand and in the need for a special class of interpreters on the other. In looking at this question, I will focus on a term that has an important role in the vocabulary of each of them: accommodation.

## III. Proclaiming the Word: Accommodation

To accommodate, *attemperare,* means to fit or adjust oneself to the needs or limitations of another. In the vocabulary of both Calvin and Erasmus, it describes the manner in which God adapts himself to human understanding, which is obviously incapable of encountering God at his level. Here are the words of Calvin describing the process in a tender image of fatherly love:

> But when [God] descends to us, adapting himself to us and prattling to us, he wishes us also to prattle back to him. And true wisdom is to embrace God, exactly as he adjusts himself to our little measure . . . Let us remember that he came down to us to raise us up to him. He does not adopt an earthly fashion of speech to keep us at a distance from heaven, but rather as a means of raising us up to heaven.[35]

There is in this relationship a double movement that is entirely initiated by God: he takes on our earthly speech, described as a form of baby talk, and we in turn respond in the only way we can with our infantile speech. Yet God does not intend us to remain at the level of infants, but ultimately to be raised to his level, to dwell with him in heaven. Thus our limitations, which are the reason for God's accommodation, are overcome in that very act of accommodation.

Chapter V of the first book of the *Institutes* begins with a discussion of the manner in which God first reveals himself to us in creation itself, in a form that is accommodated to our understanding. Nevertheless, such is the nature of human sinfulness that we do not perceive God in creation: "But although the Lord represents both himself and his everlasting Kingdom in the mirror of his works with very great clarity, such is our stupidity that we grow increasingly dull toward so

---

[34] *Institutes,* 3.2.2.

[35] Commentary on Genesis 35:7 in *Calvin: Commentaries,* 130.

manifest testimonies, and they flow away without profiting us."[36] Thus we find ourselves requiring an additional source of revelation in the form of Scripture. Calvin uses another homely analogy to explain the purpose of Scripture:

> Just as old or bleary-eyed men and those with weak vision, if you thrust before them a most beautiful volume, even if they recognize it to be some sort of writing, yet can scarcely construe two words, but with the aid of spectacles will begin to read distinctly; so Scripture, gathering up the otherwise confused knowledge of God in our minds, having dispersed our dullness, clearly shows us the true God.[37]

The veracity of Scripture is affirmed by the testimony of the Holy Spirit, speaking through the prophets but also speaking to us directly in our very hearts.[38] A person not having a heart that is so moved cannot see into the divine revelation that Scripture offers us.

So far we have an image of God reaching out to his people, who cannot possibly encounter him directly, first through his works in creation, then in Scripture. The metaphor of blighted sight is an intriguing one: the book of creation is intrinsically clear as a testimonial without Scripture, but our eyes are weak, and so we need the correction of the written word. With the clarity provided our vision through this correction we will begin to look around us and see God's hand in creation. Thus it is a book—Scripture— that enables us to read creation as the most beautiful volume that the blighted sight can only see as "some kind of writing." One question that remains, however, concerns the clarity of the visual corrective. Calvin chides the Roman theologians and priesthood for allowing the uneducated to be taught through a different means, images in the churches, rather than God's word, claiming that if the Roman church had done its job properly there would be no Christians left uneducated in God's word: "In the preaching of his Word and sacred mysteries he has bidden us that a common doctrine be there set forth for all."[39] This, of course, describes the two proper functions of the clergy, the first of which Calvin takes on himself as he expounds sacred doctrine based on Scripture for the remainder of the *Institutes*.

Yet somewhat at odds with this function is Calvin's contention that the revelation in Scripture is clear and complete in itself. In his commentary on Jeremiah, he writes:

> Here is the refutation of that impious popish blasphemy which prattles that not only the law but even the gospel is obscure. But Paul claims that the gospel is plain *except to those who are perishing* (II Cor. 4:3); over them a veil is

---

[36] *Institutes*, 1.5.11.

[37] *Institutes*, 1.6.1.

[38] *Institutes*, 1.7.5.

[39] *Institutes*, 1.11.7.

thrown because they deserve to be blind (II Cor. 3:14-15). But, as we see, Jeremiah here affirms that the law, even though it is less clear than the gospel, is set plainly before the eyes of all, and that all may learn from it exactly what pleases God and what is right.[40]

The key phrase in this passage is, of course, Paul's qualification: "except to those who are perishing." It is not Scripture itself that is veiled; rather a veil is deliberately thrown over the reprobate. To the elect of God, there will be no obscurity. Yet as we have seen, Calvin allows that the people must be taught, not simply through having the word of God read to them, but preached. As Edward Dowey puts it, "There were daily Bible studies for the populace in Geneva. The Academy and all its store of learning were directed toward Bible study. The sermons in Geneva were Bible studies. Calvin's *Institutes* is a Bible study—an aid to students in reading Scripture. All these aids to comprehension where the clarity of Scripture is a by-word!" Dowey concludes: "The situation is typically Calvinistic—it involves a paradox that issues in a dynamic."[41]

The solution to the paradox lies in the principle of accommodation, the most sublime instance of which is the incarnation: Christ, the Word made flesh. "For there has always been between God and man a distance too great for any communication to be possible without a mediator."[42] Christ's mediation is the ultimate fulfillment of all God's ways of drawing human beings to himself. We become partners in this act of communication by having faith in what God has offered: "it is by faith in the gospel that Christ becomes ours and we are made partakers of the salvation and eternal blessedness brought by him."[43]

This last passage appears at the beginning of Book IV, where Calvin introduces the outward means of salvation, the church and its ministers. It will come as no surprise that these means reflect a further accommodation that God makes to our ignorance and sloth, to which Calvin adds our fickleness of disposition:

He instituted "pastors and teachers" (Eph 4:11) through whose lips he might teach his own; he furnished them with authority; finally, he omitted nothing that might make for holy agreement of faith and for right order. First of all, he instituted sacraments, which we who have experienced them feel to be highly useful aids to foster and strengthen faith. Shut up as we are in the prison house of our flesh, we have not yet attained angelic rank. God, therefore, in his wonderful providence accommodating himself to our capacity, has prescribed a way for us, though still far off, to draw near to him.[44]

---

[40] Commentary on Jeremiah 26:4-5 in *Calvin: Commentaries,* 81.

[41] Edward A. Dowey, Jr., *The Knowledge of God in Calvin's Theology* (New York: Columbia University Press, 1952), 37.

[42] Commentary on Genesis 48:16 in *Calvin: Commentaries,* 148.

[43] *Institutes,* 4.1.1.

[44] Ibid.

Where we find the preaching of the ministry, then, as well as their performance of the sacraments, is at the end of a series of acts of accommodation, expressed in its totality through the mediation of Christ. In all cases where the term "accommodation" appears, the thrust of the meaning is to show the dynamic alternation between distance and nearness. God's accommodation to us is not so much a bridge as an activity, of drawing us close. Yet we for our part also move closer to him through the means he has devised for us. Our movement is not through our own power, but through God's power acting in us in the form of our faith in God's promises, sealed by the redemptive sacrifice of his son, Jesus Christ.

Turning our attention now to Erasmus, we find that the principle of accommodation is a vitally important principle for him as well; indeed, Manfred Hoffmann calls it "the single most important concept in Erasmus' hermeneutic."[45] Calvin's characterization of God's communication with his people as a form of baby talk could easily have been drawn from a passage in an early work of Erasmus, the *Enchiridion*:

> Divine wisdom speaks to us in baby-talk and like a loving mother accommodates its words to our state of infancy. It offers milk to tiny infants in Christ, and herbs to the sick. But you must hasten to grow so that you may receive solid food. It lowers itself to your lowliness, but you on your part must rise to its sublimity.[46]

Like Calvin, Erasmus ends with the contention that believers must not remain at the level of immaturity in which God first encounters them. One might remark on the fact that, whereas Calvin represents God as raising worshippers up to heaven, Erasmus ends with an admonishment to his *reader* to rise. This difference between the two passages is not by itself proof of a great division between them, for Erasmus would admit that it is ultimately God who enables his people to rise to his level, while Calvin would certainly utilize the language of admonishment in attempting to motivate his audience to follow where God leads. Against the background of their respective positions, however, we can recognize the two passages as marking the essential difference in their perspectives regarding the relation between God's agency and human capability.

The baby-talk analogy reappears in Erasmus's introduction to his 1518 edition of the New Testament, the *Ratio seu Methodus*, where he alleges that the divine author has lowered himself to the level of humanity as he constructed the holy writ in order to appeal to their senses, using concrete images to express spiritual meanings.[47] At another point in that work Erasmus writes that God as

---

[45] Hoffmann, *Rhetoric and Theology*, 106.

[46] CWE 66: 35.

[47] Hajo and Annemarie Holborn, *Ausgewählte werke* (München: Beck-Holborn, 1933), 274:25-27.

Christ "accommodated himself to those whom he strove to draw to himself. In order to save human beings, he was made man; in order to heal sinners, he became intimately knowledgeable about sin; to appeal to the Jews, he was circumcised, he was purified, he observed the Sabbath, he was baptized, he fasted."[48] In Erasmus's vocabulary, the word of God made flesh and the word of holy writ are the same: both are images of God and the accommodation he has made to human beings.

Like Calvin, Erasmus is also of the conviction that God reveals himself in creation. His most famous discussion of the natural world is embedded in an analogy, that of the Silenus, originally a Greek figurine of a misshapen and ridiculous drunkard that opens to reveal a god within. Thus God, the heavenly author, has written the book of nature so that what appears to be most humble and insignificant is in actuality that which is most precious: "In trees, it is the flowers and leaves which are beautiful to the eyes . . . But the seed, in which lies the power of it all, how tiny a thing it is! How secret, how far from flattering the sight or showing itself off!"[49] Two motifs are expressed in this analogy: dissimulation, in the form of an unprepossessing appearance masking the greatest power, and the hiddenness or remoteness of what is most significant. In regards to the former attribute, Christ as a Silenus figure lived a life of poverty and humility, and died a dishonorable death on the cross. As for the latter, Erasmus writes that "at the highest point of these [things not seen] there stands what is furthest removed from the senses, namely God, further than our understanding or our knowing, the single source of all things."[50] He concludes, "suffice it to say that, in both the domains of nature and faith, you will find the most excellent things are the deepest hidden, and the furthest removed from profane eyes."

Both the sacraments and holy scripture participate in this dynamic, and for this specific reason Erasmus would throughout his life admonish his readers to go beyond the ceremonial aspects of the sacraments to the underlying mysteries, just as he would have them explore the hidden meanings of Scripture within the literal sense. The ideal priest is one who helps his flock accomplish these goals. Erasmus's harshest criticisms were aimed at bishops and priests who chose worldly magnificence over servanthood: "they call priests, bishops, and Popes 'the Church,' when in reality they are only the servants of the church," Erasmus laments.[51] Later, he says, "I want [a bishop], as the vicar of Christ and the guardian of the sacred spouse, to be free from all earthly contagion, and to resemble as closely as possible the one whose place and office he fills."[52]

---

[48] Holborn, *Ausgewählte werke*, 227:11.

[49] Phillips, *Erasmus on His Times*, 81.

[50] Ibid., 82.

[51] Ibid., 86.

[52] Ibid., 89.

The office itself reflects God's accommodation of his sublimity to the humble station of humankind. As we recall, it is the priest's most important duty to impart the word of God to his flock. The Silenus-figure of scripture is such that it is accommodated to human needs by expressing God's purpose in homely terms, and yet that very accommodation necessitates the aid of a trained interpreter to penetrate to the meanings that lie hidden beneath the surface. Erasmus demands of his preacher expertise in the three tongues, in addition to a long program of study in pagan literature, to awaken the would-be exegete to a sensitivity for figurative language. The fathers of the early church play a significant role as well, for they teach the reader not just what to read but how to read. As Hoffmann explains Erasmus's method, "The movement from the visible to the invisible, so fundamental to Erasmus' thought as a whole, governs also his understanding of the exegetical process."[53]

Erasmus embraced the fourfold division of scriptural meaning into the literal/historical sense, the allegorical/Christological sense, the tropological/moral sense, and the anagogical/mystical meaning. The entire sequence describes the steps from earth to heaven that bring about in stages an ultimate unity between two entirely disparate levels of reality. God reaches out to humans through Christ and, what amounts to the same thing, through scripture. We in turn must prepare ourselves to receive God's word by cleansing our hearts of the pollution of earthly desires—desires for wealth, privilege, honors, and power—and enter into dialogue with God at the point where he meets us. Had he given us a text that is a direct mirror of himself on the surface as well as in the interior we would be unable to approach it. Had he given us a text that pandered to the desires that are at odds with his kingdom, we would sink into the gratification of those desires and fail to move beyond them. Instead he gives us language loaded with homely metaphors that can delight, instruct, and move us as we are drawn ever deeper into its divine message.

As in faith, so in nature: the natural world is constructed along lines commensurate with scripture, so that the most precious things lie hidden beneath the surface. In this way the realm of nature participates in the same dynamic of accommodation, revealing in its diversity an essential unity within itself and with its creator. At the same time Erasmus wrote the *Ecclesiastes*, he was also calling for concord within the church—indeed, his entire life's work was devoted to a plea for an end to fractious squabbling and a coming together in unity. His preference for the art of rhetoric over dialectic reflects his desire that speech should bring people together in unity and peace rather than arm them with tools for disputation. Erasmus's concern for right conduct does not limit him to the task of a mere ethical philosopher, as some would suggest, nor does his desire for peace reflect a timid individual who lacks conviction; rather, to him the hallmark of God's grace is that it brings about those behaviors that con-

---

[53] Hoffmann, *Rhetoric and Theology*, 103.

tribute to love, concord, and the reconciliation of opposites. The principle of harmony is the guiding principle of all health and well-being in the human body, in the entire created order, and in the body of Christ. The one accusation Erasmus will repeat again and again against the evangelical reformers is that they have destroyed the unity of the church and of society. The true role of the pastor is to imitate Christ in the act of accommodation, not to tear apart necessary structures of support. In Erasmus' words, as interpreters, "The meaning which we draw forth from the obscure words must correspond to the circle of Christian doctrine, to its life, and finally to the equilibrium of nature."[54]

## IV. Conclusion

In this examination of Erasmus's and Calvin's respective approaches to the spiritual formation of pastors we have tended to focus on the pastor's role as the interpreter of scripture. What we have found is a significant degree of common ground between the two, in spite of what we know to be their obvious theological and ecclesiological differences. One would expect to find that differences in their understanding of the clergy reflect the division between them. Yet even in the priest's role as celebrant of the sacraments it is important that their differences not be overdrawn, for while Erasmus never repudiated the Roman mass, he emphasized again and again the importance of the inner transformation over the mere observance of the ritual for all of the sacraments.

There is, however, one point that is a key to their respective approaches to exegesis. Calvin begins with an emphasis on the essential clarity of scripture itself; it is our sinfulness and our limitations that cause us to stumble. Pastors are God's remedy for this difficulty, men who are called and trained to help bring that clarity to the people. Along with his emphasis on clarity, Calvin would reject the allegorical approach to interpretation. As we have seen, it is this approach in particular that is the centerpiece of the program of Erasmus, who believed that scripture itself is formulated in such a way that necessitates work to "crack the nut," to get beyond the potentially misleading exterior and arrive at the inner core of meaning. Scripture is obscure by design, but not altogether inaccessible, and even the obscurity is a necessary accommodation to human limitations.

Yet even these apparent obvious levels of divergence do not necessarily bring us to the safe haven of a conclusion, for, as Ward Holder tells us, scripture for Calvin is a place where even the most seasoned interpreter can get lost.[55] In the place of a summative explanation of the differences between Calvin and Erasmus, I will end by saying that I believe the exercise of making the comparison between them opens the possibility for a better, more nuanced under-

[54] Holborn, *Ausgewählte Werke*, 286:1-4.

[55] See Ward Holder's contribution to the present work: "Calvin's Exegetical Understanding of the Office of Pastor."

standing of the thinking of each of them as individuals and within their six-teenth century context. An inquiry that would be particularly welcome would be one that could address in more detail than I have been able to do here the interrelationships between theology, ecclesiology, and exegetical method in Erasmus's and Calvin's respective approach. My preliminary insight is that the results would be neither predictable nor formulaic.

# The Apostolic and Pastoral Office: Theory and Practice in Calvin's Geneva[1]

*Darlene K. Flaming*

## I. Introduction

In the 1543 *Institutes*, John Calvin commends the necessity of human ministry, writing, "For neither the light and heat of the sun, nor food and drink, are so necessary to nourish and sustain the present life as the apostolic and pastoral office is necessary to preserve the church on earth."[2] Certainly Calvin presents a high view of the ministry, for nothing less than the preservation of the church on earth depends on it. Yet another part of the passage bears examination, that is, the description of this necessary ministry as the "apostolic and pastoral office." Why one office but two descriptors? My original project for this conference on Calvin and the Company of Pastors was to examine this intersection of "apostolic and pastoral." I planned to look at the similarities Calvin identifies between the apostles and pastors so that he can use the apostles as examples or models for contemporary pastors. Yet, at the same time, I would also look for the disjunctions Calvin finds between the apostles and pastors so that the apostles should not be "aped" or falsely imitated, a charge he often lodged against both the Romanists and the radicals.

From earlier research, I knew that Calvin's careful attention to similarities and differences was the basis on which he would build a true imitation.[3] I had intended to focus on the more theoretical side: Calvin's teachings on the subject in the *Institutes*, commentaries, sermons, and treatises. Yet last summer at the Meeter Center, I serendipitously, or perhaps providentially, happened upon a copy of the *Register of the Company of Pastors*. I picked it up for some light

---

[1] The research for this study was conducted at the Meeter Center for Calvin Studies at Calvin College and Theological Seminary and was supported by a faculty research fellowship for the Summer of 2002.

[2] *Institutes*, 4.3.2. Regardless of the year the passage was added, section numbers in the *Institutes* will be given from the easily accessible 1559 edition.

[3] Darlene K. Flaming, *The Appeal to the Apostles: The Use of the Apostolic Church in the Writings of John Calvin* (Ph.D. diss., The University of Notre Dame, 1998), particularly 19-23, 94-118, 155-157 and 203-229.

reading and almost before I knew it my project changed. I was fascinated by the glimpse into the actual practice of this group of pastors. It is one thing to set up an ideal of ministry and to castigate others for merely "aping the apostles," but it is quite another to try to put into practice a pastoral ministry based, at least in part, on the apostolic example.

So the central question has changed from "What is Calvin's theoretical model of the 'apostolic and pastoral office'?" to "How does the practice of the pastoral ministry as set up in Geneva correspond to Calvin's model of ministry as a true imitation of the apostles?" The primary resources for this study are the *Institutes*, where most of the model for ministry was in place by 1543; the *Ecclesiastical Ordinances* of 1541, which was the prescriptive plan set up for the good order of the church and ministry in Geneva; and the *Register of the Company of Pastors*, which was begun in 1546.[4]

Ephesians 4:11-12 is the central scriptural springboard for Calvin's discussion of the relationship between apostles and pastors.[5] It reads, "And [God] gave some to be apostles and some prophets, and some evangelists, and some pastors and teachers." Based on this passage, Calvin sets out in the 1543 *Institutes* a discussion of the ministry which remains virtually unchanged through the succeeding editions. In this list of five offices, Calvin groups the first three (apostles, prophets, and evangelists) together as temporary and extraordinary offices; that is, they were limited in time and outside the normal order of the church. The last two (pastors and teachers) are grouped together as permanent and ordinary offices; that is, they are always necessary for the right ordering of the church.[6] While this distinction between the temporary and extraordinary office of apostle, and the permanent and ordinary office of pastor highlights the differences between the two, Calvin immediately moves to show the similarity between the two offices. He does this by pairing the offices, writing, "For as our teachers correspond to the ancient prophets, so do our pastors [correspond] to the apostles."[7] This interpretation of Ephesians 4:11

---

[4] This present study is focused on locating the points of connection between these three different types of sources, rather than determining influence. Thomas Lambert has a helpful discussion of the sources of our knowledge about Geneva. The *Ecclesiastical Ordinances* are "prescriptive sources" setting out what should be done but often ignored in practice. See Thomas Lambert, *Preaching, Praying and Policing the Reform in Sixteenth-Century Geneva* (Ph.D. Dissertation, University of Wisconsin-Madison, 1998), 15-16. Robert Kingdon provides a readable introduction to the Company of Pastors and the Register in "Calvin and 'Presbytery': The Geneva Company of Pastors," *Pacific Theological Review* 18 (1985): 43-55.

[5] Indeed, Elsie McKee identifies it as the central scripture for Calvin's understanding of the plural ministry. Elsie McKee, *Elders and the Plural Ministry: The Role of Exegetical History in Illuminating John Calvin's Theology* (Geneva: Droz, 1988), 133.

[6] *Institutes*, 4.3.4. On the issue of Calvin's understanding of "ordinary" and "extraordinary," one might consult Benjamin Milner, *Calvin's Doctrine of the Church* (Leiden: Brill, 1970), 44 and 109.

[7] *Institutes*, 4.3.5. The evangelists are seen as associates of the apostles sharing the same charge and scope of ministry, although not being honored as highly.

according to different groups (temporary and permanent) and corresponding pairs (apostle and pastor) provides the basis for Calvin's use of the apostles as a model for pastors without promoting identity in every detail.

Elsie McKee has demonstrated that a precedent for Calvin's interpretation of Ephesians 4, particularly in terms of separating temporary and permanent offices, can be found in the exegetical history of the passage.[8] Calvin's contribution is his combination of certain exegetical traditions, his clarity, and the practical concern of finding in Scripture a workable model of church order. Calvin's pairing of apostle with pastor and prophet with teacher is not generally emphasized. Yet it is the pairing of certain offices as similar, while at the same time separating them according to temporary or permanent, which allows Calvin to create a model for "true and faithful pastors" based on first century apostles but applicable for sixteenth century Geneva.

Throughout his works, and even in his prayers, Calvin makes use of the phrase "true and faithful ministers."[9] These adjectives have very precise connotations in Calvin's thought. A true minister is one with a legitimate call. A faithful minister is one who carries out his calling or the "tasks enjoined."[10] The rest of this paper will be organized using these two ideas of a faithful minister and a true minister. Although logically it might make more sense to deal with the call of a true minister before looking at the performance of the office by a faithful minister, I will follow the order which Calvin uses in the *Institutes* which addresses first the faithful fulfillment of the office, then the true call.[11] One reason I chose to use this order (besides remaining faithful to Calvin) is that in this first category we can see both Calvin's unequivocal use and his rejection of the apostolic example for pastors.

## II. "Faithful Ministers"

### A. Shared Tasks

A faithful minister will fulfill the "two particular functions" of "the apostolic and pastoral office." Calvin finds these functions commanded of the apostles in Matthew 28:19: "The Lord, when he sent out the apostles, gave them . . . the command to preach the gospel and to baptize those who believe unto forgive-

---

[8] McKee, *Elders*, 133-170.

[9] See for instance, Calvin's prayers at the end of certain sermons on Isaiah from 1557. These prayers are excerpted in Elsie McKee, ed. and trans., *John Calvin: Writings on Pastoral Piety*, Classics of Western Spirituality (New York: Paulist Press, 2001), 226-228.

[10] *Institutes*, 4.3.10. See also *Comm. I Cor.* 1:1 (CO 49:305-6) where Calvin says that the minister "must be called by God to that office, and be faithful in carrying out its duties." Later in the same passage he gives the test for faithfulness as whether the minister was "proclaiming the pure teaching of Christ."

[11] *Institutes*, 4.3.10.

ness of sins."[12] Calvin generalizes these commands, saying, "Here is the holy, inviolable, and perpetual law imposed upon those who took the place of the apostles, by which they receive the command to preach the gospel and administer the sacraments."[13] Although Calvin adds texts from Titus 1 and I Corinthians 4, in an attempt to show that these functions are commanded of pastors as well as apostles, his central text is Matthew 28:19 where the two functions are joined.

This idea that the mandate of the "apostolic and pastoral office" is "to preach the gospel and administer the sacraments" is used primarily in two ways: 1) To oppose Roman claims of apostolic succession, and 2) to teach pastors their duty. First, the claim in the Roman church was that the bishops were the successors of the apostles. Throughout his works, Calvin makes a very standard reformers' argument that those who do not carry out this mandate to preach cannot be considered apostolic, thus disqualifying the bishops, who rarely preached.[14] However, merely preaching is not enough to fulfill the office faithfully. Faithful pastors must preach the gospel, the Word of God, rather than their own fancies.[15] Calvin rarely mentions the other possibility of someone preaching but not administering the sacraments. However, Paul's statement that Christ had not sent him to baptize does seem to cause Calvin some concern, so that he insists that as an apostle Paul received both commands but so excelled at teaching that he left baptism to those less gifted.[16]

In addition to the polemical usage of the apostolic mandate against the Roman church, Calvin also uses the idea that the functions of apostles and pastors are the same in order to teach pastors their duty. In the *Institutes,* he uses the example of Paul in Acts to show that proclaiming the gospel is not merely preaching in public but also "private admonitions," warning and teaching them "publicly and from house to house."[17] Although the example of the faithful fulfillment of the apostolic office is present in the *Institutes* to instruct pas-

---

[12] *Institutes,* 4.3.6. Cf. *Comm. Matt.* 28:19-20 (CO 45:822-826). Calvin is absolutely sure that these verses apply only to ministers of the Gospel and not to all Christians. Therefore, he uses this passage to show that women and laymen cannot perform "emergency baptisms" because they are not also given the command to preach the Word.

[13] *Institutes,* 4.3.6.

[14] *Comm. Matt.* 28:19 (CO 45:821). "No man can be a successor of the apostles who does not devote his services to Christ in the preaching of the gospel." See also *Comm. Acts* 1:21 (OE 12/1.42). Cf. Willem F. Dankbaar, "L'Apostolat chez Calvin," *Revue d'histoire et de philosophie religieuses* 41 (1961): 346-347.

[15] Léopold Schümmer sees this as evidence of a functional rather than personal succession of the Apostles in Calvin. Cf. Schummer, "Le Ministère Pastoral dans L'Institution Chrétienne de Calvin," *La Revue Reformee* 45.183 (Nov. 1994-1995), 24.

[16] *Comm. I Cor.* 1:17 (CO 49:319).

[17] *Institutes,* 4.3.6.

tors, Calvin says that "it is not [his] present intention to set forth in detail the gifts of the good pastor."[18]

The commentaries, on the other hand, are the places where Calvin sets out the model of the good pastor. Because of Calvin's conviction about the applicability of every part of scripture, the apostles are not the only ones held up as good pastors. Other models include the prophets, John the Baptist, and Jesus.[19] However, given the goal of this paper, we are going to focus on those passages where the apostles are presented as examples for faithful pastors. These passages are found mainly in the commentaries on Acts and the letters of Paul, because in the Gospels the twelve are treated more as disciples than as apostles.[20] From the beginning chapters of Acts, Calvin uses Peter as a model of the good pastor who defends the sheep from the wolves,[21] who so molds his sermon to the needs of the hearer that those who are willing, are led gently, but those who are lazy, are goaded onward.[22] The example of Paul receives greater emphasis. Like Paul, "Nobody is fit to preach the Gospel" unless he is prepared for suffering and willing to learn along with others.[23] Using Paul's example, Calvin teaches that a good pastor lives what he preaches,[24] serves rather than domineers,[25] exhorts as well as instructs both publicly and privately,[26] is grieved

---

[18] *Institutes*, 4.3.6. "Good" and "faithful" tend to be used fairly interchangeably. See *Comm. I Cor.* 4:1 (CO 49:362-363) where one is used to define the other. "Paul means by a 'faithful minister' someone who, with knowledge as well as uprightness of heart, fulfills the role of a good and genuine minister."

[19] For example in the commentary on John 10, Calvin presents Jesus as the one true Pastor and Shepherd of the sheep. But even in this case the human apostles may demonstrate more helpfully what it means to be a faithful shepherd under the authority of the Great Shepherd. See in particular *Comm. John* 10:12: "But in Himself He offers a perfect example to serve as a model for His ministers." OE, 11/2.33: Sed in sua persona absolutum exemplar proponit, ut ministris suis regulam praescribat.

[20] However, at the end of John, Calvin understands Jesus' questioning and command to Peter to show what is necessary for a pastor. A pastor can only persevere in his office if he focuses on loving Christ. The duty of the pastor is to feed the sheep; that is, to preach the Word. Calvin then uses this understanding again the Pope's claim to be the successor of Peter: "But to neglect the love of Christ and cast off the office of feeding, and then to boast of [Peter's] succession is too absurd and silly." *Comm. John* 21:15-19 (OE 11/2.309-311).

[21] *Comm. Acts* 2:40 (OE 12/1.86).

[22] *Comm. Acts* 3:17 (OE 12/1.103) and *Comm. Acts* 3:25 (OE 12/1.111).

[23] *Comm. Acts* 9:16 and 26 (OE 12/1.274-275 and 280-281).

[24] *Comm. I Cor.* 9:1 (CO 49.437) and *Comm. Acts* 20:18 (OE 12/2.177).

[25] *Comm. II Cor.* 4:5 (OE 15.74).

[26] *Comm Acts* 14:21 (OE 12/2.19), *Comm. Acts* 20:21 (OE 12/2.180), and *Comm. Acts* 27:33 (OE 12/2.298).

by the sins of others,[27] is harsh when necessary although naturally gentle,[28] perseveres in difficult situations,[29] places little value on money,[30] and always ends his teaching, warning and exhorting with prayer.[31] While Calvin sets out the basic functions shared by pastors and apostles in the *Institutes*, he uses the New Testament commentaries to inculcate what it means to discharge this office faithfully by setting forth examples from the apostles for pastors to follow.

So far we have merely looked at Calvin's theoretical model of a faithful pastor fulfilling the duties of the office shared with the apostles. How does the practice in Geneva correspond to this model? In the 1541 *Ecclesiastical Ordinances*, the duty of pastors is "to proclaim the Word of God for the purpose of instructing, admonishing, exhorting, and reproving, both in public and in private, to administer the sacraments, and to exercise fraternal discipline together with the elders or delegates."[32] This general statement of duties corresponds to Calvin's writings about the office of pastors based on the mandate given to the Apostles. It even makes use of the language of public and private admonitions seen in the *Institutes*. Beyond this statement of the basic tasks of pastors in the *Ecclesiastical Ordinances*, the focus is more how one deals with the vices which might be found in a pastor rather than inculcating the virtues of a faithful pastor as in the commentaries. This practical document sets up the days and times for fulfilling different parts of the pastoral ministry rather than stating the more abstract characteristics of faithful fulfillment of the office. For example, a weekly meeting of all the pastors is prescribed for the discussion of Scripture, along with a quarterly meeting for ministerial discipline. The times and places of preaching, baptism and the Supper are set out in detail, as are the visitation of the sick and those in prison.[33] Work on Calvin's sermons, the Consistory records and other archival sources has illuminated how these ordinances were put into practice in the areas of preaching, discipline, and baptism.

---

[27] *Comm. II Cor.* 12:21 (OE 15.207-208) and *Comm. II Cor.* 2:4 (OE 15.37).

[28] *Comm. I Cor.* 4:22 (CO 49.377), *Comm. II Cor.* 10:2 (OE 15.160) and *Comm. II Cor.* 12:20 (OE 15.206-207).

[29] *Comm. Acts* 16:11 (OE 12/2.75), *Comm. Acts* 17:1 (OE 12/2.95-96), *Comm. Acts* 17:5 (OE 12/2.100) and *Comm. Acts* 20:3-6 (OE 12/2.172).

[30] *Comm. Acts* 20:33 (OE 12/2.194).

[31] *Comm. Acts* 20:36 (OE 12/2.195-196).

[32] *Registres de la Compagnie des Pasteurs de Genève au temps de Calvin*, vol. 1, ed. Jean-François Bergier (Geneva: Librairie Droz, 1964), I.2 (36). The English translations in this paper are generally taken from *The Register of the Company of Pastors of Geneva in the Time of Calvin*, ed. and trans. Philip Edgcumbe Hughes (Grand Rapids: Eerdmans, 1966); however, at times alterations have been made to capture the French expression more closely. Hereafter cited as RCP, volume and page number, with the page of the English translation in parentheses, as in the passage listed earlier in this footnote.

[33] RCP I.5, 9-10 (40, 44 and 46). Thomas Lambert has also compiled statistics of the number of baptisms each of the pastors in Geneva performed in a year. The administration of this sacrament is closely tied to the particular time and location of the usual service of each pastor

*The Register of the Company of Pastors* may yield some other ways to think about how the office of the faithful pastor was carried out in Geneva. First, the *Register* bears testimony to the goodness of some pastors. The death of a pastor usually merited some mention with a statement of his service. For example, we hear that Mathieu Malesier "had always fulfilled his office with faithfulness."[34] On occasion positive statements were also made about living pastors. On 9 November 1552, the secretary of the Company records an announcement by the Council that Calvin "was esteemed as a good and true minister of this city."[35] About a year later, the *Register* records a number of citizens coming before the Council to testify that "they esteemed Farel as a true servant of God and his preaching as good and godly, and had received profit and edification from his exhortations." The Council itself recognized Farel "as a true pastor, as he had always been, and it was declared that he had preached and fulfilled his office faithfully."[36] Later we hear that the Messieurs of Berne "esteemed M. Jean Calvin as a good and faithful servant of God and his doctrine as good and godly."[37] While these may seem to be glowing statements about the faithfulness and goodness of some of the pastors, the common thread in all of these cases is that the affirmations were made when the ministers were under attack either for their writings or their preaching.

The other way to look at the practice of the model of faithful pastor would be to look at the failure of pastors to live up to the standard. Although Calvin says in the *Institutes* that those pastors who do not preach the word of God do not deserve the title of pastor, in practice this is a difficult standard to enforce. In the *Ecclesiastical Ordinances* attached to the beginning of the *Register of the Company of Pastors*, outright heresy, schism, and "rebellion against ecclesiastical order" (along with drunkenness, usury, dancing) are considered intolerable vices for a pastor. However, things like "negligence in study" and "negligence in performing all the duties of one's office" come under the category of "vices which can be endured provided they are rebuked."[38] Few of the pastors in Geneva during Calvin's time are deposed for neglecting their duties; indeed

---

[34] December 1557. RCP II.79 (336). See also the statement at the death of Claude du Pont who was "constant to the end in the same faith which he had preached, mourned by all the brethren because he was a man of learning and godliness. RCP II.85 (343).

[35] "Bon et vray ministre," RCP I.144 (201). Calvin dedicates his 1553 *Commentary on John* to the Syndics of Geneva confessing that he is "very far from possessing the careful diligence and other virtues which the greatness and excellence of the office require in a good pastor," although he does "not lack a faithful and sincere will" (OE 11/1.5).

[36] 1 November 1553. RCP II.53 (292).

[37] 28 March 1555. RCP II.62 (308). The sincerity of this testimony may be brought into question because the Messieurs of Berne subsequently sent a letter to their churches indirectly charging the Genevan doctrine "with showing too much curiosity and with wishing to enter too deeply into the secrets of God."

[38] RCP I.4 (38-39).

they cannot be, but rather the main charges will be issues of morality (committing usury, fornication) or rebellion/stubbornness. Ultimately the Small Council, rather than the Company of Pastors, was responsible for the dismissal of pastors, which sometimes made for conflict.

In one early case, Pastor Vandert was deposed for not visiting the sick and not doing the other things necessary for his office. However, it was the magistrates who moved for his quick removal against ministerial opposition.[39] In a later case, beginning in 1549 the Company of Pastors pushed for the dismissal of Philippe de Ecclesia because of his rebelliousness in persisting in "a number of ineptitudes and absurdities and even erroneous teaching," although he had received several warnings.[40] The Council was slow to move this time so that it took four years and numerous other charges before de Ecclesia was finally deposed. Although the Company of Pastors cannot dismiss ministers who do not fulfill their duties, the Company serves a warning function, not only warning those who are negligent but also warning public authorities about these pastors. In the earliest letter recorded in the *Register of the Company of Pastors*, they warn the Bernese of the faults of several pastors who were deposed by Geneva but were welcomed in the territory of Gex. Among these faults they include "The negligence of those who show no care for the charge which they hold and who preach only as a formality and as seldom as they can, involving themselves in profane affairs rather than in the duties of their office."[41]

William Naphy has ably demonstrated the distinction between the pastors hired from 1541 to 1545 and those hired later.[42] In this earlier group, Calvin found much to lament about in colleagues who seemed to be of lower caliber and certainly had shorter tenures in office. Naphy comments that the reality of the situation in Geneva was that "upon his return Calvin and Geneva were so desperate to fill the ministerial vacancies that men of lesser ability were hired and would be replaced as better men became available."[43] Unfortunately the *Register of the Company of Pastors* is not able to provide insight into either the hiring or the dismissal of most of these earlier pastors because these records were not begun until December of 1546. The later group of pastors is more stable and the pastors tend to be more educated and of higher social status. These men certainly come closer to Calvin's understanding of a faithful pastor.

---

[39] William G. Naphy, *Calvin and the Consolidation of the Genevan Reformation* (Manchester and New York: Manchester University Press, 1994), 70. This incident took place before the Company of Pastors began keeping records.

[40] 15 February 1549. RCP I.47 (92).

[41] 3 June 1547. RCP I.20 (61). According to the editors' notes, although not mentioned by name, these charges are likely referring to Champereau, de la Mare, and other pastors who had been compelled to leave Geneva. Champereau was deposed for indecency at the public baths. For an extended narration of the treatment of de la Mare by Calvin, see Naphy, *Consolidation*, 60-68.

[42] Naphy, *Consolidation*, 53-79.

[43] Naphy, *Consolidation*, 59.

Calvin sees apostles and pastors sharing the same mandate to preach the Gospel and administer the sacraments. This idea is used both to oppose the Roman claims of apostolic succession and to teach reformed pastors their duties. In the commentaries, Calvin uses the Apostles to demonstrate the ideal of a faithful pastor. In practice, however, only the basic functions are built into the ecclesiastical order of Geneva. Even then, neglecting the duties of a faithful pastor is not cause for dismissal. The gap between theory and practice may be due to the exigencies of the time, such as the political context and the scarcity of ministers. This office is, according to Calvin, so "necessary to preserve the church on earth" that many officeholders may be tolerated who do not live up to the ideal of the faithful pastor modeled by the Apostles.

## B. Different Extents

Calvin uses the pairing of the office of apostle and pastor to show the faithful fulfillment of the shared tasks of word and sacrament found in Matthew 28:19. However, even within this verse he makes a distinction between what is temporary, applicable only to the apostles, and what is the permanent norm for pastors. The command to make disciples of "every nation," or in Mark's version of the saying, "to preach the gospel to every creature," was, according to Calvin, specific to the apostles and evangelists in the extraordinary circumstances of the first century.[44] The ordinary order is that pastors were assigned to perform in a particular church what the apostles had been sent to do in the whole world.[45] Although apostles and pastors share the same mandate, they differ on the *extent* of the mandate. Once again, there was an exegetical tradition on this distinction going back to Chrysostom and Theodoret.[46] However, Calvin places special emphasis on a settled ministry in opposition to the mendicant monks and itinerant Anabaptist preachers, both of whom were claiming the apostolic example.[47]

While the emphasis on a settled ministry was part of the *Institutes* from the beginning, in the 1543 edition Calvin added a discussion that a pastor is not so absolutely bound to a particular church that he cannot move if "public welfare demand it." He goes on to say,

> But he who is called to one place ought not to think of leaving or to seek release (considering it to be to his advantage). Then, if it be expedient for

---

[44]*Institutes*, 4.3.4.

[45] This distinction between apostles and pastors on the extent of their ministries is also found throughout the commentaries. See *Comm. Acts* 14:23 (OE 12/2.21-22), *Comm. Acts* 15:36 (OE 12/2.63), *Comm. Acts* 16:16 (OE 12/2.72), *Comm. Rom.* 1:5 (*Romanos*, 16), and *Comm. I Cor.* 12:28 (CO 49.506).

[46] McKee, *Elders*, 141.

[47] These freelance preachers were evidently a significant problem because a number of synods of the French churches included lists of vagrant preachers about whom churches should be warned. John Quick, ed., *Synodicon in Gallia Reformata*, (London, 1692) I.42, 46-7, and 74.

anyone to be transferred to another place, still he ought not to attempt this on his own private resolve, but to await public authority.[48]

This addition may have been a response to Calvin's own struggles in determining whether it was right for him to leave Strasbourg to return to Geneva.

The exception to this rule of waiting for public authority to leave one place to go to another is in the event of persecution. In the New Testament commentaries, Calvin deals with this issue of whether faithful pastors may flee persecution. In interpreting Jesus' words to the Apostles, "when they persecute you in this city, flee into the next," Calvin opposes the extremes that a pastor may never flee or that pastors may flee persecution for any reason.[49] Instead he follows Augustine and takes the moderate view that the actions of the good pastor depend on the particular circumstances. Calvin addresses this topic again in reference to Acts 8 where the apostles stay in Jerusalem when the other believers flee because of persecution. Calvin's general rule is that a pastor may be permitted to flee, "if he alone is being attacked, and if there is no fear of the church being scattered because of his absence. But if the struggle involves him and the flock in common, he is deserting his office treacherously, if he does not hold on right to the bitter end."[50] What is ironic in this whole discussion is that since the apostles have the world as their parish (so to say), it is not a problem if they were to leave. Calvin actually has to defend the Apostles for staying in Jerusalem, using them as the model for good pastors in many instances of persecution.

The issue of a settled ministry with the exception of persecution is not merely a theoretical exercise for Calvin, it is an integral part of the practice of faithful ministry in Geneva. Within the *Register of the Company of Pastors*, we can see the emphasis on a settled ministry both in the call of a pastor to a specific church and the release of a pastor. The ministers in Geneva were elected (by the Company) to fulfill specific charges or posts. Although the pastors sent to France beginning around 1555 are sometimes called missionaries in the secondary sources, they were viewed as pastors rather than apostles or evangelists.[51] They were sent to specific churches at the request of the church. They were not sent to evangelize in general.

---

[48] *Institutes* 4.3.7.

[49] *Comm. Matt.* 10:23 (CO 45:284-285).

[50] *Comm. Acts* 8:1 (OE 12/1.232).

[51] Robert M. Kingdon, *Geneva and the Coming of the Wars of Religion in France: 1555-1563*, Travaux D'Humanisme et Renaissance, LV (Geneva: Droz, 1956). Throughout the work, Kingdon refers to these pastors sent to France as missionaries. However, in the *Register of the Company of Pastors*, the men are referred to simply as pastors and the indication is that they were sent at the request of the church to have charge of a particular church. There is some indication that part of the task would have been to visit those with reformed leanings in nearby communities to encourage them to organize formally. See Pierre Imbart de La Tour, *Les Origines de la Réforme* (Melun: Librarie d'Argences, 1914-1948) IV.447-452.

The faithful exercise of the pastoral office also included staying at the particular church until one was released from that church or moved to another one by legitimate authority. In fact, one of the "intolerable vices" listed in the *Ecclesiastical Ordinances* is "leaving one's church without lawful permission and genuine vocation."[52] In the *Register*, we see an example of a pastor leaving his congregation on his own and the reaction of the Company to it. On 10 February 1553, Louis Treppereau sent a letter to the Company of Pastors saying, "the fact is that I was neither able nor obliged to concern myself with the care and administration of the church at Céligny, and so I commended that church to Christ, the true and supreme Pastor of all churches, who will rule you by His Spirit and guide you in the choice of a suitable minister for that church."[53] Evidently the Company of Pastors thought that they had already chosen a "suitable minister" and professed not to know the reasons for his leaving. They sent him a verbal message that "it was impossible to excuse him as he requested in the letter."[54] When one digs deeper, it is clear that this change was initiated by the public authority of Berne, but without the agreement of either the Company of Pastors or the Council of Geneva.

Even within Geneva there was a question about who exercised the legitimate authority for reassigning pastors. As the case of François Bourgoin illustrates, it is not clear whether the Council or the Company of Pastors had the real authority.[55] In March of 1552, the Small Council instructed the Company of Pastors to fill a vacancy at Jussy, one of the country parishes. The Company chose Philippe de Ecclesia. He refused to go unless he was ordered to do so by the Council. So evidently de Ecclesia thought that the Council had the ultimate authority to determine the charge of pastors. When he appealed to the Council, he was not forced to go to Jussy; instead the Company was told to choose someone else. When the Company of Pastors refused, the Council sent word to François Bourgoin, one of the other pastors in Geneva, that he was to go to Jussy. His reaction is instructive:

> Bourgoin now informed the brethren that, as he had no testimony to this call other than the wish of the Messieurs, he could not vacate his present post to go to the country, and that the assurance which he had had hitherto in the exercise of his office was entirely the result of his legitimate calling in accordance with ecclesiastical order; if this was lacking, he could not continue to exercise his ministerial office with a good conscience. He therefore requested the brethren to consider this and give him their counsel, protest-

---

[52] RCP I.4 (38).

[53] RCP I.154 (212).

[54] RCP I.154 (213).

[55] Lambert says that the Small Council had the final authority in hiring and firing ministers. However, most of the time the Council went along with the recommendations made by the Company of Pastors. Lambert, *Preaching, Praying and Policing the Reform*, 222-223.

ing that if he was not sent with their approval and consent he would resign from the ministry.[56]

Although the Council had the political authority to send him where they wanted, their authority alone was not sufficient to assure his conscience of his legitimate call. On the other hand, it is also not clear whether the Company alone would have had the authority. In the end, the Company urged Bourgoin not to resign but to go to Jussy under constraint even though the pastors did not agree with the decision. Almost a year later, Bourgoin was still in Jussy and seems to have learned the lesson that the Council is the authority for the moving of pastors. He sent a request for a transfer directly to the Messieurs, and without notifying the Company of Pastors, the Council ordered Bourgoin to come back to the city and ordered Nicolas des Gallars to go to Jussy.[57] Although the Company had not approved of sending Bourgoin to Jussy in the first place, they are angry at the way he secured his own return without consulting them. Eventually they tell the Messieurs that they "would acquiesce in this change for the sake of peace, yet [they] could not accord it [their] approval."[58]

Outside of Geneva, there was not the same tension between Council and Company over who had the final authority for appointing and moving pastors.[59] Yet even then, the pastor had to be officially released by his church; he could not merely leave on his own. Robert Kingdon gives the example of a letter from the Noyers Church about Pierre Collet: " 'And because the sanctimony of the life of the aforesaid, manners, and sane doctrine merit indeed that he be employed in the Ministry,' the church released him to accept any post open."[60] The issue of whether a pastor could leave a church because of persecution was a very real one for these French pastors. Pastors who had become "too discovered" risked their own lives and all those with whom they came in contact.[61] In these cases, usually the pastor did not decide on his own to flee, but rather the church sent him back to Geneva to be reassigned.

In a long letter to the Church in Paris, the Company of Pastors lamented the persecution faced by this church, but drew on the same distinctions from Augustine about when a pastor could flee that Calvin had used in his commentaries. Although the choice is left in the hands of the church, the general tenor of the letter seems to counsel the church to send the minister back to Geneva as they are asked to "consider whether it would not be more expedient

---

[56] RCP I.133 (189).

[57] 12 May 1553. RCP I.160 (220-221).

[58] July 1553. RCP II.1-2 (223).

[59] Kingdon, *Geneva and the Coming of the Wars*, 26. For these pastors sent to France, the Company of the Pastors had the authority to appoint without the need for approval by the Genevan government or the people of Geneva.

[60] Ibid., 49.

[61] Ibid.

that such arrangement, which could inflame the fury of your enemies, should be discontinued."[62] The pastor (Nicolas des Gallars), on the other hand, received a letter encouraging him to stay if he saw that his leaving would cause the collapse of the church.[63] In the end, the Company of Pastors does not make the decision for the Church of Paris or its pastor; they provide counsel based on the distinction drawn by Augustine but leave it to those closest to the situation to determine how that rule might apply in their current circumstances.

Calvin's theory and practice of the faithful pastor is informed by his understanding of the similarities and differences between apostles and pastors. Like the apostles, the pastors must faithfully carry out the tasks of preaching the gospel and administering the sacraments, although there is the understanding that few pastors could live up to the high standard in the performance of these duties. However according to Calvin, "what the apostles performed for the whole world, each pastor ought to perform for his own flock, to which he is assigned."[64] Therefore those ministers who "gad about the countryside" claiming the apostolic example are merely "aping" the apostles, for they have not discerned what parts of the apostolic witness are permanent and what parts are temporary. A true imitation of the Apostles would mean then that pastors would stay in one place, not arrogating to themselves a universality of ministry which belonged only to the Apostles. On the extent of the ministry, the practice in Geneva corresponds much more to the theory based on the distinction between pastors and apostles.

### III. True Ministers

Now if it seems that Calvin was making some rather fine distinctions between what was temporary and what was permanent in talking about a faithful minister, his discussion about the true minister as one with a lawful call becomes even more complex. Calvin understands the apostles (as mentioned in Ephesians 4) to include, strictly speaking, only the twelve and Paul.[65] When he is discussing the function of the apostles and the extent of their task, he is clear that all of the apostles are told to preach and administer the sacraments, and that all of them are assigned the whole world. However, when he comes to the issue of the "true minister," Calvin tends to divide the apostolic example so that the twelve represent the temporary and extraordinary needs of the first century, but Paul provides an apostolic example which can serve as a model for the permanent order of the calling of a true pastor. In the *Institutes*, Calvin con-

---

[62] 16 September 1557. This letter found in the English translation of the *Register* (333-335) is published in CO XVI.629.

[63] CO XVI.628 (332).

[64] *Institutes* 4.3.6.

[65] *Institutes* 4.3.5.

siders four questions under the topic of calling: "(1) what sort of ministers they should be, (2) how, and (3) by whom they should be appointed, and (4) by what rite or ceremony they should be installed."[66] In the *Ecclesiastical Ordinances*, the points are narrowed to three, with "what sort of ministers" and "how" being replaced by a discussion of the "examination" which is said to be "the most important."[67] In both works, Calvin passes over the secret call which each minister should have, in order to focus on the outward call by the church.[68]

## A. Qualifications of Pastors ("What sort of ministers they should be")

In the *Institutes,* people are told to choose those "fit and competent" to exercise ministry or "adequate and fit to bear the burden imposed upon them, that is, that they be instructed in those skills necessary for the discharge of their office."[69] It is not surprising that Calvin refers to qualifications given in the pastoral epistles which he summarizes as "sound doctrine and . . . holy life, not notorious in any fault which might both deprive them of authority and disgrace the ministry."[70] Perhaps as an echo of doctrine and life, Calvin says, "For, to be sure, learning joined with piety and the other gifts of the good pastor are a sort of preparation for it. Those whom the Lord has destined for such high office, he first supplies with the arms required to fulfill it, that they may not come empty-handed and unprepared."[71] Here he gives the apostles as an example because Jesus equipped them before he sent them out to preach.[72]

Yet when we look at the *Commentary on the Harmony of the Gospels*, there is a clear statement that the contemporary church should not choose people like some of the apostles. According to Calvin, although Jesus "chose unlearned and ignorant persons, he did not leave them in that condition; and, therefore, what he did ought not to be held by us to be an example, as if we were now to ordain pastors who were afterwards to be trained to the discharge of their

---

[66] *Institutes* 4.3.11.

[67] RCP I.2 (36).

[68] According to Calvin, a secret call and one's own recognition of gifts for ministry are not enough; one must have the public call to the office. See *Comm. Luke* 24:49 (CO 45.819).

[69] 4.3.11-12.

[70] *Institutes*, 4.3.12. In the *Commentary on Acts* 1:24, Calvin added a line in the 1560 edition stressing the importance which must be given to integrity because without it learning and eloquence are nothing (OE 12/1.44).

[71] *Institutes*, 4.3.11

[72] *Institutes*, 4.3.12. Calvin does not specify the "arms and tools" the apostles received but if one checks the scripture passages given, the list would include "words and wisdom," "power from on high," the Holy Spirit, exorcism, tongues, snake handling, and healing the sick. The passages referenced are Luke 21:15, 24:49, Mark 16:15-18, and Acts 1:8. One supposes that at least some of these gifts are not necessary for all pastors! In *Comm. Mark* 6:12, Calvin does say that the gift of healing was temporary (CO 45:298).

office."[73] Later in the same passage, Calvin holds up the fact that Christ also chose Paul, who had been educated from childhood. The choosing of the rude and ignorant as in the first twelve is seen as a temporary measure to humble the proud.[74] The later selection of the educated Paul is seen as the norm for contemporary selecting of pastors. Calvin's interpretation of this passage takes place in the context of Anabaptist pastors whom he describes as fanatics "who are delighted with their own ignorance, and fancy that, in proportion as they hate literature, they approach the nearer to the apostles."[75] The problem with these opponents is not that they have falsely imitated the apostles but that they imitated the twelve rather than Paul.

The *Ecclesiastical Ordinances* give more specific instructions about the kind of person the Genevans were to look for in a pastor and the way these qualifications should be ascertained. The two main parts are once again sound doctrine and holy life.[76] The holy life is important because ministers are to set a good example for the congregation. Under the idea of the gifts necessary to be a good pastor, the Company of Pastors is to look for those who are "fit to teach,"[77] who demonstrate a "good and sound knowledge of Scripture," and who can "communicate it to the people in an edifying manner."[78] The ability to communicate means, among other things, that he has a voice loud enough to be heard.

Most of the entries in the *Register of the Company of Pastors* in reference to the election of pastors are very short statements that this person was elected as pas-

---

[73] *Comm. Luke* 5:10 (CO 45:150-151).

[74] Cf. *Comm. Luke* 10:16 (CO 45.314). God "frequently selects the ministers of the Word from among the lowest dregs of the people." It is hard to see the truth of the statement in the Geneva experience. Kingdon looked at the social class of the 88 pastors sent to France by the Company of Pastors. Of the 42 whose class can be determined, there were 14 nobles, 24 bourgeoisie and 4 artisans. None was peasant born (*Geneva and the Coming of the Wars*, 6-8). However, one might connect this to Naphy's findings about the earlier and later groups of pastors in Geneva. Before 1545 the pastors were certainly of a lower quality and also came from lower social ranks. See Naphy, *Consolidation*, 53-79.

[75] *Comm. Luke* 5:10 (CO 45:150-151).

[76] The examination of teaching and life does not stop when one has been called to public office but rather is given as a continuing "mark of a good pastor." *Comm. I Cor.* 4:3 (CO 49.363). Calvin insisted on a congruence between a pastor's preaching and his own life. See Andrew Pettegree, "The clergy and the Reformation: from 'devilish priesthood' to new professional elite," in *The Reformation of the Parishes: The Ministry and the Reformation in Town and Country*, ed. Andrew Pettegree (Manchester and New York: Manchester University Press, 1993), 9.

[77] RCP I.2 (36). Cf. the Argumentum to *Comm. I Cor.* (CO 49:299). No one is fit to teach who has not absorbed the Gospel so that he can speak from the heart and not merely from the lips.

[78] RCP I.2 (36). Karin Maag points out that the establishment of the academy in 1559 does not change the requirements for pastors in the 1576 *Ecclesiastical Ordinances*"; see her "Education and training for the Calvinist minister: the Academy of Geneva, 1559-1620," in *The reformation of the parishes: The ministry and the Reformation in town and country*, ed. Andrew Pettegree (Manchester and New York: Manchester University Press, 1993), 135.

tor to that place. However, there are three rather full accounts of the elections of pastors during Calvin's time. One of these accounts is especially interesting in terms of the gifts desired in a pastor but the willingness to work with lesser gifts. In June of 1557, the Company of Pastors had the task of electing three new pastors. Several names were put forward, including François de Morel (a pastor coming from Paris) and Mathieu Grandjean (the school master from the hospital). When Grandjean expounded a passage for the Company, it was clear that he was "too timid and as yet lacking in style,"[79] but they decided to proceed with the examination. They found his knowledge good but his answers slow. The next time the pastors assembled they "agreed to wait some time longer to see whether God would send us someone more adequate than those whose names were before us." Grandjean was given some assurances so he would not "lose heart" and was told to "do all he could to equip himself."[80] When de Morel finally arrived and expounded Psalm 125, they were "well pleased with his acuteness and skill."[81] In the end, Grandjean, de Morel, and Claude du Pont were all three elected as pastors. The recognition of Grandjean's lack of style, however, prompted a movement of a number of pastors so that Grandjean could be sent to a country parish and one of the other country pastors brought to Geneva. The juxtaposition of these three elections gives us some insight into the practical consideration of having to choose pastors with vastly different gifts and trying to find appropriate places for them. Some of these pastors may have been closer to the twelve originally chosen by Jesus than Calvin would have wanted!

## B. How Pastors Are Chosen

This situation of the scarcity of pastors and the conviction of the absolute importance of the pastoral office may shed some light on the small but significant discussion in the *Institutes* of how or rather with what "religious awe" pastors were chosen. Calvin mentions the example of Acts 14 with the fasting and prayers tied to the appointment of presbyters: "For, since they understood that they were doing the most serious thing of all, they dared attempt nothing but with the highest reverence and care. But they especially applied themselves to prayers in which they besought from God the Spirit of counsel and discretion."[82] Throughout the commentaries, Calvin finds examples of how the church should choose ministers drawing on Jesus' praying before appointing

---

[79] RCP II.75 (324).

[80] RCP II.75 (325). Kingdon discusses the case of Grandjean, but indicates that because of the less than stellar performance he was returned to the school; see his *Geneva and the Coming of the Wars*, 26-27.

[81] RCP II.76 (326).

[82] *Institutes*, 4.3.12.

the apostles and the church at Antioch at prayer when they appointed Paul and Barnabas.[83]

Although these instructions are not given in the *Ecclesiastical Ordinances*, we do see the group at prayer in the *Register of the Company of Pastors*. Although we might assume that prayer was a normal part of the meeting of the Company, the *Register* mentions prayer specifically in connection with the election of pastors: "After having earnestly invoked the name of God, several good candidates were nominated."[84] "After invocation of the name of God, all unanimously elected Maitre Jean Fabri."[85] Sometimes after nominations were made, the pastors agreed to meet the following week so that they would have time to "give thought to the matter and commend it in prayer to our Lord."[86] In the case mentioned earlier where the Company of Pastors and the Council did not agree on who should fill the position at Jussy, the *Register* states explicitly that the decision to send de Ecclesia to Jussy was made "after calling on the name of God." This may help to explain why the Company was convinced that "they could not have acted better and more conscientiously than they had done" and why, therefore, they refused to choose another.[87] On this issue of how pastors should be chosen or the care with which they are chosen, the actual practice in Geneva corresponds well to the prayerful model Calvin finds in Jesus choosing the apostles, the church at Antioch choosing Paul and Barnabas, and the Apostles appointing elders.

## C. Who Should Choose Pastors

Calvin's next point about the true call of a minister in both the *Institutes* and in the *Ecclesiastical Ordinances* is the question of who should choose or elect a pastor. In the *Institutes*, Calvin says that "The election of the apostles provides no sure rule in this matter, for it was somewhat different from the calling of the rest."[88] In this passage, he is referring specifically to the twelve. Because it was an extraordinary ministry, it needed the notable mark of being ordained by

---

[83] "Now, this example ought to be regarded by us as a perpetual rule, to begin with prayer, when we are about to choose pastors to churches: otherwise, what we attempt will not succeed well. And certainly our Lord prayed, not so much on his own account, as to lay down a rule for us." *Comm. Luke* 6:12 (CO:45:157-8). See also *Comm. Acts* 1:24 (OE 12/1.44) with the choosing of Judas' replacement, and *Comm. Acts* 14:23 (OE 12/2.22-23) with Paul and Barnabas appointing elders. In this passage there is a two-fold reason for the prayer: 1) "that God would direct them with the Spirit of wisdom and discretion to choose all the best and most suitable men," and 2) "That God might endow with the necessary gifts those elected to be pastors."

[84] RCP II.75 (324).

[85] RCP I.61 (113). See also RCP I.149 (207) where the formula is used twice.

[86] RCP I.61 (113).

[87] RCP I.132 (188).

[88] *Institutes* 4.3.13.

Christ alone. Calvin takes seriously Paul's claim in Galatians 1 not to have been made an apostle by man nor through man so that he has the same status as the other apostles.[89] Yet from Acts' description of the setting apart of Paul and Barnabas by the church at Antioch, Calvin is able to find a model which should be followed: "God, then, could not approve this sort of order by a clearer example than, after having declared that he had appointed Paul apostle to the Gentiles, he nevertheless would have him designated by the church."[90]

This section on the churchly call was added in the 1539 *Institutes* in response to the radicals who emphasized the apostolic example of a direct call by God, what Calvin would refer to as the "secret call." Even within the church, the question remains: Who should elect the pastor: a single official, the pastors, the elders, or the entire congregation?[91] Calvin takes as his key example Acts 14:23 where Paul and Barnabas create presbyters in every church. The Greek word χειροτονέω plays a critical role here. It is usually translated as "by the laying on of hands," but Calvin finds that it can also mean "by the show of hands" or by a vote of the people. In the *Institutes*, he comes to the conclusion that the "call of a minister is lawful according to the Word of God, when those who seemed fit are created by the consent and approval of the people; moreover, that other pastors ought to preside over the election in order that the multitude may not go wrong either through fickleness, through evil intentions, or through disorder."[92]

Before we go on to the practice in Geneva, it will be useful to look more closely at the 1543 *Institutes*. Beginning in this edition, Calvin systematically incorporates into his discussion of ministry an historical progression of the corruption of the church. He begins with the order for governing the church as instituted by Christ and shown in the practice of the apostles; then he moves to the ancient church as it mainly followed the model from Scripture but introduced some changes; and finally he shows the total corruption of the practice under the papacy. In connection with the type of candidate and the "religious awe" with which he is chosen, Calvin says clearly that "the ancient church followed Paul's prescription and the examples of the apostles."[93]

However, in terms of who should choose the minister, Calvin finds much more variety in the ancient church. He makes use of statements by Leo I and

---

[89] Cf. *Comm. Acts* 1:23 (OE 12/1.43). Paul and Matthias both have dual status since their call was indicated directly by God and that they received a churchly call. Therefore, Calvin is able to use these call stories as partial examples for the calling of pastors. The other eleven apostles do not really give an example for the call of pastors because they were directly appointed by Christ.

[90] *Institutes*, 4.3.14.

[91] Kingdon helpfully sets the context of this decision in a rejection of the Roman practice of ordination by a bishop. The focus on the Company of Pastors is a commitment to "collegial leadership." See Kingdon, "Calvin and 'Presbytery'," 48.

[92] *Institutes*, 4.3.15.

[93] *Institutes*, 4.4.10.

the decrees from the Council of Laodicea to show the part played not only by the clergy and people, but also by the civic leaders in the election of a bishop. Calvin gives one such scenario:

> First, the clergy alone made their choice; they then offered the one they had chosen to the magistrates or senate and leading citizens. The latter, after deliberation, ratified the election if it seemed just; if not, they chose another whom they preferred. Then they brought the matter before the people, who, although not bound by the previous decisions, nevertheless could not raise a tumult.[94]

When it came to the election of presbyters, Calvin says that the people generally trusted the other clergy to make wise choices, and therefore, the consent of the inhabitants was only needed "when new presbyters were assigned to parishes."[95] Calvin usually sees practices in the ancient church which differ from the model in scripture as beginning a process of corruption. However, Calvin does not have any negative statement in the *Institutes* about the new roles played by civic leaders in the election of ministers.

When we come back to the question of how Calvin's theoretical model corresponds to practice in Geneva, we see that in the *Ecclesiastical Ordinances,* the issue of who chooses pastors is based more on the ancient church than on the apostolic church. In fact, at the beginning of the section the claim is made that "it will be advisable to follow the order of the ancient Church, seeing that it is but the putting into practice of what we are shown in Scripture."[96] First, the Company of Pastors examines the candidate for holy life and sound doctrine through interrogation and hearing him expound a passage of scripture. Then he is to be presented to the Council for their commendation. Once approved, he is presented to the people in preaching and if there are no objections he is commended to God by prayer. Finally, he is to swear an oath of office before the Council.[97] The Company of Pastors plays the largest role in the selection of new pastors in Geneva. The Council or public authority has a significant role, possibly because they provide the salary for pastors. The people's role is silent acceptance, although, in theory, objections can be raised by the congregation.

In the *Register of the Company of Pastors,* we see a fuller picture of how this procedure was practiced in Geneva, as in the case of Jean Macar. In December of 1552, when the position at Russin became open, on Friday after prayer, the Company of Pastors nominated several people. The next day the Company met again and after prayer elected Jean Macar as minister to Russin.[98] He was

---

[94] *Institutes,* 4.4.12.

[95] *Institutes,* 4.4.10.

[96] RCP I.2 (36).

[97] RCP I.2-3 (36-37). There is some variation of the pattern here. Ministers sent to the rural parishes generally took the oath before they were presented to the people.

[98] It is somewhat curious that the "election" takes place before the examination.

brought in, told of his election and "admonished concerning the nature and obligation of the ministry, and also its difficulties."[99] He accepted the charge and was given Psalm 110 to expound which he did on the following Monday. His exposition was critiqued by the Pastors, then they began his examination on the articles of religion which lasted around two weeks. As part of the examination he preached on Hebrews 4 before the Consistory and representatives from the Syndics.[100] He took the oath before the Council on January 5. Only afterwards was he presented by another minister and civil representatives to the congregation at Russin. The whole procedure occupied about three weeks.

What is most notable is the diminished role of the congregation. According to Calvin's examination of the apostolic church, ministers were elected by the votes of the people; now they are only called upon for their silent approval. In the case of a minister sent to a rural parish, he is presented to the congregation only after he has taken the oath so that any effective veto power is negated. The presence of the syndics at the examination sermon, however, offers some lay representation early in the process. In the 1561 version of the *Ecclesiastical Ordinances* a change is made so that the name of the minister-elect is presented one Sunday and then the people have until the next Sunday to raise objections.[101] Their silence is taken as approval. It would be interesting to take a look at the Register after this revision to see if there are cases where the people did indeed have objections.[102]

On the issue of who should choose the ministers, Calvin rejects the calling of the twelve as a model but embraces, in theory, both Paul's call by the church at Antioch and the way Paul appointed presbyters by the vote of the people in the churches he visited. In practice in Geneva, the pastors and the Council play a much larger role than the people, but some sort of popular approval (at least by silence) is included. Geneva with its Christian magistrates found the model seen in the ancient church to be more appropriate to their context. Yet in the *Institutes*, Calvin does not insist upon this model which included civil authorities. The key point for him in the apostolic church and the ancient church is not the presence or absence of magistrates in ministerial election, but rather that the people have some voice in the election of ministers. Therefore, a reformed order such as that of Valerand Poullain which gives the people much greater power in choosing their ministers [103] and the Genevan model which

---

[99] RCP I.149 (207).

[100] Most often the candidates preach only before the company and one or two representatives of the Council. See Kingdon, "Calvin and 'Presbytery,' " 48.

[101] CO X.94.

[102] Kingdon remarks that he knows of no cases where the congregation rejected the candidate; see Kingdon, "Calvin and 'Presbytery,'" 49.

[103] In Poullain's order, the elders assemble the whole church and propose two or three candidates they have found worthy; then the church votes on the one they want (led by God, of course). A public examination of this candidate takes place after the election. See Valerandus Pollanus, *Liturgia Sacra*, ed. A. C. Honders (Leiden: Brill, 1970), 220-225.

gives the congregation the limited role of raising objections would both be appropriate ways to put into practice the apostolic model.

## D. The Ceremony for Installing a Pastor

In the *Institutes*, Calvin commends the laying on of hands in ordination for the ministry. He says, "although there exists no set precept for the laying on of hands, because we see it in continual use with the apostles, their very careful observance ought to serve in lieu of a precept."[104] Although in theory Calvin approves of the laying on of hands based on the example of the Apostles, actual practice is another story. In the original draft of the *Ecclesiastical Ordinances*, laying on of hands is approved, but the qualification is made that "because there has been a great deal of superstition in former times, and it may be the occasion of scandal, the practice may be omitted because of the infirmity of times."[105] While following this example of the apostles is recommended, it is not absolutely necessary. In the final 1541 version of the *Ordinances*, any explicit mention of the imposition of hands was deleted, and instead it was claimed that "it will suffice that a declaration explaining the office to which he is being ordained should be made by one of the ministers, and then that prayers and intercessions should be offered to the end that the Lord may grant him grace to acquit himself faithfully in it."[106]

The *Register of the Company of Pastors* provides very little information in terms of the installation of pastors. In July 1549, after the account of the examination of Jean Fabri, there is a brief statement that "Fabri was received as a minister of the church of Geneva and took the oath before Messieurs in the customary manner."[107] The other entries concerning the election or change of pastors usually include a mention that the person "was presented to the people" of the particular congregation by another minister.[108] Ministers in Geneva were usually presented at St. Pierre and St. Gervais at different services. Ministers in the country were generally presented to the people by the previous pastor with a representative of the Council present. These statements about presentation do not differ between a newly appointed pastor and one moving from another charge. There is no mention of the reception of the pastor by the people or any particular form of presentation.

---

[104]*Institutes*, 4.3.16.

[105] RCP I.3; note 1 (37; note 2).

[106] RCP I.3 (37). See Comm. Acts 13:3 (OE 12/1.366) for the possible content of such a prayer: "that the Lord would provide with the Spirit of wisdom and courage those whom He had already chosen for Himself; that by His power He would make them invincible in the face of all the attacks of Satan and the world; that He would bless their labors so that they might not be unfruitful; and that He would open a door for the new promulgation of the Gospel."

[107] RCP I.63 (115).

[108] August 1554, RCP II.56-57 (297); May 1556, RCP II.67 (316);18 July 1557, RCP II.77 (327).

A form for ordination or installation is not given in Calvin's *Form of Prayers*. Although I have tried to find a sermon preached on one of these days of the presentation of a minister, so far I have not found anything at all resembling an ordination sermon. My colleagues have alerted me to some other liturgies which might be useful for comparison.[109] In the liturgy of Poullain, after a suitable candidate has been elected by the people, the minister-elect is examined publicly. On the following Sunday, after a prayer and a psalm, he is asked a series of questions which seems to take the place of an oath. Then the elders lay hands on him praying that God would send the Holy Spirit on him in order that he might serve faithfully in this ministry to the glory of His name and the edification of the Church.[110]

The 1556 Genevan Service Book of John Knox contains a combination of practices—some similar to Calvin's form and others closer to Poullain. Among the English congregation in Geneva, two or three candidates were put forward by the congregation. These candidates were examined by the other ministers and one was chosen. The name of the most excellent candidate was published to the people with the space of at least eight days for objections to be raised about his life. The election and ordination occur in the morning service after the presiding minister has used at least part of the sermon to set forth the duties of a minister. After a prayer by the minister, the people proceed to elect the qualified candidate. However, like the Genevan practice, there is no laying on of hands. Finally, "the minister gives thanks to God with the request of such things as shall be necessary for his office. After that he is appointed minister, the people sing a psalm and depart."[111]

In the end, these two liturgies do not necessarily bring us closer to the practice in the regular Genevan churches. Their explicit discussions of the ceremonies of installation in front of the entire church may serve to highlight a rather weak congregational ceremony in Geneva. The real moment of installation into office may be the oath before the Council or the passing of the examination of the Company of Pastors. In any case, the clear apostolic example of the laying of hands which Calvin promotes in the *Institutes* was edited out of the *Ecclesiastical Ordinances* and even the practice of the commendation through prayer is missing from the records.

## IV. Conclusion

In the sixteenth century, a number of groups were making claims about the truth of their religion based on apostolic succession or apostolic restoration.

---

[109] Michael Springer was of special assistance in identifying these liturgical sources.

[110] Pollanus, 220-225.

[111] William D. Maxwell, ed., *John Knox's Genevan Service Book, 1556: The Liturgical Portions of the Genevan Service Book* (Edinburgh: Oliver and Boyd, 1931), 166-168.

Calvin's delineation of the "apostolic and pastoral office" was made within the context of both the Romanists and the radicals claiming apostolic succession or to be imitating the example of the apostles. It is conceivable that Calvin could have insisted that the apostles were unique and their actions were not to be replicated. He could have taken his church order solely from the teachings about pastors. He could have sought only to restore apostolic doctrine but not the practice of the apostles. However, he does not adopt any of these alternatives.

In his theological and exegetical works, Calvin makes careful distinctions between the permanent aspects of the apostolic office which must be shared by the pastor, and the temporary aspects which were unique to the apostles. Thus, a true imitation of the apostles comes from perpetuating the functions intended for all times and eschewing the characteristics intended only for the first century. Pastors absolutely must fulfill the same tasks commanded to the apostles of preaching the word and administering the sacraments. If they do not fulfill these tasks, then they cannot even be considered pastors. Yet the universal extent of the apostles' ministry was limited to the beginning of the gospel so that now faithful pastors must stay in one place and not use the example of the apostles to roam from place to place.

Calvin also makes distinctions about how the apostolic example is to be used to understand the legitimate call of the true pastor. Calvin is more likely to use the educated Paul rather than the unlettered twelve as an example of the kind of person who should be chosen as pastor. The reliance on the example of Paul is also necessary in understanding who should choose the pastor. The direct calling of the twelve by Jesus without a churchly call was unique. Of course, at all times prayer is necessary for the choosing of apostles and pastors. Finally, in the *Institutes* and commentaries, Calvin sees the constant example of the laying on of hands as an appropriate way to set apart those chosen for ministry. The distinctions that Calvin makes in these more theoretical works are hammered out in the polemical context against those he sees as false imitators or "apes" of the apostles.

Calvin also tries to incorporate these same distinctions into a workable model of the church and ministry in Geneva. Many of these ideas are included the *Ecclesiastical Ordinances*, although without making direct reference to the apostles. The shared tasks of Word and sacraments are set out as the basic duties of pastors. A settled ministry is assumed because leaving one's charge without legitimate authority was an intolerable vice. Pastors were to be chosen who already exhibited the gifts necessary for ministry. The people were to have some role in the call of a pastor. The major differences between this church order and the more theoretical works would be the added role of the Council in authorizing pastors, and the exclusion of the laying on of hands as a ceremony for installing pastors.

The *Register of the Company of Pastors* gives almost no explicit references to an apostolic model for ministry; yet if it is compared to the model set up in the *Institutes*, one can still discern the underlying arguments about how the apostolic ministry is to be enacted in the present. The genre of the *Register* makes it more likely that we will hear about the pastors when they are less than faithful in the fulfillment of their office. There is a clear emphasis on a settled ministry. The thought and prayer put into the choosing of pastors on the part of the Company certainly is in keeping with the apostolic model set out in the *Institutes*. In the actual candidates for ministry, few "Pauls" were available and for a while, at least, Geneva had to make do with some pastors who might have been closer to the twelve. Of course, the apostles did not have to work with Christian city officials.

By merely looking at the actual practice of ministry or even the prescriptive *Ordinances*, one would not immediately come to the conclusion that the Genevan ministry was patterned after the apostolic example. The language and the scriptural texts are not there. However, if one starts with Calvin's careful description in the *Institutes* of a true imitation of the apostles, then it is possible to see the imprint of Calvin's model of the apostles on the ministry in Geneva. With the exception of the laying on of hands, those things which Calvin understands to be a permanent part of the calling to, and exercise of, the office shared by the apostles and pastors are prescribed for pastors in Geneva. Those things which were unique to the apostles, such as a universal ministry, are excluded. Items unique to the Genevan context, such as the role of the civil authorities, may be added. For Calvin, trying to replicate every detail of apostolic practice would be a senseless "aping" of the apostles. Instead, he strives for a true imitation of apostolic ministry embodied in his particular context in Geneva. He prays for the "true and faithful" pastors needed to fill this "apostolic and pastoral office" which is so necessary for the preservation of the church on earth and in Geneva.

# A Response to "The Apostolic and Pastoral Office: Theory and Practice in Calvin's Geneva"

*Thomas J. Davis*

Professor Flaming has provided us with an analysis of the apostolic and pastoral office in Calvin's thought and in Calvin's Geneva, examining in the process the relationship between theory and practice. In a paper that meets the standards of "brevity and clarity," she has scoped out Calvin's position on the pastor's office, showing the nuances of his thought on the matter and the deft movements of his mind while gleaning from the sources available how well, in fact, theory and practice lined up one with the other. The result is a presentation that is quite useful, I would argue, not only for its exegesis of a particular topic that was of theological and pastoral concern for Calvin, but also for its underscoring of a method of interpretation Calvin used, something that one must grapple with as one explores Calvin's approach to Scripture.

Professor Flaming has shown that, drawing upon Ephesians 4:11, Calvin posits a correspondence between especially apostle and pastor, but he does so in such a way that distinguishes the two offices without separating them. Some traits are shared; others are not. The key for a true imitation of the apostles by pastors is to understand what aspects of the office of apostle is "permanent" and shared, and what aspects are "temporary" and not held in common. Preaching the word and administering the sacraments are the tasks that apostle and pastor share, and insofar as pastors truly engage in these acts of ministry, they are "faithful" ministers. The universality of ministry is not shared, so for pastors a settled ministry (a local church) should be the mark that distinguishes them from apostles, whose mandate to preach included going out into all the world. Calvin insisted on this distinction—a settled ministry—as the norm for Geneva.

In the next section of her presentation, Professor Flaming presents the guidelines for what constitutes a "true" minister, that is, what makes for a properly installed pastor. In this regard, she argues that, for Calvin, Paul and his situation within the early church serve as the model for the apostolic and pastoral office more so than the Twelve. Pastors are to be educated, and they are to be chosen with "religious awe," exhibited in a prayerful attitude. Because a secret call is not enough to establish one as a true minister, candidates must be examined by the Company of Pastors, presented to the Council for approval, and then "silently accepted" by the congregation. Though Calvin sees the role of the Company of

Pastors and the congregation as scripturally warranted in terms of public call to office—again modeled after the work of Paul and Barnabas, who created presbyters in every church, who then were accepted by a show of hands—he also understands the role of the Council to be scripturally warranted as well, though not really showing how. Finally, although Calvin, in the Institutes, accepts in principle the laying on of hands as part of the ceremony of setting the pastor apart for his work, this seems perhaps to be lost, or at least obscured, in practice and was edited out of the ordinances as a requirement.

As Professor Flaming has set out for examination these aspects of Calvin's thought on the office of pastor and the way theory and practice coincided, she has throughout demonstrated Calvin's concern for making distinctions while still managing to hold together things that should not be separated. Rather than simply say pastors are not apostles, or that pastors are apostles, we get a both/and with qualifications rather than a blunt either/or. Throughout, Professor Flaming has, at least implicitly, pointed to the expansiveness of Calvin's mind in the way he is able to hold together concepts despite logical tensions that result from so doing.

This approach by Calvin contributes to his ability to think through what amounts to a "true" imitation: capturing the essence or the inward spiritual aspect of a thing without being controlled or overcome, so to speak, by its temporal, outward attributes. A true imitation of the apostles, then, gets at the heart of what they are about: proclaiming the gospel and administering the sacraments; a false imitation simply apes the apostles outward and temporal movements—for example, an itinerant ministry, free from an established parish.

But it is through closer attention to the permanent aspect of the Apostles' work that I want to focus a set of questions. In her presentation, Professor Flaming has done a nice job of distinguishing without separating aspects of Calvin's work on the office of pastor and how he tried to implement that model. If her goal has been to bring clarity to Calvin's material, mine is now to muddy the waters a bit and wonder about things that might complicate today's presentation.

One of the places where one can legitimately spring off into questions has to do with the very role of pastor and apostle. The permanent aspect that is shared is preaching and administration of the sacraments. Calvin, I think, assumed readers knew what he meant by both of these things, so at the point of discussion about offices he does not expand on what it is exactly that is held in common by apostle and pastor. But the assumption is there. For Calvin, word and sacrament both offer Christ to the congregation, and with him, his benefits. Through these things, Christ is made visible to believers. In regard to the sermon, Dawn DeVries has nicely summarized the event: "[it] conveys, or is the medium of, the presence of Christ in the church."[1] When preaching on John

---

[1] Dawn DeVries, *Jesus Christ in the Preaching of Calvin and Schleiermacher* (Louisville: Westminster/ John Knox, 1996), 95.

1:1-5, Calvin states, "When the gospel is proclaimed to us, it is a manifestation of Jesus Christ."[2] Thus, in preaching (as in the sacrament), Christ is made visible, as it were; and the presence of Christ makes palpable the presence and goodwill of God. Indeed, in the *Institutes* (4.3.1), Calvin says that Christ "uses the ministry of men to declare openly his will to us by mouth."[3]

So, if we are to grasp Calvin's view of the office of pastor, it is important to keep in mind that his view of ministry is a high one—not simply that pastors truly imitate the apostles (pretty high in and of itself), but also that, within that true imitation, both offices (apostle and pastor) serve as the mouthpiece of Christ himself.

Thus, the task, if one is going to correlate theory and practice, boils down to, essentially, how humans can serve as the very representatives of Christ, and how that ends up being acted out in the life of the church.

Again, to complicate the scheme a little bit, much of Calvin's understanding of why humans serve as speakers on behalf of the divine can be found, not in reference to the Apostles, but to the prophets, especially Moses. Even in his commentary on Ephesians 4:11, Calvin indicates that the work of the Apostles was preceded, at least in part, by Moses.[4] Professor Flaming has rightly pointed out in her paper that others, not just the Apostles, serve as models for pastors. And since Calvin himself in the very passage on the apostolic and pastoral office makes mention of Moses—muddying up his own scheme—perhaps we should look to Moses as well.[5]

In his commentary on Deuteronomy 5 (the chapter where Moses, as intermediary between God and the people, proclaims the Ten Commandments), Calvin has an extended discussion of how God speaks through humans. And although he follows the pattern of correspondence he devised (and Professor Flaming has pointed out) of equating apostles with pastors but prophets with teachers,[6] he quickly moves on to mix the function of teaching and preaching,

---

[2] John Calvin, *Sermons on the Saving Work of Christ*, ed. and tr. Leroy Nixon (Grand Rapids: Eerdmans, 1950; repr. Hertfordshire, England: Evangelical Press, 1980), 14; CO 47:466.

[3] *Institutes*, 4.3.1; CO 1:776.

[4] *Institutes* 4.3.4 (CO 1:780) indicates that the three offices under consideration—apostle, prophet, evangelist—carried over (*traducendae*) from Moses to Christ.

[5] Indeed, Calvin not only seems to push backwards in time the functioning of the apostolic office to Moses, thus making the category of "temporary" as applied to the office problematic; he also in this self-same passage (*Institutes* 4.3.4, CO 1:780) makes veiled reference to Luther as an apostle in his own time (*nostro tempore*), which again renders the category "temporary" problematic. Maybe in this case it is best to follow Calvin himself, as he uses the word "extraordinary" to refer to apostolic work outside the time of the apostles which does not, under normal circumstances, apply to pastors in the modern day.

[6] Preaching on Deuteronomy 4:44 – 5:3, Calvin explains how God ordained Moses to be as a mirror to all prophets, and to all those charged with the task of teaching in God's church: Et puis Dieu l'a constitu, cumme un miroir … tous Prophetes, et … tous ceux qui ont la charge d'enseigner en l'Eglise de Dieu. CO 26:237.

and Moses becomes the model for preachers, and what it is they do; which, in the end, is to proclaim the Word so that Christians are joined to God and thereby saved.[7]

At this point, then, what Calvin sets before ministers, in their imitation of the apostles, is not simply a hard task, or even an awesome one, but an ideal which seems impossible to meet in practice. That is why one must look at the broader context of Calvin's treatment of the Ephesians passage that Professor Flaming has emphasized, viz. 4:11. It is set within the framework of "gifts of the spirit," but then Paul moves from gifts to offices. Calvin explains the move:

> Now, we might be surprised that, when he is speaking of the gifts of the Holy Spirit, Paul should mention offices instead of gifts. I reply, however, whenever men are called by God, gifts are necessarily connected with offices. For God does not cover men with a mask in appointing them apostles or pastors, but also furnishes them with gifts, without which they cannot properly discharge their office. Therefore, he who has been appointed an apostle by God's authority does not bear an empty and bare title; for he is endued at the same time with both command and faculty.[8]

Calvin goes on to say that ministers, their gifts from God, and the execution of their duties are all gifts from Christ.

I would suggest that it is here—the conjunction of human and divine—that serves as the way Calvin at least thought he had worked out the proper relationship of theory to practice. For Calvin, the Holy Spirit works to make present Christ and his benefits through the use of material instruments: bread, wine, voice, the text of Scripture. Those instruments are not to be disdained; they are the tools of the Spirit. But neither are those instruments to be exalted; without the Spirit, they are useless. But God has willed their use, the Spirit empowers their use, and Christ is present through their use. In the end, God works God's purposes through vessels chosen by God.

But since God works in such an accommodative manner, Calvin takes seriously the role human beings have been assigned in the economy of salvation. Thus, though the final working depends entirely on God, human beings are to prepare themselves for that work, discern that work, and lift it up through the ordinary means God has laid out for the governance of the church—all the processes Professor Flaming has laid out for us in the Genevan context.

---

[7] Preaching on Deuteronomy 5:28-33, Calvin says: Or cependant Dieu montre ice, que quand il nous envoye sa parolle, c'est afin d'estre conioint ... nous, et que nous soyons aussi unis ... luy; qu'il se monster nostre Pere, voila donc ... quelle intention Dieu veut que sa parolle nous soit preschee: c'est que nous soyons reduits comme sous ses ailes, qu'il nous garde, qu'il nous sauve ... (CO 26:410).

[8] John Calvin, *The Epistles of Paul the Apostle to the Galatians, Ephesians, Philippians and Colossians,* tr. T. H. L. Parker (Edinburgh: Oliver and Boyd, 1965; repr. Grand Rapids: Eerdmans, 1985), 178; CO 51:196. The translation has been slightly altered.

And at least allowing that God can and does accomplish God's work of salvation in the manner that God chooses, and by whom God chooses, Calvin says, "This is the best and most useful exercise in humility, when [God] accustoms us to His word, even though it be preached through men like us, and sometimes even by those of lower worth than we are."[9] Lower than we are. As Professor Flaming has so successfully pointed out, there are times in Calvin when the practice does not quite seem to match the theory, at least from our perspective, centuries later. But perhaps we make distinctions that verge on separation that Calvin would have considered suspect. For him, fruit follows blessing, and God's word does not return to God in vain. A faithful pastor is one who does in fact fulfill his calling; if he does not fulfill his duties, the pastor was, by definition, never faithful to begin with.

[9] *Institutes*, 4.3.1; CO 1:777.

# Calvin's Exegetical Understanding of the Office of Pastor

*R. Ward Holder*

## I. Introduction

In 1984, Robert M. Kingdon noted that it was more than a little puzzling that scholars had not devoted considerably more time to understanding the class of people most affected by the Reformation changes, the clergy.[1] While that is a trenchant observation, the explanation may be rather straightforward. This may be due to the kinds of artifacts that pastors leave behind, or rather fail to leave behind. Sermons were frequently not written down, and even more frequently were not maintained.[2] Letters of spiritual counsel might be kept, but only if the minister were recognized as important during his lifetime. As most of us will realize, that is rare. Counseling parishioners, exhorting the indolent to greater efforts at a pure lifestyle, advising couples about wedding arrangements and the baptisms of their children—all of these and dozens of other tasks which a pastor might perform in a week are generally transparent to the gaze of history, unless something goes spectacularly badly.[3]

But as theologians and historians, we do have resources for considering what Calvin thought of the office of the pastor. Certainly some of these have already been considered, such as his four-fold pastoral offices of doctor, pastor, elder and deacon.[4] In fact, some of that ground has been more than ably covered. We

---

[1] Robert M. Kingdon, "Calvin and the Government of Geneva" in *Calvinus Ecclesiae Genevensis Custos*, ed. Wilhelm Neuser (New York: Peter Lang, 1984), 51: "The fact that the Reformation produced several different new types of clergy, furthermore helps explain why there were several different kinds of Protestantism. Full demonstration of this argument, of course, would require extensive studies of the role of the clergy during the Reformation. It puzzles me a bit that more studies of this sort have not already been undertaken, since obviously no social class was as directly affected by the Reformation."

[2] Lee Palmer Wandel notes this in "Switzerland," in *Preachers and People in the Reformations and Early Modern Period*, ed. Larissa Taylor (Leiden: Brill, 2001), esp. 221-233. This contains a particularly helpful consideration of the difference between the sermonic event—which ties together preaching, hearing, pastor and people—and printed sermons.

[3] An example is the case of the baptism noted by William Naphy in "Baptisms, Church Riots and Social Unrest in Calvin's Geneva," *The Sixteenth Century Journal* 26 (1995): 86-97.

[4] *Institutes*, 4.3.4-9. Commentary on Ephesians 4:11.

know what Calvin believed about the various offices of the Church and what tasks he attached to each. But what did Calvin believe about the practice of ministry? To put this another way: if we were to shift Calvin out of the systematics faculty (even though he might have believed that he belonged in the Bible specialty), and placed him in the practical division of our modern seminary, what might he have to say? Further, upon what would he base his teaching?

These are the questions I am trying to get at in this study: Where does Calvin come up with his doctrine of the pastor, speaking exegetically? Second, what is the character of that doctrine? To do this, I will run the following course. First, to lay the groundwork, I will consider the doctrine that Calvin sets forth in the *Institutes* for the pastor. This will be somewhat cursory, as this material from the fourth book of the *Institutes* is rather familiar. After that material is set, I will consider some of Calvin's comments upon the pastoral task found in his commentaries. I will concentrate my efforts upon the Pauline commentaries. This will not come as a great surprise to those who know I have been working at these for some time, but I believe the argument for beginning there is rather sound and straightforward. Calvin finished his Romans commentary in 1539, completing it while exiled from Geneva. From that beginning, he tackled the Pauline commentaries as a set,[5] which takes up the greatest part of his time commenting upon scripture until 1551, when the set is published by Jean Gerard in Geneva.[6] Thus, not only were these the first commentaries that Calvin wrote, but these were also the commentaries that he wrote while his own early pastoral formation occurred.

After having set out the material from the *Institutes* and the commentaries, I will be able to demonstrate several important differences. The material in the *Institutes* concentrates far more upon setting forth the pastoral offices and defending these as the divinely ordained offices against the depredations of Rome. While that same polemical strand can be found in the commentaries, and sometimes at such great length that one wonders how Calvin could have believed that he was writing with any brevity, there are also significant moments of pastoral formation. Frequently, and almost always in passing, Calvin offers the reader a glimpse of what the true pastor will be, or do, or how he will act. This kind of material is almost wholly absent from the treatment of the pastoral office in the *Institutes*. I will not consider the reasons for that difference until I have set both before us.

## II. The Pastoral Office in the *Institutes*

Calvin addresses the question of the pastoral office in the fourth book of the *Institutes*, taking this up in the third section. Having set out in the first section

---

[5]T. H. L. Parker notes this in his *Calvin's New Testament Commentaries*, 2nd edition (Westminster John Knox Press, 1993), 16.

[6]Parker, 26.

of the fourth book the definition and marks of the true church, and in the second section an argument why the church of Rome is not to be considered a church, Calvin arrives at the third section needing to explain what kind of ministers must be provided to the Church.

Calvin begins by noting the divine choice to grace the ministry of humans, rather than the necessity of this option. He calls this an exercise in humility, that we should "obey [God's] Word, even though it be preached through men and sometimes even by those of lower worth than we."[7] Further, Calvin uses Paul's letter to the Ephesians to make his case that this human ministry is the chief way which God has chosen to hold the Church together.[8] Thus, the high prestige of the preaching office is also, in Calvin's opinion, secured by scripture.[9]

Having set forth these issues, Calvin turns to the pastoral offices themselves. He writes that pastors (*pastores*) were part of the permanent offices of the church, along with doctors or teachers.[10] Calvin famously sets the ordering of the Church into four offices, those of doctor, pastor, elder and deacon. I am only considering the pastoral office. Calvin draws upon the fourth chapter of Ephesians again and differentiates between those ministerial offices which were and are occasional at God's command, such as apostles, prophets and evangelists, and the permanent offices of pastor and doctor.[11] Calvin ends the fourth paragraph by delineating between pastors and doctors. Doctors or teachers have the sole task of scriptural interpretation, the maintenance of pure doctrine.[12] (It is a mark of the difference of our time and purpose from those of Calvin's that biblical and theological faculties see themselves as pursuing different disciplines.) Pastors teach doctrine as well, but are also in charge of discipline, administering the sacraments, and giving the faithful warnings and exhortations. The role of doctor thus can be more universal, but that of pastor is necessarily attached to a particular church.[13]

Pastors were charged with "discipline, administration of the sacraments, exhorting the congregation, and scriptural interpretation – to keep doctrine whole and pure among believers."[14] Calvin binds pastors to a church in order

---

[7] *Institutes*, 4.3.1.

[8] *Institutes*, 4.3.2. "Paul shows by these words that this human ministry which God uses to govern the church is the chief sinew by which believers are held together in one body." Calvin draws upon Ephesians 4:8, and 4:10-16.

[9] *Institutes*, 4.3.3.

[10] *Institutes*, 4.3.4.

[11] Ibid.

[12] Ibid.

[13] *Institutes*, 4.3.7.

[14] *Institutes*, 4.3.4, 6.

to maintain good order.[15] After considering the various biblical terms for the pastor, Calvin affirms that these terms for those who rule the church such as bishop, presbyter, pastor and minister all signify the same thing.[16] Calvin covers the calling of ministers,[17] the manner of choosing and electing pastors,[18] and ordination.[19] The whole of the discussion in the 1559 edition of the *Institutes* is actually quite succinct, especially when one considers the kind of spiritual and moral authority the pastors of Geneva wielded.[20]

But does this short discussion in the *Institutes* exhaust what Calvin believed about the pastorate? Those who believe that it does may have a rather adumbrated idea of the ministry in Calvin's theology, as well as a skewed understanding of what pastors do. Some have written that for Calvin, almost the whole of the pastor's task is being a preacher.[21] This idea fails to note the hint in the sixth paragraph of this section which modifies Calvin's insistence upon preaching the Word and the administration of the sacraments. After setting these out as the particular functions of the pastor, Calvin qualifies his statement by noting that "The manner of teaching not only consists in public discourses, but also has to do with private admonitions."[22] This will be considered far more amply in the Pauline commentaries.

Even so, at the end of this brief consideration of the doctrine of the pastor in the *Institutes*, there is a problem. Calvin's pastor seems lifeless, a bloodless form that may deny certain choices of the church of Rome, but is hardly robust enough to take on the charge placed upon him. Consider Geneva itself for an example. In 1534, approximately four hundred religious filled the city, employing possibly another six hundred. The total makes up roughly ten percent of the populace of the city.[23] In the reformed Geneva of only a few years later, a

---

[15] *Institutes*, 4.3.7. It is just as likely that this is a swipe at the clerical absenteeism of the Roman Church.

[16] *Institutes*, 4.3.8. Bishops, presbyters, pastors, and ministers. Calvin claims that he interchanges these terms in the same manner as scripture.

[17] *Institutes*, 4.3.10-11.

[18] *Institutes*, 4.3.12-15.

[19] *Institutes*, 4.3.16.

[20] William Naphy notes that preaching was one of the most significant forms of mass communication in Calvin's Geneva in his *Calvin and the Consolidation of the Genevan Reformation* (Manchester: Manchester University Press, 1994).

[21] Lee Palmer Wandel writes that "For Calvin, the pastors were a distinct office, whose primary activity was preaching—not the range of pastoral activities parish priests had held." Wandel, "Switzerland," 242.

[22] *Institutes*, 4.3.6.

[23] Kingdon, "Calvin and the Government of Geneva," 53-54. Kingdon notes that the 97.5% reduction is misleading, as many of those religious prior to the reform were not directly involved in strictly pastoral duties.

mere twenty pastors filled most of the functions of the much larger number, while being called upon to lead the city in a revolution of piety, worship and common morality. Without considerable personal charisma, this is flatly impossible, especially considering the manner in which the city government could blow hot and cold in support of the pastors.[24] What flesh and blood advice does Calvin provide to fill out these patterns?

If that question is not enough, further issues push themselves into our field of view. For instance: did Calvin's doctrine of the pastor change according to his audience? Did he state a different message in his writings that were aimed at ministers, from those messages he placed in his commentaries to the laity, which might include the artisans, the nobility, and the working class of Geneva? Finally, we may ask why the doctrine or tone of the doctrine of the pastor in the commentaries should differ at all from that in the *Institutes*? Is the ministry not central enough so that the whole of the doctrine about pastors should be found in this guide to the scriptures? Answering these questions, attempting to get at those things left unsaid in Calvin's *Institutes*, as well as coming to a greater understanding of the commentaries in their purpose and doctrine, will be my aim.

### III. The Pastoral Office in the Pauline [25] Commentaries and the Types of Pastoral Advice

Calvin frequently addresses ministerial concerns in the Pauline commentaries. Now, obviously, all concerns of theology, ecclesiology and anthropology are ministerial concerns, if one means by "ministerial" those things which ministers should know for their ministry. But that is not what I mean here. Instead, I have discerned a class of statements about the ministry in the commentaries which are about the practice of ministry itself. In fact, there are two general types of guidance in the commentaries. First, there are those moments when Calvin breaks the train of thought to speak about the necessary actions or characteristics of the minister. Second, there are the paradigmatic ministry moments of the main character, Paul. While the second category is fascinating, I have chosen not to consider it in this paper. Instead, I will concentrate our attention upon those moments when Calvin gives advice helpful to the practice of ministry in the Pauline commentaries. As I have said before, these seem to

---

[24] These differences could occur through new elections, or from the council's seeing the rights of the civil and ecclesiastical spheres differently from the company of pastors. See William Naphy, *Calvin and the Consolidation of the Genevan Reformation* (Manchester: Manchester University Press, 1994).

[25] The term "Pauline" is certainly the most appropriate for the set of commentaries which Calvin first produced. Calvin always intended the book of Hebrews to be among this set, but it is entirely clear from the text of the commentary and his custom of not calling the author "Paul" that Calvin does not hold with any tradition of Paul's authorship of that epistle. His inclusion of this text in the set seems to have been a sort of bowing to the Church's tradition, not a statement of its appropriateness for inclusion.

be moments when Calvin leaves the systematics faculty for the practical faculty, moments when he explains the lives and tasks and necessary character of ministers. It is, paradoxically, almost as if Calvin is offering the breadth of his experience to other ministers.[26] I shall consider what that advice consists of, where it is found in the commentaries, and the kinds of patterns into which it falls. Finally, I shall offer up some reasons for the patterns of evidence.

Calvin's advice can be set forth according to type. In no particular order, those types include his moral advice on the character of the minister; his concrete advice on the demeanor of the minister and practical advice on the life of the minister; his practical guidance on doing ministry; his advice on the preaching ministry; his specific advice on the doctrine a minister must have; his observations on the general ministry of the word; his notes on the office of the presbyter or bishop or pastor, and, finally, his suggestions to congregations on how they must relate to the ministers. As the notes on the office of the presbyter or bishop most closely resemble the material from the *Institutes*, I shall skip that in order to focus on the other sections.

## A. The Demeanor of the Minister

Calvin frequently takes up the opportunity in the commentaries to address the temperament, moral fiber, and integrity of the minister. This was evident even in his first commentary on Romans when he stated, "The preachers of the Gospel are also characterized by friendliness and a pleasant manner, but this is combined with a freedom of expression which prevents them from wheedling men with empty praise or being complaisant to their faults."[27] When one considers Calvin's own ministry, one assumes that he had more personal experience with freedom of expression than the friendliness and pleasant manner portions of this advice. But joking aside, what does this insertion tell us about Calvin's style of commenting? The text upon which he is commenting is Romans 16:18, in which Paul castigates those false teachers who entice the hearts of the faithful away from the true doctrine. There is no necessity to balance the consideration of the false teachers with the positive advice to the true teachers of the Gospel. The passage is clear enough without the antithesis being supplied. In other words, it seems that Calvin finds the formation of pas-

---

[26] Paradoxical, because when Calvin was first writing the Romans commentary in 1539, he had only had one brief period of ministry, which ended astonishingly poorly. More than two-thirds of his pastoral comments come from the first edition version of the commentary.

[27] For citations to the commentaries, I shall adopt the following style. First, the Epistle, comm., chapter and verse. Then the citation to Calvin's New Testament commentaries, volume and page number. Finally, a Latin edition, with page and line numbers, or in the case of the Calvini Opera, column and line numbers. Thus, Romans Comm. 16:18, CNTC 8:325. *Iohannis Calvini Commentarius in Epistolam Pauli ad Romanos*, edited by T.H.L. Parker (Leiden: E.J. Brill, 1981), 326.85-87 "Habent etiam Euangelii praecones suam comitatem et suavitatem, verum cum libertate coniunctam, ut neque homines vanis laudibus demulceant, neque vitiis blandiantur:"

toral consciousness significant enough so as to make it worthy of stepping out-side his normal pattern in order to address it.[28]

Calvin writes a similar passage in consideration of the minister's demeanor in his next commentary, commenting upon 1 Corinthians 4:14. Paul, having made a devastating critique of the Corinthians who are held in honor by speaking of the disrepute in which the apostles are held, then writes, "I am not writing this to make you ashamed, but to admonish you as beloved children."[29] Commenting, Calvin declares

> Now, teachers should learn from this, that such moderation must always be used in reproofs, so as not to hurt men's feelings by excessive harshness; and, as the well-known proverb puts it, honey or oil must be mixed with vinegar. But, most of all, they must take care not to appear to taunt those whom they are reproving, or to be taking a delight in their disgrace. No! and more than that, they must take pains to make it plain that they are out for nothing but the promotion of their welfare. For what will a teacher accomplish by mere shouting, if he does not season the sharpness of his rebuke with that moderation of which I spoke? Therefore if we want to do any good by correcting men's faults, it is right to make it plain to them that our criticisms come from a friendly heart.[30]

What we have here, other than an obvious glossing over Paul's apparent nastiness, is rather significant. First, the insertion of a lengthy comment on how to minister breaks the flow of the argument. Calvin had just observed that Paul's whole point in this extended Corinthian bashing was to get the Corinthians to set aside any arrogance and high ideas and to place true value on Paul's ministry, set before them truly by Paul's sufferings in his ministry among them. Calvin goes so far as to call these sufferings "stigmata of Christ" (*stigmata Christi*). The aim of exalting the humility of the apostle's suffering and the denigration of the pseudo-apostles is rather side-tracked by this addition. This side-tracking signals the reader about this feature's significance for study and consideration.

---

[28] I am not proposing an exegetical principle for reading Calvin's commentaries, namely that it is extraordinary for Calvin to abandon his lucid brevity. This is not unusual for Calvin. Rather, it is a mark that something is important to Calvin.

[29] 1 Corinthians, 4:14, New Revised Standard Version.

[30] *Comm. 1 Corinthians 4:14*, CNTC 9: 96; CO, 49:371-372. "Hinc autem colligant doctores, tale in correctionibus semper adhibendum esse temperamentum, ne immodica acerbitate vulnerent animos, et (ut vulgari proverbio dicitur) mel aut aleum aceto miscendum esse: in primis vero esse cavendum, ne videantur insultare iis quos castigant, aut eorum pudore delectari: quin potius dandam esse operam ut nihil aliud quaerere intelligantur quam ut ipsorum saluti sit consultum. Quid enim vociferando proficit doctor, nisi illa quam dixi moderatione acrimoniam obiurgationis condiat? Ergo si quid prodesse volumus hominum vitia corrigendo, testatum illis facere convenit, ab amico animo correctiones nostras profisci."

Second, Calvin is again offering very practical advice. "Be gentle and sweet," states the teacher. We may chuckle to ourselves that this is another case of the adage that "those who can, do; those who can't, teach." However, it is worth noting the quality and character of the advice. This is hardly advanced theology, but it touches directly upon advanced ministry. Experienced pastors know that there are some messages which cannot be given until the congregation is convinced of the love and concern of the pastor for that body of the faithful. It is normally young pastors who have not figured this out and whose ministry suffers grievously for that lack of understanding.

Finally,[31] Calvin thunders that there is no room for coldness in the office of minister. This may be one of the more stunning passages in Calvin's corpus, as the Reformer perhaps most famous for his dour attitude denies the possibility of serving truly in the office of pastor with a cold or indifferent heart. Commenting upon 2 Corinthians 11:2, Calvin differentiated between two types of jealousy, one that represented a petty sin, and another which was a holy zeal:

> All ministers are "friends of the bridegroom", as the Baptist says of himself (John 3.29), and so they should all be concerned that the fidelity of the holy marriage [between Christ and the Church] remains entire and inviolate. This they can do only if they share the love of the Bridegroom for the Church, so that each is as concerned for her purity as a husband is for the chastity of his wife. Away with all coldness and indifference in this matter, for he who is cold cannot be suited for this office, but at the same time let ministers beware of pursuing their own interests rather than Christ's and of intruding themselves in His place, lest, while they pretend to be the bridegroom's friends, they are in fact adulterers who seduce the bride's love to themselves.[32]

See the necessity of fire in the minister! Only those who can offer a true passion are able to be about the business of the Church. Only those who enter into this task with all of their faculties, which includes their passions, will be able to take on the difficult duties which a minister must perform. The scholar-pastor, who brings a depth of knowledge and learning to the leading of the Church is perhaps the ideal in Calvin's conception of the ministerial office. But some of the virtues of the scholar, such as detachment, must not be carried over into pastoring.

---

[31] Other passages in which Calvin considers the demeanor of the minister include Calvin's comments upon 2 Corinthians 2:2, Colossians 4:2, 1 Timothy 4:7 and 6:12, 2 Timothy 1:7 and 4:2, Titus 2:9 and 3:11, and 1 Thessalonians 2:11 and 4:1.

[32] *Comm. 2 Corinthians 11:2*, CNTC 10: 140; *Ioannis Calvini Opera Exegetica, Commentarii in Secundum Pauli Epistolam ad Corinthios*, edited by Helmut Feld (Geneva: Droz, 1994), 174.12-21. "Ministri omnes amici Sponsi sunt, quemadmodum Baptista de se testatatur. Curare igitur debent omnes ut fides sacri coniugii salva et illibata maneat. Id facere nequeunt, nisi Sponsi affectum induant, ut non secus ac maritus de uxoris suae castitate unusquisque eorum de Ecclesiae puritate sit solicitus. Facessat hic frigus et ignavia. Nam qui frigidus est, nunquam erit ad hoc officium idoneus. Sed caveant interea, ne suum ipsi negotium agant potius quam Christi: ne se eius loco obtrudant; ne dum eius paranymphos se esse simulant, sponsam in amorem sui pelliciendo, revere sint adulteri."

This passage introduces another facet of Calvin's pastoral advice in his commentaries. Here, we see the way that Calvin enjoys getting "double-duty" out of his advice. This piece of advice was about the demeanor of the minister, but it also served as a warning against improper ambition in the pastor and therefore speaks to the character of the minister. This must be understood for three reasons. First, analytically, this habit of Calvin makes the creation of a tidy typology of his advice difficult or even impossible. Second, this should act as a caution against modern page-counters. Yes, Calvin's total amount of space given to these comments is not great, but the amount of advice given over-reaches the amount of lines he devotes to it. Finally, and I believe most importantly, the intertwining of various types of advice to ministers in Calvin's commentaries gives us a clue to Calvin's conception of the pastoral task. It was not a labyrinth, but the parts of the task did touch each other, meaning that no man could simply change a single feature of his ministry without considering how that affected the totality of his service to the Church and to God.

## B. The Character of the Minister's Life

Calvin frequently will speak to the moral character which ministers must possess. Given what we know of the actions of the Consistory, it seems wholly harmonious with Calvin's general concern for morality that he should have a high set of standards for preachers.[33] This is the case. One significant topic recurs throughout the commentaries: the denial of ambition as an appropriate characteristic for a minister. We see this in the 1 Corinthians commentary in the first chapter. In commenting on the twelfth verse, Calvin notes

If anyone is mastered by ambition, he wins followers, not for Christ, but for himself. Therefore this is the source of all evils, this is the most harmful of all diseases, this is the deadly poison in all churches—when ministers are devoted to their own interests rather than to Christ's.[34]

Calvin uses the opportunity given by the Corinthians' desire for factionalism to turn and lecture the ministers. Should it happen, or rather especially when it happens, that a congregation begins to prefer one or another pastor, thus opening the door to possible self-seeking ambition, the minister's own moral character must be there as a safeguard. See how strongly he attacks this moral

---

[33] Indeed, Calvin encourages the Church to hold ministers to a high moral standard, stating that a severe discipline must be exercised against pastors in his comment on 1 Timothy 5:20. There are those who seem to want to flay Calvin for being hypocritical in his morality. This is hardly new. See Francis Higman's article, "The Origins of the Image of Geneva," *The Identity of Geneva: The Christian Commonwealth 1564-1864*, edited by John B. Roney and Martin Klauber (Westport, CA: Greenwood Press, 1998), 21-38.

[34] *Comm. 1 Corinthians 1:12*, CNTC 9:28; CO, 49:316 "Si quis ambitione ducitur, ille iam non Christo, sed sibi discipulos colligit. Hic ergo fons est omnium malorum, haec nocentissima omnium pestis, hoc exitiale ecclesiarum omnium venenum, quum sibi potius quam Christo ministri student."

flaw—it is the font of all evil, the worst of all the plagues which can befall a church. Simple ambition is not a small issue, but the heart of the matter.

Calvin does not only take one swipe at the sin of ambition. He attacks those who would play to the crowd in his comments upon 1 Corinthians 3:8,[35] and in explaining 2 Corinthians 12:14, he excoriates two types of pastors who take up the office out of their own desires. He claims, "It is a bad thing to be devoted to gain or to undertake the office of pastor for the sake of making profit from it, but it is much worse to divert the loyalty of disciples to oneself for reasons of personal ambition."[36] Here, the penetration into the psychology of ambition has been sharpened. Certainly, most will acknowledge the sinfulness of over-weening ambition for money and worldly gain, and the significant danger having such a pastor presents to a congregation. But the desire to nurture the cult of personality is a far more subtle sin, seldom recognized by the churches, even more seldom disciplined. In the age of mega-churches, it is easy to point to ministries that seem to have fallen under a particular personality. What is interesting is that Calvin noted it in a time when the evangelical pastorate had the reputation of withdrawing from some of the excesses of wealth with which Rome had become entangled. That monetary loss did not blind him to the prestige which some ambitious pastors might seek.[37]

Further, Calvin was not above constructing a nuanced standard for the paying of ministers. He berates churches that will not pay pastors a living wage.[38] (Presbyterians were ever thus…) He notes further that there is nothing which keeps a pastor from being wealthy.[39] However, Calvin knows the human heart

---

[35] *Comm. 1 Corinthians 3:8*, CNTC 9:71: "Paul teaches here what goal all ministers should have before them: not being on the look-out for the applause of the crowd, but pleasing to the Lord." CO, 49:351: "Hic docet quem in finem respicere debeant omnes ministri: non ut applausus populi aucupentur, sed ut Domino placeant."

[36] *Comm. 2 Corinthians 12:14*, CNTC 10: 65; *Secundam ad Corinthios*, edited by Helmut Feld (Geneva:Droz, 1994), 204. 21: "Malum est lucro esse addictum, aut quaestus faciendi causa Pastoris munus obire; sed discipulos abducere post se ambitionis causa multo peius."

[37] Calvin also notes the impropriety of pastoral seeking through ambition in his comment upon 1 Timothy 3:1, where he does allow a holy zeal, but worries about any self-seeking.

[38] *Comm. 1 Timothy 5:18*, CNTC 10:262-263. "Thus it follows that those who allow cattle—to say nothing of men—whom they make to sweat for their own interests, to go hungry are cruel and forgetful of all the claims of equity. How much more intolerable is the ingratitude of those who refuse a livelihood to their pastors, who do for them something that it is quite impossible worthily to repay." CO, 52:316. "Ergo crudeles sunt et omnis aequitatis immemores, qui iumenta, nedum homines, esurire sinunt, quorum sudorem exsugunt in suum commodum. Quanto autem minus ferenda eorum ingratitudo qui victum pastoribus suis negant, quibus nullam satis dignam mercedem possunt rependere?" See also *Comm. 2 Thessalonians 3:6-9*.

[39] *Comm. 2 Corinthians 6:4*, CNTC 10:86. "Afflictions include more than necessities, for I take the latter to mean poverty. This is shared by many ministers, since there are few who are not poor, but not by all. For why should the possession of moderate riches prevent a man from being considered Christ's servant, if in other respoects he is godly, of upright mind and honorable life and otherwise

well enough to know the effect of wealth upon pastors or candidates for the pastorate. The desire for wealth is very dangerous in a minister![40] So time and again, Calvin condemns the sins of ambition and avarice in pastors. Taken together, these passages form a fine set of pastoral distinctions. Churches cannot comfort themselves in being niggardly with their pastors by telling themselves that this is somehow the will of God. There is no scriptural attack on pastoral wealth, but if there is ambition, this can be the deadliest sin for a pastor.

Calvin did hold pastors to a high moral standard. He demanded that their lives should be a demonstration of the gospel. Thus, the preacher's life is a key to not only how he is received, but the effectiveness of his ministry: "The first thing in a preacher is that he should speak, not with his mouth only, but by his life, and procure authority for his doctrine by rectitude of life."[41] Calvin understood only too well the effect of a pastor's moral failings on a congregation. We can argue that he might have listened sympathetically to the complaints that this creates the exact kind of clerical elite against which he labored. But he was too realistic in his hard-won knowledge to deny the actual effect of a minister's moral failings on the congregation's health.[42] So he pours forth advice, attempting to form pastors who can meet this standard.

## C. Practical Advice on the Performance of Ministry

Calvin spends a great deal of energy setting out both the demeanor and personal character of the minister. But ministry is not only about the presence which the pastor creates among the people, either by his moral manner of life

---

excellent? A man is not considered a good minister just because he is poor, and he should not therefore be rejected just because he is rich." *Secundum ad Corinthios*, 110.3-10. "Afflictiones latius patent quam necessitates; siquidem necessitatis nomine hic inopiam accipio. Haec porro multis ministris est communis, quod pauci sunt, qui non egeant; non tamen omnibus. Cur enim obstarent mediocres dividiae, ne Christi servus habeatur, qui alioqui pius est, recto animo, honesta vita aliisque virtutibus excellit? Quemadmodum qui pauper est, non ideo protinus bonus est minister, ita qui dives est, non propterea est repudiandus."

[40] *Comm 1 Timothy 6:9*, CNTC 10:275, "This evil is universal, but it shows up more conspicuously in pastors of the Church, for they are so maddened by greed that they will stop at nothing, however foolish, as soon as the glitter of silver or gold dazzles their eyes." CO, 52:327. "Hoc quidem malum est universale: sed in ecclesiae pastoribus magis conspicuum eminet. Ita enim eos dementat avaritia, ut nihil quantumvis absurdum refugiant, simulatque auri fulgor vel argenti oculos perstrinxit."

[41] *Comm. Philippians 4:9*, CNTC 11:291; *Commentarii in Pauli Epistolas Ad Galatas, Ad Ephesios, Ad Philippenses, Ad Colossenses,* edited by Helmut Feld (Geneva:Droz, 1992), 376.63. "Hoc vero primum est in concionatore, ut non ore tantum loquatur, sed vita, doctrinaeque suae fidem vitae probitate conciliet."

[42] Other passages in which Calvin considers the moral character of the pastor include Calvin's comments upon 1 Corinthians 1:17, 3:5, 3:7, 9:1, and 14:31; 2 Corinthians 7:2; Galatians 1:10 and 6:16; Philippians 2:21 and 3:20; 1 Timothy 3:1, 3:2, and 6:12; Titus 1:6, 1:11, and 2:7; and 1 Thessalonians 2:5.

or by his chosen deportment among the members of his congregation. Ministry also is a technical skill. As in other fields of endeavor where one learns through practice, such as law and medicine, in ministry one can see that there are frequently-made choices that can be judged better, worse, or even, finally, wrong. Calvin notes this character of ministry and addresses some of his advice to the practical side of the education of the pastor.

Calvin's practical advice can come in the form of informing the pastor of an important teaching technique. Commenting upon 1 Corinthians 3:2, "I fed you with milk," Calvin writes

> Here one may ask if Paul presented a different Christ to different people. I answer that this refers to his manner or form of teaching, rather than to the substance of what he taught. For the same Christ is milk for babes, and solid food for adults. The same truth of the Gospel is handled for both, but so as to suit the capacity of each. Therefore the wise teacher has the responsibility of accommodating himself to the power of comprehension of those whom he undertakes to teach, so as to begin with first principles when instructing the weak and ignorant, and not to move any higher than they can follow. In short, he must instill his teaching bit by bit, for imparting too much would only result in loss. But these rudiments will contain whatever is necessary for knowledge, no less than the fuller instruction given to the stronger.[43]

The technique or principle of accommodation is rather well-known in Calvin's interpretation of the scriptures, as well as a principle of his theology.[44] It is

---

[43] *Comm. 1 Corinthians*, CNTC 9:66. CO, 49:347. "Hic quaeritur num Christum transfiguraverit Paulus pro auditorum varietate. Respondeo, ad docendi modum vel formam id potius quam ad doctrinae substantiam referri. Christus enim idem lac est pueris, et adultis solidus cibus: eadem evangelii veritas utrisque, set pro suo modo administratur. Prudentis ergo doctoris est, eorum, quos docendos suscipit, captui se attemperare: ut apud infirmos et rudes ab elementis incipiat, nec altius conscendat quam sequi possint: ut denique paulatim instillet doctrinam, ne largius infusa superfluat. Sed nihilo minus quidquid cognitu necessarium est continebunt haec rudimenta quam absolutior doctrina, quae robustioribus traditur."

[44] It is so common, that simply listing the important references becomes cumbersome. See Edward Dowey, *The Knowledge of God in Calvin's Theology*, 3rd ed. (Grand Rapids: Wm. B. Eerdmans, 1994), 3-7; Francois Wendel, *Calvin: Origins and Development of His Religious Thought*, trans. Philip Mairet, (Durham, NC: Labyrinth Press, 1987), 229-230; H. Jackson Forstman, *Word and Spirit: Calvin's Doctrine of Biblical Authority*, (Stanford, CA: Stanford University Press, 1962), 13; Ford Lewis Battles, "God Was Accommodating Himself to Human Capacity," *Interpretation* 31 (1977): 19-38; Olivier Millet, *Calvin et la dynamique de la parole: Etude de Rhétorique réformée* (Geneve: Editions Slatkine: 1992), 247-256; Dirk Jellema "God's 'babytalk': Calvin and the 'errors' in the Bible," *Reformed Journal* 30, 4 (1980):25-27; Vincent Bru, "La notion d'accommodation divine chez Calvin: Ses implications theologiques et exegetiques," *La Revue Reformee* 49 (1998): 79-91. Finally, David F. Wright has considered accommodation in Calvin in several articles. See his "Calvin's Pentateuchal Criticism: Equity, Hardness of Heart, and Divine Accommodation in the Mosaic Harmony Commentary." Calvin Theological Journal 21 (1986): 33-50; "Accommodation and Barbarity in John Calvin's Old Testament Commentaries," *Understanding Prophets and Poets: Essays in Honor of*

important to note that this was not only for God to use in condescending to humanity, but for the pastor or teacher in approaching the faithful. Considering how important Calvin believed teaching the young of Geneva would be to the success of the evangelical cause there,[45] it seems safe to assume that this is more than merely rhetoric, or boilerplate ideals of education. Instead, Calvin advises pastors that this technique is vital.

The reason that this is so important, accommodating rather than obfuscating or changing doctrine for different people, is clear. Without a consistent practice, made possible by accommodation, the possibility of teaching truth to children as well as adults is well-nigh lost. The resulting pedagogical catastrophe strikes at the heart of the Church. Calvin writes

> So this proves false the trumped-up excuse of some who, because they fear danger, make only some stammering and indistinct reference to the Gospel, and allege that in this Paul is their example. In the meantime they make known a Christ so far away, and indeed hidden by many coverings, that the result is that they are always keeping their followers in a state of fatal ignorance.[46]

Only solid teaching, fitted to the capacities of the audience, can hope to advance the cause of Christ in Geneva and the world.

That solid teaching will be facilitated by a well-considered plan, according to Calvin. Perhaps resting on his own experience of having the town to which he was called to teach rise up against his teaching, Calvin advises the teacher to prepare a method of teaching, and to remain steadfast to that plan. Accommodation is good, but the minister must be seen to be acting in a consistent manner:

> It is very likely that Paul had been attacked by the misrepresentations of the false apostles, as though he claimed more power for himself over the Corinthians than over others, or conducted himself quite differently in other places; for he had good reason for wanting this to be made known to them. Therefore a wise minister ought to determine what his method of

---

*George Wishart Anderson*, 413-427, edited by A. Graeme Auld (Sheffield: Journal for the Study of the Old Testament Press, 1993); and most recently in his "Calvin's Accommodating God," in *Calvinus Sincerioris Religionis Vindex*, edited by Wilhelm Neuser and Brian Armstrong, (Kirksville, MO: Sixteenth Century Journal Publishers, 1997), 3-20. This last article contains a brief overview of the literature.

[45] "Articles concerning the Organization of the Church and of Worship at Geneva proposed by the Ministers at the Council, January 16, 1537," *Calvin: Theological Treatises*, translated by J.K.S. Reid (Philadelphia: Westminster Press, 1954), 54: "The third article concerns the instruction of children, who without doubt ought to make a confession of their faith to the Church."

[46] *Comm. 1 Corinthians 3:2*, CNTC 9:66; CO, 49:347. "Ita refellitur focosa quorundam excusatio, qui, quum timore periculi aliquid tantum obscure balbutiant de evangelio, praetendunt hoc Pauli exemplum. Interea Christum ita procul indicant, et quidem multis involucris tectum, ut suos discipulos perpetuo detineant in exitiali ignorantia."

teaching is to be and to persist with this plan, so that no such objection could be brought against him, without his having a ready defense, based on the actual situation, as Paul had.[47]

The minister has to be ready to demonstrate his firmness in the manner of life and doctrine. It is too easy for him to be attacked, otherwise. Though Calvin does not mention that this plan will also force the minister to have actual plans about his teaching, it does have that added virtue!

In his commentary on 2 Corinthians, Calvin further develops what that plan ought to be. He finds in Paul the method which all Christian teachers should employ: "All Christian teachers should make this their invariable method, first to strive with gentleness to bring their hearers to obedience and to appeal to them kindly, before they go on to visit punishment on rebelliousness."[48] This may be of little comfort to those who found themselves before the cold stare of the Genevan Consistory, but Calvin did at least teach the priority of sweetness and kindness over the rod of correction.

Calvin makes substantial contributions to the pastor's educational ministry. But he knew that not everything the pastor did, or would be called to do, could be handled under that rubric. Other topics come up as well. For instance, Calvin knew as well as anyone else that remaining in a church could be a daunting challenge for a pastor. Yet, he does not always speak of the problems with the individual churches. Instead, he frequently points out the difficulties that pastors introduce into their own relationship with churches. Commenting upon 2 Corinthians 7:2, Calvin noted three ways in which ministers estrange people from themselves. He lists incorrect use of authority, leading the people into error, and greediness.[49] He qualifies that warning with his advice to pastors

---

[47] *Comm. 1 Corinthians 4:17*, CNTC 9:100; CO, 49:374. "Verisimile autem est, pseudoapostolorum calumniis fuisse impetitum, quasi plus sibi iuris sumeret in Corinthìos quam in alios, aut aliter se gereret in aliis locis: neque enim frustra testatum hoc illis esse vult. Prudentis ergo ministri est, suas ita rationes constituere, et hanc tenere docendi regulam, ne quid tale obiici illi queat, quin promptam abeat defensionem ex re ipsa, sicut habuit Paulus."

[48] *Comm. 2 Corinthians 10:6*, CNTC 10:131. *Secundam Pauli Epistolam Ad Corinthios*, 164.12-15. "Quare hunc ordinem diligenter tenere debent omnes Christiani doctores, ut prius studeant placide obedientiam ab auditoribus impetrare, eousque ut comiter invitent, quam prosiliant ad poenam rebellionis."

[49] *Comm. 2 Corinthians 7:2*, CNTC 10:95. "It is usually in one of these three ways that pastors estrange their people from them. Either they behave unreasonably and use their authority as a pretext for tyrannical cruelty or oppression, or they lead away into error those they should have guided aright and infect them with the corruption of false doctrine, or they give evidence of immoderate greed by coveting what belongs to another. To put it briefly, the first offence is harshness and abuse of power by over officiousness, the second is unfaithfulness in doctrine and the third avarice." *Secundam Pauli Epistolam Ad Corinthios*, 121.11-19. "Haec tria sunt, quibus utplurimum solent Pastores plebis animos a se alienare. Nempe vel quum petulantius se gerunt et authoritatis suae praetextu erumpunt in tyrannicam saevitiam aut importunitatem, vel quum eos abducunt a recta via,

that pastors are to stay with a particular church and not see themselves as drifters.[50] What is rather telling about that piece of advice is the way in which it mirrors the present studies coming from seminaries and institutes like the Alban Institute. It is not uncommon that Calvin's sensibilities about practical ministry summarize what practitioners are currently finding to be effective.

Even in his doctrinal advice to pastors, Calvin seasons it with the spice of practicality. Of course, ministers are to teach correct doctrine. But should they simply put it forward without care for its reception? Just the opposite! Commenting upon 2 Corinthians 6:1, Calvin declares, "Here ministers are taught that it is not enough merely to propound doctrine. They must labor that those who hear it should also accept it, and not once but continually."[51] Do we almost see the rueful shaking of the head of a more experienced Calvin, looking back at his early days in Geneva?

Likewise, considering the proper manner for correcting faults, Calvin suggests that the model of Paul's own ministry "teaches … that pastors should always seek moderate remedies for correcting faults before they have recourse to extreme severity; by advising and reproving, final rigour can be avoided."[52] Here we see Calvin taking up one of the more difficult tasks any pastor faces: the correction of faults in the congregation. This is so difficult that many seminaries avoid the topic more assiduously than they do sin. But see the basic and candid path which Calvin sketches. Begin the task with the lesser remedies,

---

quibus duces esse debuerant, eosque perversae doctrinae corruptelis imbuunt, vel quum alienis bonis inhiando immodicam cupiditatem produnt. Si quis malit brevius: primum est ferocia et potestatis abusus, praeter modum sinsolescendo; secundum infidelitas in docendo; tertium avaritia."

[50] *Comm. 1 Corinthians 12:28*, CNTC 9:271. "The office of teacher (*officium doctoris*) belongs to the first class, that of apostle to the second. For the Lord appointed (*creavit*) the apostles, so that they might spread the Gospel throught the whole world. He did not assign any particular boundaries or parishes to them but wanted them to act as ambassadors for Him, wherever they went, among people of every nation and language. In that respect they differ from the pastors, who are bound, so to speak, to their own churches. For the pastor does not have a mandate to preach the Gospel all the world over, but to look after the church, that has been committed to his charge." CO, 49:506. "Ex priore genere est officium doctoris: ex secundo officium apostoli. Nam apostolos creavit Dominus, ut evangelium spargerent per totum orbem: nec singulis attribuit certos fines aut parochias: sed quocunque venissent, fungi legatione voluit apud omnes gentes et linguas. In quo ab illis differunt pastores, qui suis ecclesiis quodammodo alligantur. Pastor enim non habet mandatum praedicandi per orbem universum evangelii, sed curandae ecclesiae quae eius fidei commissa est."

[51] *Comm. 2 Corinthians 6:1*, CNTC, 10:83. *Secundum ad Corinthios*, 107.20-22, "Hinc docentur ministri non sufficere, si doctrinam simplicem proponant, sed elaborandum, ut recipiatur ab auditoribus, neque id semel, sed assidue."

[52] *Comm. 2 Corinthians 12:20*, CNTC, 10:167. *Commentarii in Secundum Pauli Epistolam ad Corinthios*, 207.5-8. "Ergo suo exemplo docet moderata semper remedia quaerenda esse Pastoribus, quibus vitia corrigant, priusquam ad praecisam severitatem ferantur, et simul monendo et obiurgando antevertendum esse ultimum rigorem."

hoping to avoid the harsher penalties. It may be simple, but it is also helpful and generally correct.[53]

## D. Advice on the Ministry of the Word

As we might have guessed, Calvin spends a significant portion of his pastoral advice on preaching.[54] While preaching is not the only task of the minister, it certainly seems to be the central task. Our own language of identifying Reformed ministers as "preachers" betrays these roots. Some of Calvin's material here is on the generic ministry of the Word. I do not mean to say that Calvin believed that there was such a thing as a "generic" sermon, though certainly the modern age seems to have made that leap! Rather, Calvin divides his consideration of preaching and the ministry of the Word into general comments upon the preaching ministry, and practical comments upon the ways that pastors should preach. I will begin with the first category.

Given the centrality of the ministry of the Word,[55] it is no great surprise that Calvin frequently lauds the explication of God's Word in sermonic form. This takes on a doctrinal character, rather than the nature of pastoral formation, like the theological underpinnings of the importance and function of preaching that is the necessary propaedeutic to instruction in homiletics. As we have seen before, Calvin's separation of topics is not rigid but fluid, and correlative rather than differentiating. We see this immediately in the first chapter of Romans, when in commenting upon Romans 1:9, Calvin notes:

---

[53] Other passages in which Calvin offers practical ministry advice to the pastor include Calvin's comments upon Galatians 4:12, Ephesians 4:14, Colossians 1:23, 1 Timothy 3:1, 1 Timothy 3:4, 1 Timothy 4:15, 2 Timothy 3:1, 2 Timothy 4:2, and Titus 2:9.

[54] Of the various sections addressed, this is perhaps the most widely considered in the literature. The number or articles is simply too vast to survey here. Those given are only a useful sampling. See especially James Thomas Ford, "Preaching in the Reformed Tradition," *Preachers and People in the Reformations and Early Modern Period*, edited by Larissa Taylor (Leiden: Brill, 2001), 65-88; Lee Palmer Wandel, "Switzerland," *Preachers and People in the Reformations and Early Modern Period*, edited by Larissa Taylor (Leiden: Brill, 2001), 221-247; T.H.L. Parker, *Calvin's Preaching* (Edinburgh: T. & T. Clark, 1992); Jean-Marc Berthoud, "La formation des pasteurs et la predication de Calvin." *La revue reformee* 49 (1998): 19-44; Erik A. de Boer, "Hermeneutische Schlüssel zur alttestamentlichen Prophetie in Calvins Hesekiel Predigten." *Calvinus Sacrae Scripturae Professor.* International Congress on Calvin Research, edited by Wilhelm Neuser (Grand Rapids: Eerdmans, 1994), 199-208; Max Engammare, "Calvin connaissait-il la Bible? Les citations de l'Ecriture dans ses sermons sur la Genese," *Bulletin de la Societe de l'Histoire du Protestantisme Francais* 141 (1995): 163-184; and "Calvin: A Prophet without a Prophecy." *Church History* 64 (1998), 643-661; Daniele Fischer, "L'Element Historique dans la Predication de Calvin." *Revue d'histoire et de philosophie religieuses*, 64, (1984), 365-386; Rodolphe Peter, "Rhétorique et prédication selon Calvin," *Revue d'Histoire et de Philosophie Religieuses* 55 (1975): 249-272.

[55] Brian Gerrish has spoken of the "sacramental character" of the preached word in his *Grace and Gratitude: The Eucharistic Theology of John Calvin* (Philadelphia: Fortress Press, 1993).

We deduce from this some useful teaching which ought to add no small encouragement to ministers of the Gospel when they hear that in preaching the Gospel they are rendering an acceptable and valuable service to God. Is there anything that should prevent them from doing so, when they know that their labours are so pleasing to God and approved by Him as to be considered an act of the highest worship?[56]

The preaching of the Gospel serves God. Calvin (perhaps inadvertently) introduces a meritorious action for preachers! But joking aside, even this doctrinal point is given such a trajectory as to be comforting to preachers. Their work of preparing sermons, of learning Greek and Hebrew and working at walking the fine line between crude and overly loquacious speech, embodies true service to God.

But Calvin hardly ever tires of speaking of the doctrinal character of Christian preaching in his Pauline commentaries. In his next commentary, on 1 Corinthians, Calvin uses Paul's language about the preaching of the cross to take up the consideration of Christian preaching:

Therefore, what he says must be explained in this way: 'No knowledge was of such importance to me, as to make me desire to know anything other than Christ, even if He was crucified.' This little phrase is by way of being an addition to cause more irritation to those arrogant teachers, who already had a poor opinion of Christ, for their great desire was to be applauded for their reputation for some sort of higher wisdom. This is a beautiful verse, and from it we may learn what faithful ministers ought to teach, and what we must be learning throughout our life; and in comparison with that everything else is to be counted as dung.[57]

Truly faithful ministers preach Christ. Crucified or not, an embarrassment or not, this is what they must preach, this must be the object of their sermons.[58] Further, Christ is only to be found in the words of scripture, at least for the

---

[56] *Comm. Romans 1:9*, CNTC, 8:23; *Ad Romanos* 21.46-49. "Sed hinc colligimus utilem doctrinam, quae Euangelii ministris non parum animi addere debet, quum audiunt se cultum Deo gratum et pretiosum impendere, Euangelium praedicando. Quid enim est quod eos impediat, ubi Deo sciunt laborem suum placere et probari, ut eximius etiam cultus censeatur?"

[57] *Comm. 1 Corinthians 2:2*, CNTC, 9:49; CO, 49:333-334. "Ac si diceret, non faciet ignominia crucis ut non suspiciam eum a quo est salus, vel ut me pudeat totam in eo sapientiam meam icludere: illum, inquam, quem propter crucis probrum superbi homines fastidiunt ac repudiant. Ideo sic resolvenda est oratio: nulla mihi scientia tanti fuit, ut aliud cognoscere appeterem quam Christum, licit crucifixum. Facit haec particula ad αὔξησιν, ut stomachum magis moveat arrogantibus illis magistris quibus propemodum sordebat Christus, quum ex altioris cuiusdam sapientiae opinione plausum captarent. Pulcher locus, unde intelligimus et quid docere debeant fideles ministri, et quid nobis discendum sit tota vita, et prae quo nihil non pro stercore habendum."

[58] This familiar theme is also brought out in Calvin's comments on 2 Corinthians 1:19.

homiletician: "God wants his Church built up by the pure preaching of the Word,"[59] not adulterated with other building materials, nor garishly decorated with other embellishments.

Calvin sets forth a model of preaching that is absolutely riveted to the biblical text. Calvin's own sermons were basically expository offerings, setting out the meaning of the chosen pericope for the people of Geneva. That method was supported by a reliance on the scriptural witness. Though we can see that Calvin was well aware of the newsworthy events of his own day and city,[60] these do not take center stage, but rather the doctrine of the scripture.

The pastor's main task, for Calvin, is edifying teaching. But what is the nature of that teaching? Furthermore, is that a necessary task, in an age of expanding literacy, a time of expanding availability of scriptures in vulgar languages, and given the common emphasis on personal devotion and private scripture reading? Calvin was not unaware of the possible contradictions that arise out of this mix. Thus, he chooses to address these questions in his comment upon 2 Timothy 2:15. The translated text reads: "Give diligence to present thyself approved unto God, a workman that needeth not to be ashamed, dividing aright the word of truth." It is Calvin's comment upon the phrase "dividing aright the word of truth" which is of importance for this study. Calvin feels that this phrase captures well the preacher's task:

This is a fine metaphor which accurately explains the main purpose of teaching. For since we should be satisfied only with God's Word, what purpose is there in having daily sermons and even in the office of pastor itself? Does not everybody have a chance to read the Scriptures for himself? But Paul assigns to teachers the duty of carving or dividing the Word, like a father dividing the bread into small pieces to feed his children. He advises Timothy to 'divide aright' lest, like men without skill, he succeeds only in cutting the surface and leaves the inmost pith and marrow untouched. But I take what is said here to have general application to refer to a judicious dispensing of the Word which is adapted to the profit of those that hear it. Some mutilate it, some dismember it, some distort it, some break it in pieces, some, as I have said, keep to the outside and never come to the heart of the matter. With all these faults he contrasts a right dividing, that is, a manner of exposition

[59] *Comm. 1 Corinthians 3:12*, CNTC, 9:75; CO, 49:355. "Pura enim verbi sui praedicatione ecclesiam suam institui vult Deus, non hominum figmentis: qualis est etiam quae nihil ad aedificationem facit, ut sunt curiosae quaestiones, quae ostentationi magis vel stultae cupiditati, ut plurimum, quam hominus saluti serviunt."

[60] A recent study by Wilhelmus T. H. Moehn has set out how contextually sensitive Calvin's sermons could be, and how the modern reader so frequently misses that fact. See his *God Calls Us to His Service: The Relation Between God and His Audience in Calvin's Sermons on Acts* (Genève: Droz, 2001).

adapted to edify. This is the rule by which we should judge every interpretation of Scripture.[61]

Clearly, Calvin has extracted a tremendous amount of doctrine from a single metaphor. But consider what he gains from this exposition. The more radical Reformers are answered in the protest against privileged pastoral readings of scripture. However, no particular line is crossed, by which Calvin would be granting an authoritative and definitive exegesis to all pastors by virtue of ordination to an office.

Calvin does have a vast amount to say about the content of sermons. But just as importantly, Calvin sees himself giving true advice to the crafter of sermons. We see this in his concern for the art of rhetoric. True preaching must not be loquacious. Human eloquence must give way to that of the Holy Spirit. Perhaps Calvin's longest treatment of this comes in his comments upon 1 Corinthians 1:17, which take up three whole columns in the Calvini Opera.[62] Calvin writes that "The preaching of the cross of Christ is bare and simple; therefore it ought not to be obscured by an overlying disguise of words."[63] Calvin decries the use of human eloquence, pointing out that if it is the "brilliance of words" that people seek in a sermon, then the Gospel is denied.[64] Calvin holds, apparently, for a rough and simple style.

Apparently, for that is false. In Calvin's own person, we see one of the better linguistic stylists of his day. Did he include himself in his condemnation? There really is not a condemnation, rather a careful line is being walked. He recognized the issue, and addressed it immediately upon raising it:

> But what if someone in our day speaks in rather brilliant fashion, and makes the teaching of the Gospel sparkle with his eloquence? Should he be rejected on that account, as if he spoiled it, or obscured the glory of Christ? I answer first of all that eloquence is not in conflict with the simplicity of the

---

[61] *Comm. 2 Timothy 2:15*, CNTC, 10:313-314; CO, 52:367-368. "Pulchra metaphora, et quae scite exprimit praecipuum docendi finem. Nam quum solo Dei verbo contentos esse nos oporteat: quorsum quotidianae conciones et ipsum quoque pastorum munus? Nonne in medio posita est scriptura? At Paulus secandi partes doctoribus assignat: ac si pater alendis filiis panem in frustra secando distribueret. Commendat autem rectam sectionem Timotheo, ne in secando cortice occupatus (ut solent inepti homines) ipsam interiorem medullam intactam relinquat. Quamquam generaliter hoc nomine prudentem verbi distributionem, et quae rite ad auditorii profectum attemperatur, intelligo. Alii enim mutilant, alii discerpunt, alii contorquent, alii disrumpunt, alii in cortice (ut dixi) haerentes non perveniunt ad ipsam animam. His omnibus vitiis opponitur recta sectio: hoc est explicandi ratio ad aedificationem formata. Est enim quasi regula ad quam exigere convenit omnem scripturae interpretationem."

[62] Actually, three and a half. CO, 49:319-322.

[63] *Comm. 1 Corinthians 1:17*, CNTC, 9:34. Changing the translation from "Christ," to "cross of Christ." CO, 49:321. "Christi enim crucifixi praedicatio simplex est ac nuda: obfuscari ergo verborum fuco non debet."

[64] *Comm. 1 Corinthians 1:17*, CNTC, 9:33-34; CO, 49:321-322.

Gospel at all, when, free from contempt of the gospel, it not only gives it first place, and is subject to it, but also serves it as a handmaid serves her mistress. … We must not condemn or reject the kind of eloquence which does not aim at captivating Christians with an outward brilliancy of words, or at intoxicating them with empty delights, or at tickling their ears with its jingle, or at covering up the Cross of Christ with its ostentation. No, we must not condemn or reject it, because, on the other hand, its aim is to call us back to the original simplicity of the Gospel, to set on high the preaching of the Cross and nothing else by humbling itself of its own accord, and finally, to carry out, as it were, the duties of a herald.[65]

Thus, there is a balance, which is preserved most especially by the simple eloquence of the Holy Spirit. Yes, the preacher can be properly eloquent. But his efforts and human inventions must never be allowed to interfere with the true eloquence which moves the hearts of believers, and that is the property of the Holy Spirit alone.

But Calvin can go much further than simply speaking of homiletic eloquence in such abstract manner. In his comments on the first verse of the third chapter of Galatians, Calvin sets forth a practical aesthetic for the preacher.

[Paul] suggests that the actual sight of Christ's death could not have affected them more than his preaching. … Paul's doctrine had taught them about Christ in such a manner that it was as if He had been shown to them in a picture, even crucified among them. Such a representation could not have been effected by any eloquence or tricks of oratory, had not that power of the Spirit been present, of which he spoke in both the epistles to the Corinthians.

Let those who want to discharge the ministry of the Gospel aright learn not only to speak and declaim but also to penetrate into consciences, so that men may see Christ crucified and that His blood may flow. When the Church has such painters as these she no longer needs wood and stone, that is, dead images, she no longer requires any pictures. And certainly images and pictures were first admitted to Christian temples when, partly, the pastors had become dumb and were mere shadows, partly, when they uttered a

---

[65] *Comm. 1 Corinthians 1:17*, CNTC, 9:34-35; CO, 49:321-322. "Quid autem si quispiam hodie paulo nitidius disserendo, evangelii doctrinam eloquentia illustret? an propterea repudiandus erit, quasi vel eam contaminet, vel obscuret Christi gloriam? Respondeo, primum nihil pugnare cum evangelii simpliitate eloquentiam, quae sine fastidio illi non tantum cedat et se subiiciat, sed etiam tanquam ancilla dominae serviat.

… Haec ergo eloquentia nec damnanda, nec adspernanda est, quae non huc spectat ut Christianos in externo verborum colore detineat, ut eos inebriet vana oblectatione, ut suo tinnitu aures feriat, ut sua pompa tanquam involucro obruat Christi crucem: sed potius ut ad nativam evangelii simplicitatem nos revocet, ut ipsa sponte se in ordinem redigens solam crucis praedicationem extollat, …"

few words from the pulpit so coldly and superficially that the power and efficacy of the ministry were utterly extinguished.[66]

Examine for a moment the crafting Calvin pours into this comment.[67] Certainly, he wants to maintain his central point that the efficacy of preaching comes from the Holy Spirit, rather than from a false or attention-grabbing human eloquence. But having set that forth, Calvin moves directly into useful discussions of preaching tactics. If the point of preaching is to make Christ's blood flow in the sight of believers, then the preacher must develop the rhetorical skills which will allow him to penetrate consciences, to make people feel the pain of their sin, and to generate empathy. Such preachers are the true artists, whose words create the most moving canvasses, which are far better than any pictorial art. One is reminded that it was said of the Grand Itinerant of the Great Awakening, John Whitefield, that he could bring congregations to tears simply by stating the word "Mesopotamia." While that level of brilliance generally tends to escape preachers in our own day, and most likely in Calvin's, the ideal remains firm.

This is true because for Calvin the stakes for failure are so high. When the preacher fails to achieve this intimacy of impact, when he skims lightly over the surface of the human soul and conscience, the door is thrown open to other, lesser forms of communication. It was only through the coldness (*frigide*) of the preaching that this abomination of iconic art entered the sanctuaries, drawing people's minds away from the spiritual aspect of worship. It matters little whether this was the actual history of Christian art,[68] rather what matters is how much importance Calvin attaches to this ministry through earthen vessels. Yes, the efficacy of preaching remains wholly in the power of the Holy Spirit. Yes, the credit for the salvific power of Christian preaching must always be attrib-

---

[66] *Comm. Galatians 3:1*, CNTC, 11:47. *Commentarii in Pauli Epistolas, Ad Galatas*, edited by Helmut Feld (Geneve: Librairie Droz, 1992), 60.9-61.5. "Quo signifcat non debuisse plus affici praesenti mortis Christi aspectu quam sua praedicatione. ... Retineamus ergo sensum illum: non aliter Pauli doctrina edoctos fuisse de Christo, acsi fuisset illis ostensus in tabula, imo inter ipsos crucifixus. Talis repraesentatio nulla eloquentia, nullis rhetorum coloribus fieri potest, nisi adsit illa Spiritus efficacia, de qua dictum fuit in utraque ad Corinthios. Itaque qui rite Euangelii ministerio defungi volent, discant non tantum loqui et declamare, sed etiam penetrare in conscientias, ut illis Christus crucifixus sentiatur et sanguis eius stillet. Ubi tales Ecclesia pictores habet, minime amplius indiget ligneis et lapideis, hoc est mortuis simulachris; minime picturas ullas requirit. Et certe tunc primum simulachris et picturis apertae fuerunt templorum fores apud Christianos, quum partim obmutuissent Pastores essentque mera idola, partim ita frigide et perfunctorie pro suggestu pauca verba facerent, ut penitus extincta esset vis et efficacia ministerii."

[67] I have considered this text also in my response to John Witvliet, "Images and Themes in Calvin's Theology of Liturgy," in *The Legacy of John Calvin*, Calvin Studies Society Papers 1999, ed. David Foxgrover (Grand Rapids, Michigan: CRC Publications Services, 2000), 156.

[68] We are assured that it was not. See Robin Margaret Jensen, *Understanding Early Christian Art* (London: Routledge, 2000).

uted to God. But the preacher is able, radically, to obstruct the power of the gospel through an inability to preach.[69]

## E. The Minister's Doctrine

This might seem the oddest section of my entire paper. Certainly, the whole point of the *Institutes* and the commentaries is to give advice on correct doctrine! That is the case. However, two reasons restrict me from dropping this section completely. The first is the frequency with which Calvin notes to pastors and teachers just what kind of doctrine they must hold if they wish to edify the Church. The second reason is more significant, because Calvin continually offers the practical consequences of faulty and sound doctrine. Thus, the commentaries become not only storehouses of reliable doctrine, but also a constant reminder of the possible result of leaving such teaching. Because of the obvious character of this section, I will restrain myself and consider only two passages.

An excellent example comes to us from the commentary on 1 Corinthians, reading the comment upon 1 Corinthians 3:11, which states that "no one can lay any foundation other than that which is laid, that is, Jesus Christ." Calvin believed that two points were important, that Christ is the only foundation, and that Paul had properly set forth that foundation. He then expands upon the dangers of leaving that underpinning.

> To sum up: the Church must quite definitely be founded on Christ alone; and Paul had carried out his role in this respect among the Corinthians so faithfully that his ministry could leave nothing to be desired. It follows that whoever may come after him cannot serve the Lord conscientiously, or be heard as ministers of Christ, in any other way than by taking pains to make their teaching like his, and to maintain the foundation which he has laid.

> From this we can come to a certain conclusion about those who, when they follow true ministers, do not trouble to adapt themselves to their teaching, and to follow up a good beginning in order to make it perfectly plain that they are not undertaking something new. We can conclude that they are not working faithfully to build up the Church, but rather are its demolishers. For what is more destructive than confusing believers well grounded in pure doctrine, with a new kind of teaching, so that they are not sure where they stand and turn this way and that?[70]

---

[69] Further citations for preaching are legion. Some are Romans 1:9, and 2:16; 1 Corinthians 1:17, 2:2, 2:3, 3:6, 4:20, 9:1, and 13:12; 2 Corinthians 1:18, 2:17, 3:6, 4:5, and 13:5; Galatians 6:12; Ephesians 1:8, 1:13, 3:10, 4:10, and 4:12; Philippians 2:17; 1 Timothy 3:15; Titus 1:9, and 2:1; 1 Thessalonians 2:12; 2 Thessalonians 2:8, and Hebrews 4:12.

[70] *Comm. 1 Corinthians 3:11*, CNTC 9:74; CO, 49:353-354. "Summa est, ecclesiam nonnisi in solo Christo fundatam esse oportere: Paulum his partibus ita fideliter perfunctum fuisse apud Corinthios, ut nihil desiderari possit in eius ministerio: proinde quicunque succedent, non aliter posse bona fide servire Domino, nec audiendos esse pro Christi ministris, nisi illius doctrinae suam coaptare studeant, ac retineant fundamentum quod posuit.

Ministers must follow the same doctrine which was already in place when they arrive at a call! They cannot think that their honeymoon period is free for their expression of their own slant—if that is permissible at all, it must be very much tertiary or quaternary to the priority of demonstrable fealty to the true foundation. This is all considered from the point of view of the good of believers, and the edification of the Church.

Purity of doctrine must be extended in the life of a congregation. In fact, it must be extended beyond the life of the pastor, if that should be possible! Calvin notes that good pastors are called to "perpetuate and conserve the remembrance of the doctrine entrusted to them." This requires especially faithful ministers. In fact, Calvin writes that Paul's example in writing to Timothy demonstrates "how much trouble a servant of Christ should take to preserve and guard the purity of his teaching not only in his own lifetime but for as long as his care and labor can extend it."[71] Here we see Calvin addressing himself to the issue of pastoral transmission of doctrine, realizing the ticklish area of transitional moments, and attempting to mine the Bible for advice about these times.[72]

## F. Advice to Congregations

After so much advice to ministers, it is perhaps not surprising that we find Calvin turning to give practical advice to believers or to congregations about the ministry. Note that I am not speaking here about general moral or doctrinal teaching. That would, of course, be the warp and weft of any commentary on the epistles. Rather, not infrequently, Calvin turns and gives a piece of advice to the congregation, so as to make their cooperation in the tasks of ministry more fruitful. We first see him do this in the Romans commentary, commenting upon the fifth verse of the first chapter. Calvin has been clarifying the necessity of obedience to the ministry of Paul. He writes that Paul had the duty to preach, and the Romans had the responsibility to hear and obey. His amplification, however, is strictly a modern application. Calvin states, "We deduce from this that those who

---

Hinc colligimus, non esse fideles operarios ad aedificandam ecclesiam, sed potius eius dissipatores, qui dum succedunt veris ministris non se acccommodare student eorum doctrinae, ac persequi quod bene inchoatum est, adeo ut prorsus appareat, nihil eos novi operis aggredi. Quid enim perniciosius quam fideles probe institutos in pura doctrina turbare non genere docendi, ut fundamenti incerti vacillent?

[71] *Comm. 2 Timothy 2:2*, CNTC 10:306; CO, 52:360-361. "Hinc discimus quantum laborare debeat servus Christi pro conservanda ac tuenda doctrinae puritate: neque solum quamdiu vivit, sed quam longissime eius cura et studium extendere se poterit."

[72] Other passages in which Calvin considers the doctrine of the pastor include Calvin's comments upon Romans 2:16, 1 Corinthians 4:15, 9:2; 2 Corinthians 1:19, Galatians 2:2, 6:12; 1 Timothy 1:19, 4:1, 4:6, 6:3; 2 Timothy 1:7, 2:14, 3:14; Titus 1:10, 2:7; 1 Thessalonians 2:3; and 2 Thessalonians 2:8.

irreverently and contemptuously reject the preaching of the Gospel, the design of which is to bring us into obedience to God, are stubbornly resisting the power of God, and perverting the whole of His order."[73] The analysis of this comment is not historically easy. The rejection of preaching is a charge which Calvin levels against the church of Rome and against the Radicals. It will not be too great a stretch of the historical imagination to believe that Calvin was thinking of Geneva when he wrote these words. There is sufficient broadness of language to cover all of these possibilities. Pastorally speaking, the difficulty vanishes. No matter whom Calvin might have in his mind, he knows the difficulty of having people hear sermons and then rejecting them as the living word. He rebukes that tendency in the strongest language, making such a choice tantamount to the rejection of faith.

While this is the first piece of advice to congregations which Calvin included in his commentaries on the Pauline epistles, it was hardly the last. Further, this advice to congregations did not always take the side of the pastor. For instance, consider this remarkable passage from the commentary on 1 Corinthians 3:22. "We must, on the whole, maintain that all who exercise the office of the ministry, from the greatest to the least, are ours, so that we are at liberty not to accept what they teach until they make it plain that it is derived from Christ. For they must all be tested and obedience must be given to them only when they have shown that they are true servants of Christ."[74] The congregations are given the power of discernment here! The pastors derive all their authority from the clear presence and foundation of Christ in their teaching. Should that be found lacking, they are utterly without warrant. Calvin sets out as the cornerstone of his theology of the pastorate, not the chrism of ordination, but the warrant of Christ. Further, he demands that this be demonstrable to the Church.

One might hope, if one were an indolent pastor, that this was an uncommon theme in Calvin's commentaries, that he rarely places the church in the place of judging the pastor. One would hold this hope in vain. Commenting upon 1 Thessalonians 5:12, Calvin praises ministers, but then takes away any extra praise: "It may, however, be inferred from Paul's words that judgment is entrusted to the Church so that it may distinguish true pastors. It would have been to no purpose to attribute these distinctions to pastors had Paul not wanted believers to take notice of them."[75] Likewise, in 1 Corinthians 4:3, Calvin

---

[73] *Comm. Romans 1:5*, CNTC 8:18, *Ad Romanos*, 16.70-73. "Unde [colligimus, Dei imperio contumaciter resistere, ac pervertere totum eius ordinem,] qui Euangelii praedicationem irreverenter et contemptim [respuunt, cuius finis est nos in obsequium Dei cogere.]"

[74] *Comm. 1 Corinthians 3:22*, CNTC 9:82; CO, 49:361. "Caeterum hoc generaliter habendum est, quicunque ministerio funguntur, eos a summo ad infinum usque esse nostros: ut liberum nobis sit ipsorum doctrinam non amplecti, donec a Christo esse ostendant. Probandi enim sunt omnes, et tum demum praestanda illis obedientia, ubi se fideles esse Christi servos demonstraverint."

[75] *Comm. 1 Thessalonians 5:12*, CNTC 8:372; CO, 52:172. "Verum ex Pauli verbis colligere licet, iudicium ecclesiae mandari, ut veros pastores discernat. Nam frustra notae istae adscriberentur, nisi vellet a fidelibus eas animadverti."

again states that the church must judge whether ministers are good or bad workmen according to the Word of God. The church must be careful not to forward the ministry of those who are full of empty show, but should not be overly harsh, instead considering the circumstances of ministry.[76]

Sometimes, Calvin's comments on the nature of congregations can be harsh. Calvin castigates congregations for following empty shows of eloquence, for desiring to have their "own" teachers,[77] for their "itching ears,"[78] and for their commercial character.[79] Calvin leaves few stones unturned, warning churches that their rejection of faithful ministers is actually a rejection of God.[80] However, at other times, Calvin simply gives advice to the congregations about one of their most significant relationships, that which they share with the pastor. Churches should be concerned about the lives of their ministers,[81] they should pay their ministers fairly;[82] these expectations are right and good and fair.

What is the usefulness of this advice to congregations? This type of counsel seems to have a two-fold audience and a two-fold purpose. The two-fold audience is obvious, pastors and lay believers. But the messages which the two audiences will take from these are not exactly the same. For the congregations, the message is clear about the necessity for formation as the body of Christ. The individual members should take these moments of guidance to heart, seek to amend their ways where appropriate, and return to their tasks helped by this direction. The pastors, on the other hand, are reminded of their tasks and pledges made to congregations, whether implicit or explicit, and the necessity of fulfilling them. But they are also reminded that sometimes congregations can simply be difficult to serve, and that if God could afflict Paul in such a manner, they should be comforted to share such discomfort.

---

[76] *Comm. 1 Corinthians 4:3*, CNTC 9:88: "Therefore he does not prevent us from making up our minds about those whom we have come to know to be faithful, and whom we commend as such; nor does he forbid our deciding who are bad workmen according to the Word of God. But he condemns the effrontery that is evident when some, governed by ambition, are put before others, not because they deserve it, but because proper account is not take of all their circumstances." CO, 49:364-365. "Non ergo vetat quin eos, quos fideles comperimus, sentiamus esse tales ac praedicemus: quin malos etiam operarios iudicemus ex verbo Dei: sed temeritatem illam damnat, ubi alii aliis ambitiose non pro suo merito, sed causa incognita praeferuntur."

[77] *Comm. 1 Corinthians 3:1*, CNTC 9:65-66; CO, 49:346-347.

[78] *Comm. 1 Corinthians 3:11*, CNTC 9:73; CO, 49:353. "pruriebant aures."

[79] *Comm. 1 Corinthians 3:1*, CNTC 9:65-66; CO, 49:346-347.

[80] *Comm. 1 Corinthians 10:10*, CNTC 9:210; CO, 49:459-460.

[81] *Comm. 1 Corinthians 16:10*, CNTC 9:353-354; CO, 49:569.

[82] *Comm. 1 Corinthians 9:7* and *9:11*, CNTC 9:187, 189; CO, 49:441, 442.

## IV. Conclusion: Summations and Trajectories

From the material considered, and from the far greater amount of material from which you have been spared, some conclusions appear warranted, as well as some considerations for further study. First, let us ask some questions of this evidence. What was Calvin doing in commenting upon scripture? What might have been his aim in including so frequently these snippets of pastoral advice? What is the distribution of this material in his Pauline commentaries, and what reasons might we put forward to explain those patterns of distribution? Finally, how does this fit into Calvin's pastoral theological project?

Let us begin with what is most easily demonstrated: the distribution of pastoral commentary within the Pauline commentaries. The distribution of the advice does not follow a simple pattern. In the Romans commentary of 1540, the amount of this kind of material is quite small. In the next effort, the 1 Corinthians commentary of 1546, Calvin more than quadruples the amount of practical advice to the pastor, as well as considerations of the congregation. This is followed by a similar amount, if slightly less, in the 2 Corinthians commentary of 1547. Surprisingly for the pattern, the Galatians group, published in 1548, holds even less, though not so little as Romans. In fact, this group holds some of the most trenchant observations for the minister, so that their quality outstrips their quantity. The Timothy commentary appears next in late 1548, and is drenched with pastoral advice. This is followed by the publication in 1549 of the commentary on the Hebrews; although Calvin did not consider this to be written by Paul, it seems that he never believed that the Pauline commentaries would be complete without it. The pastoral advice in the Hebrews commentary is the slightest of all, not reaching to the level of that which is in Romans. Jean Gerard prints the Titus commentary in French in 1550, so we may assume that Calvin wrote it separately. It represents the same high level of advice of the Timothy commentary of 1548. The Thessalonians commentaries and Philemon seem never to have been separately printed, appearing only with the collected commentaries in 1551.[83] Thessalonians provides little, and Philemon less, in the way of pastoral advice.

One is tempted to offer a sweeping answer to the differences in Calvin's commenting upon the various books. A possibility such as the necessity of paying attention to the character of the books not only offers a ready guide, but also allows us to keep our hero worship of Calvin intact, as we can demonstrate again Calvin's iron-willed determination to follow where the voice of the Holy Spirit led. But as both theologians and historians should know, sweeping answers to such problems seem tempting because of the weakness of character of their authors and the wideness of the road down which they would lead us.

---

[83] See T. H. L. Parker, *Calvin's New Testament Commentaries*, 15-35 and 206-222, for the history of the printing of the commentaries.

It seems that, instead of a single explanation of this phenomenon, a variety of impulses, working in concert, are probably behind the varied distribution of pastoral advice in the Pauline commentaries. Certainly, the character of the scripture did change some of the commentaries. The Epistle to the Romans more nearly resembles a theological treatise than a truly pastoral epistle, and that would be reflected in the kind of commentary which a sensitive reader like Calvin would produce. This same explanation goes for the Epistle to the Hebrews.

Standing beside the issue of the character of the scripture, however, must be the experience of the commentator. This may seem strange, but we must remember that Calvin begins his theological career, in some ways, woefully short of experience. Never having completed a theological degree may not have been a great obstacle to a brilliant and extraordinarily facile mind. The lack of actual experience under mentors who could guide a young and perhaps timid personality through periods of turbulence so as to gain wisdom from those storms is a wholly different matter. For an example that this difference seems to have been the case in at least some of this variegation, let us consider only the first two commentaries, those on Romans and 1 Corinthians.

The Romans commentary is perhaps the second most lightly noted with these materials of advice for the pastor.[84] However, in Calvin's next commentary, on 1 Corinthians,[85] that lacuna is more than filled.[86] As we know, the time between the publishing of the Romans and 1 Corinthians commentaries is the longest gap in the whole of the production of the Pauline set. Both were published by Wendelinus Rihelius in Strasbourg, but the Romans commentary came out early in 1540, while 1 Corinthians did not appear until 1546. To put that in perspective, the gap between no other two publishing dates is longer than eighteen months, and occasionally multiple commentaries were published within a single calendar year.[87] To some of Calvin's friends, it may have seemed that the call to Geneva meant that Calvin's vision of commenting upon a great number of biblical books was to go unfulfilled.[88]

---

[84] Counting these pieces of advice is difficult; for instance, does a single line, which makes an entry, make the same impact as a whole page, which also counts as a single entry? Obviously not. However, given that Romans is one of his longest commentaries in this set, the paucity of pastoral comments raises questions.

[85] See his reply to Sadoleto in their debate. *A Reformation Debate: Sadoleto's Letter to the Genevans and Calvin's Reply*, ed. John C. Olin (San Francisco: Harper and Row, 1966).

[86] The scarcity of pastoral comments in the Romans commentary is made far more clear by comparison to the 1 Corinthians commentary. Here, page after page of the commentary urge specific actions and specific disciplines upon the one who would be a minister.

[87] Romans was published in 1540, 1 Corinthians in 1546. After that long drought, 2 Corinthians was published in 1547, the Galatians group and Timothy in 1548, Hebrews in 1549, a French version of Titus in 1550, and the whole set including Philemon and 1 and 2 Thessalonians in 1551.

[88] T.H.L. Parker, *Calvin's New Testament Commentaries*, 17.

But may that almost certainly unintended long break between the two commentaries have given an opportunity for more change in the character of pastoral advice, and in the amount of pastoral advice in the second commentary? Certainly, there was no reason that such comments could not have been written quickly, and I am not suggesting that the time period of the composition of the 1 Corinthians commentary was lengthened by adding advice to ministers! However, it is significant that this second commentary is not started until Calvin has begun to mature as a minister. Calvin's time in Geneva was stormy and brief. However, his time in Strasbourg had a different character. In a reforming town, with colleagues and a senior mentor in the person of Martin Bucer, and a congregation whom he seems to have loved, Calvin's own ministry may have come of age.[89] This provides a partial explanation of the pattern of pastoral advice in the Pauline commentaries—Calvin's own level of experience. In the Romans commentary, he is drawing on very little experience of his own, and his only significant ministry has been darkened with the cloud of banishment. By the time the 1 Corinthians commentary is published, he is an established pastor who has had success in two pastorates, if one counts his second stay in Geneva.

However, Calvin's pastoral experience alone is not a complete explanation. Another factor must be seen in the time factor of the production of the commentaries. Yes, Calvin took longer to write some of the longer commentaries. But he literally races through the Galatians group, which includes Galatians, Ephesians, Colossians and Philippians. This is a set; they are never published separately. But even the most cursory glance demonstrates that these books contain many significant theological issues, and that as a group they outweigh either of the two epistles to the Corinthians, at least in the number of chapters and pages. Why then are they treated so quickly?

The answer may have to do with Calvin's aim in creating a set of Pauline commentaries, his goal of having his guide to the scriptures, the *Institutes*, accompanied by a more or less full set of commentaries upon the scriptures, and his luck with publishing commentaries to that point. We know that early on, Calvin believed that he was setting forth a Pauline set. Just as certainly, we know that he had hoped to write commentaries to work with the *Institutes* for the edification of the Church. What we must realize is the difficulty with which the commentary on 2 Corinthians was printed.[90] For a time, the sole manucript was lost, having been sent from Geneva to Strasbourg. Calvin for a time despaired—though eventually it was found, and he found himself a new printer—Jean Gerard of Geneva.

---

[89] See Cornelius Augustijn, "Calvin in Strasbourg," *Calvinus Sacrae Scripturae Professor.* International Congress on Calvin Research, ed. Wilhelm Neuser (Grand Rapids: Eerdmans, 1994), 166-177.

[90] See Parker, *Calvin's New Testament Commentaries*, 19-22.

My point is that Calvin had received the most brutal of messages about his writing of the Pauline commentaries. No further delay could be brooked, if he should fulfill the task which he set before himself. Because of this, and certainly not because of any leisure in Geneva from 1546 to 1548, Calvin alters his style. He sets aside other tasks, such as the writing of *De Scandalis*, and depends upon the nature of the set to cover those pieces of ministerial advice except where absolutely demanded by the text. The commentaries on Timothy and Titus obviously give ample opportunity for that kind of advice, and it is far less frequent in the Thessalonians and Hebrews commentaries.

Having commented upon the distribution of these snippets of pastoral advice, we can begin to see things in this study that we may have known before, but now know more certainly, or from different sources. First, Calvin's commenting upon scripture represents a significant effort not only at textual understanding, but also at the training of godly readers of scripture and, at least at times, especially pastors. The comments are too frequent, especially in 1 and 2 Corinthians, and in the commentaries on Timothy and Titus, to be careless inclusions. When Calvin comments upon the scripture, he is holding forth the necessity of the placement in the Church, and the edification of that body through a formed piety of both pastors and parishioners.

Therefore, we see in Calvin not only a discussion of the key theological ideas of the Pauline corpus for the most erudite scholars and doctors, but also for pastors and lay believers. The commentaries are Calvin's model seminary, until he can accomplish that goal in a more concrete fashion. Let me elaborate. In 1541, Calvin had expressed the desire for the formation of a college for the training of pastors.[91] Throughout the next two decades, that desire would remain, at best, a frustrated one. Calvin did not receive the support which might have caused that dream to come to fruition any earlier than the elections of 1555.[92] Without that political support to gain financial and administrative cooperation from the town, the ordinances remained very much a hope, rather than any kind of reality.[93] This may have been one of the greater frustrations

---

[91] Draft Ecclesiastical Ordinances: September and October, 1541. *Calvin: Theological Treatises*, trans. J.K.S. Reid (Philadelphia: Westminster Press, 1954), 62-63: "The degree nearest to the minister and most closely joined to the government of the Church is the lecturer in theology, of which it will be good to have one in Old Testament and one in New Testament.

"But because it is only possible to profit from such lectures if first one is instructed in the languages and humanities, and also because it is necessary to raise offspring for time to come, in order not to leave the Church deserted to our children, a college should be instituted for instructing children to prepare them for the ministry as well as for civil government."

[92] See Naphy, *Calvin and the Consolidation*, 189-193.

[93] Karin Maag, *Seminary or University? The Genevan Academy and Reformed Higher Education, 1560-1620* (Brookfield, Vermont: Ashgate, 1995), 8.

which Calvin faced, as he possessed a truly fine education himself, and had witnessed firsthand the Strasbourg school system created by Johannes Sturm.[94]

But certainly, Calvin's desire for a godly and well-trained pastorate did not wane during that period. Here we have our next conclusion. After the printing of the Romans commentary, the greater amounts of pastoral advice inserted into the Pauline commentaries are Calvin's first seminary. Granted, this must be a "distance-learning seminary." But the formation of a trained pastorate, which had received models of reading the scripture and had also been given practical advice on the performance of the pastoral task, was too vital a goal to leave until Calvin received political support sturdy enough to found his academy.

Another point that is worthy of consideration is the factor of the various audiences for the commentaries. Certainly, Calvin wrote these commentaries expecting to be entering into the lists with the other top scholars of his day, and he makes polemical points about the correct interpretation of key passages which only the diligent work of the history of exegesis school has begun to put before us. However, turning aside from that, consider that Calvin opens a dialogue between pastors and congregations about the form of the Church. Yes, pastors are to be held to high standards. But churches are not to be left in their way of simply ignoring the sharp points of the gospel, nor are they to be coddled when their itching ears attempt to force useless disputations or shows of vain eloquence.

We miss a vital point if we do not see this as a dialogue! Calvin did not write only to pastors, nor, of course, only to congregations. Instead, at this point he is trying to shape a true *schola Christi*, which believers and pastors accept as their goal, even should they know the impossibility of reaching that goal while living in the present age. Both sides, pastor and people, have responsibilities in that effort. Further, the responsibilities of the people do not end with accepting a teachable spirit! While the lack of that quality on the part of congregations was the cry of pastors in the 16th century, and remains the cry of pastors in the 21st century, Calvin does not end there! Rather, believers have the task of considering the preaching of the pastor against the purity of the gospel. They have the task of providing a secure income for the pastor. They have the job of turning themselves teachable and incarnating the *schola Christi*.

Similarly, pastors are not the new ecclesiastical lords come to replace the bishops so recently escaped! But we see how much their success lies outside their grasp. Calvin frequently turns to the ministry of the Holy Spirit, never letting his readers forget that all the success of any ministry has to do with the power of God. But beyond that, the pastor must equip himself with endurance, with patience, with a comely demeanor, and with a holy practicality. He must pursue daily and yearly and by decade the goal of edifying the Church entrusted to his care.

---

[94] Steven Ozment, *The Age of Reform 1250—1550: An Intellectual and Religious History of Late Medieval and Reformation Europe* (New Haven: Yale University Press, 1980), 364.

This dialogue is the formation of an intentional textual community.[95] Both pastor and people place themselves under the direction of God, as represented in the scripture. Both seek to understand its most basic meanings by continual learning. For some, that learning will be shallow, for they are ill-equipped either by mental gift or by lack of time. For others, it will be deep, nurtured by faculties given by God to the individual for the benefit of the community. The union of deeper and shallower reading comes together in the community, to form the imperfect incarnation of the Bride of Christ, in which all seek the more perfect instance of the Church.

A final point can be made about Calvin's aim in commenting upon scripture and his overall theological project. The very practicality of the level of some of this pastoral advice signals to us that although Calvin was, in his own way, a "scripture-ophile"; he never lost sight of the realistic and functional ideal. For Calvin, scripture and theology must be devoted to edifying the Church. That building up may take many forms, but it cannot take a form that is so divorced from the necessary context of the Church that it becomes foreign to it. Occasionally, in our twenty-first century search for the "heart" of Calvin's theological project, we have forgotten that. We have replaced his ideal of edification which is rather too simple and straightforward with a variety of models.[96] Fortunately, Calvin's text tugs us back, and we are left with a picture of a brilliant scholar who can never forget that the humble congregation is the true home of all Christian dialogue.

---

[95] Brian Stock has written of this concept in *Listening for the Text: On the Uses of the Past* (Philadelphia: University of Pennsylvania Press, 1990).

[96] Hermann Bauke, in his *Die Probleme der Theologie Calvins*, (Leipzig:Hinrichs'schen, 1922), noted the tendency to reduce Calvin to a single doctrine. Bauke replaces the central doctrine idea with three formal principles, which are rationalism, *complexio oppositorum*, and biblicism; see p. 20. Mary Potter Engel's *John Calvin's Perspectival Anthropology*, American Academy of Religion Series, no. 52, ed. Susan Thistlethwaite (Atlanta: Scholars Press, 1988), ix-xi, gives a thumbnail sketch of a variety of the impulses. Christology is Wilhelm Niesel's contribution; see his *The Theology of Calvin*, trans. Harold Knight, (Philadelphia: Westminster Press, 1956); the doctrine of faith is Peter Brunner's; see his *Vom Glauben bei Calvin*, (Tübingen: Mohr, 1925); Brian Gerrish has argued for Calvin's coherence through a concentration on the sacramental nature of the Word; see his *Grace and Gratitude: The Eucharistic Theology of John Calvin*, (Philadelphia: Fortress Press, 1993).

# A Response to "Calvin's Exegetical Understanding of the Office of Pastor"

*Tom Trinidad*

Anyone who might still want to argue that "Calvin is a man of one book"[1] and that everything anyone wanted to know about Calvin's theology can be found in the *Institutes* will benefit from R. Ward Holder's investigation into Calvin's exegetical understanding of the office of pastor. Prof. Holder shows that Calvin's teaching on the office of pastor in the *Institutes* is relatively sparse and straightforward. It may display systematic coherence and good doctrinal theology, but it fails to render practical direction for the wandering pastor.

In his paper, Prof. Holder has explored that other great corpus of Calvin's writings, his commentaries on the scriptures. It is in the commentaries on scripture that Prof. Holder has found Calvin offering practical advice on various topics of interest to pastors. Calvin envisioned these two guides, the *Institutes* and the commentaries, to contribute equally to the task of interpreting scripture. As seminary curricula will attest, however, it is the *Institutes* that commands the greatest study among would-be pastors. One consequence is that students receive Calvin's doctrinal teaching on the pastorate, but not much practical guidance. Imaginatively, Prof. Holder asks what Calvin would say as a faculty member in today's seminary—not in the systematics department, however, but rather in the practical department.

Prof. Holder sketches the beginnings of an answer to this question from his study of the commentaries. To place limits on his investigation, he has kept to the commentaries on the Pauline letters, and attempted to categorize, as much as is possible, the various strands of counsel Calvin offers his readers.

Prof. Holder identifies six headings under which Calvin's comments on the Pauline texts may be organized.[2] In his investigation, Prof. Holder discovered that Calvin's thoughts on pastoral matters are quite complex. This complexity

---

[1] Cf. T. H. L. Parker, *Calvin's New Testament Commentaries* 2nd ed. (Louisville: Westminster/John Knox Press, 1993), pp. 6-7.

[2] These are: 1) the demeanor of the minister; 2) the moral character of the pastor; 3) practical advice concerning the ministry; 4) comments pertains to preaching; 5) exhortations to maintain sound doctrine; 6) advice concerning congregations.

makes any attempt to categorize them difficult and the character of such classification somewhat arbitrary. Whereas Prof. Holder finally settled on six categorical headings, certainly other classifications could have been used. For example, gathering Calvin's polemical remarks together, or his comments on worship, may suggest new directions. And, one wonders how many additional categories might emerge after considering Calvin's comments outside of the Pauline letters.

The method Prof. Holder employs in his study deserves attention. Calvin placed a premium on "lucid brevity" as a commentator of scripture.[3] He modeled this principle by staying close to the text and eschewing renegade speculative or overly spiritualized interpretations. T. H. L. Parker summarizes Calvin's approach by stating, "when the commentator reveals, clearly and succinctly, the mind of the writer expressed in the text, he is fulfilling almost his only duty."[4]

Even so, as Prof. Holder has demonstrated, Calvin seasons his exegesis with pastoral advice whose direct relationship to the text at hand is more obvious in some instances than in others. Prof. Holder's first example, using Calvin's comments on Romans 16:18,[5] demonstrates his method well. As Prof. Holder observes, "it seems that Calvin finds the formation of pastoral consciousness significant enough so as to make it worthy of stepping outside his normal pattern in order to address it." Prof. Holder uses several such passages in which Calvin appears to compromise "lucid brevity" in order to take advantage of an opportunity to advise pastors.

Prof. Holder's method for identifying significant indications of Calvin's thought on the office of pastor is intriguing. One can imagine only one case in which the evidence would be stronger. For those Pauline letters in which we have both Calvin's commentaries and his sermons, one could compare Calvin's comments with his preaching. If the commentaries included pastoral advice (observable as a departure from the genuine sense of the passage) but his sermons did not, it would suggest a higher commitment on Calvin's part to include his pastoral advice. In other words, it would be clear that Calvin reserved his remarks on the pastorate for the commentaries, whose audience consisted of pastors and the laity, and not for the sermons, whose audience was strictly lay. This approach would exclude the pastoral epistles, since these texts naturally lead to remarks on the pastoral ministry in both commentaries and sermons.

But in fact, drawing from the references used by Prof. Holder or listed in his notes, this criterion, when applied, leaves no passages under consideration.

---

[3] Cf. Calvin's dedicatory letter to Simon Grynaeus introducing the commentary on Romans.

[4] Parker, 108.

[5] "For such people do not serve our Lord Jesus Christ, but their own appetites, and by smooth talk and flattery they deceive the hearts of the simple-minded" (NRSV).

This is to say, whenever Calvin inserts pastoral advice into those biblical passages that do not themselves lead naturally to such comments, the same remarks appear in his sermons. Thus, the passages Prof. Holder examines are the best these commentaries have to offer in determining Calvin's understanding of the office of pastor.

In the conclusion of his paper, Prof. Holder offers an interesting insight as to why the distribution of Calvin's practical pastoral remarks is so uneven throughout the commentaries on the Pauline letters. The easy solution is, of course, that the commentator was simply following the arguments of the texts. But Prof. Holder identifies other contributing factors as well.

The first is that between the commentaries on Romans and 1 Corinthians (the first two written), Calvin had been expelled from Geneva, gained some experience in Strasbourg under the guidance of Martin Bucer, and had returned to a more successful pastorate in Geneva. In their first calls, many seminary graduates today are disappointed to hear that, "It takes three years to go to seminary, and another three years to get seminary out of you." Calvin's "field education" under Bucer appears to have equipped him to better advise pastors by the time he commented on 1 Corinthians.

A second factor is that Calvin was eager to finish the commentaries on the Pauline letters. Thus, in writing the group of commentaries that begins with Galatians, for example, Calvin appears to have skimped on pastoral comments, depending instead on the Pauline set as a whole—which includes the pastoral epistles, of course—to address such matters.

Another of Prof. Holder's valuable insights is the observation of the role of the commentaries, especially when considered in relation to the *Institutes*. The commentaries, according to Prof. Holder, represent Calvin's "model seminary," a provisional measure Calvin used in conjunction with the *Institutes* to train pastors in the right interpretation of scripture. Randall Zachman has argued that "by 1549 all elements of Calvin's plan of instruction for the school of Christ were emerging in print: the *Institutes* and commentaries for pastors, and the catechism and sermons for ordinary Christians."[6] He finds evidence of this plan as early as 1540, the year of the commentary on Romans.

Finally, our appreciation of Calvin's understanding of the pastoral office would be enhanced further by consideration of Calvin's actual practice of pastoral duties. As both teacher of the church and preacher in Geneva, Calvin himself epitomized his understanding of the office of pastor. Thus one place to

---

[6] Randall C. Zachman, "Do You Understand What You Are Reading?" *Scottish Journal of Theology* 54.1 (2001), p. 7. Although both Zachman and Holder recognize that the audience for the commentaries includes both the learned, that is, doctors and pastors, and the unlearned laity, Zachman lays emphasis on the pastoral audience for the commentaries (cf. p. 6, n. 20). Cf. also Zachman, "Gathering Meaning from the Context: Calvin's Exegetical Method" *Journal of Religion* 82.1 (Jan., 2002), 5.

begin would be to consult his letters offering pastoral care and advice. But above all other of what might be considered to be secondary witnesses to Calvin's exegetical understanding of the office of pastor, one should consider his prayers.

Calvin's prayers in worship and during his lectures were influenced by the passages of scripture upon which he had just preached or taught. There are some inherent limitations with such considerations, however. First, many of the prayers related to sermons are lost, and few of those that survive deal with biblical texts having to do with the office of pastor. Second, only a very limited number of prayers following Calvin's lectures survive, and these follow lectures only on the Old Testament prophets (excluding Isaiah).

Still, within these limitations, the prayers that do survive suggest how Calvin as pastor actually practiced what Calvin as commentator understood about the pastorate. According to Elsie Anne McKee, "Calvin's great pastoral goal was to bring peace to troubled hearts, to preach God's acceptance of sinners."[7] The prayer following Calvin's final lecture on Malachi demonstrates how Calvin's prayers exemplify his exegetical understanding and practice of the office of pastor.[8] It reads:

> Grant, Almighty God, that as nothing is omitted by thee to help us onward in the course of our faith, and as our sloth is such that we hardly advance one step though stimulated by thee,—O grant, that we may strive to profit more by the various helps which thou has provided for us, so that the Law, the Prophets, the voice of John the Baptist, and especially the doctrine of thine only-begotten Son, may more fully awaken us, that we may not only hasten to him, but also proceed constantly in our course, and persevere in it until we shall at length obtain the victory and the crown of our calling, as thou hast promised an eternal inheritance in heaven to all who faint not but wait the coming of the great Redeemer.—Amen.[9]

Though Parker disagrees with McKee that Calvin's New Testament commentaries also originated as lectures,[10] it is not too difficult, bearing in mind what Prof. Holder has taught us, to imagine a prayer similar to this one accompanying Calvin's comments on the office of pastor in the Pauline letters. Many of Calvin's other prayers in worship and lectures also demonstrate the close

---

[7] Elsie Anne McKee, ed., trans., *John Calvin: Writings on Pastoral Piety*, (New York: Paulist Press, 2001), p. 23.

[8] I have chosen the prayer for this passage in Malachi because in his comments Calvin does exactly what Prof. Holder observes—he inserts comments about the pastoral office.

[9] John Calvin, *Commentaries on the Twelve Minor Prophets* vol. 5, John Owen, trans., in *Calvin's Commentaries* vol. XV, (Grand Rapids: Baker Book House, 1996), 632.

[10] Parker, p. 28; McKee, p. 240.

relationship between his exegetical understanding of the office of pastor and its practice.[11]

In summary, Prof. Holder invites us to give due consideration to Calvin's exegetical understanding of the office of pastor. He proves the value of the commentaries as a source beyond the *Institutes* for this understanding. He offers us a method to use when approaching the commentaries, and one system with which to organize Calvin's exegetical understanding of the office of pastor. This method and organizing principle invite further application and modification. In other words, it would be worthwhile to apply the method to the other commentaries and to consider how else Calvin's comments could be organized.[12] Prof. Holder suggests how Calvin's experience may have influenced his pastoral advice, hinting at the autobiographical dimension of theology. In so doing, Prof. Holder opens the door to other data which could be considered, including, for example, sources representing how Calvin himself practiced his exegetical understanding of the office of pastor.

---

[11] For example, Calvin's prayers for illumination and sealing prior to preaching exemplify the pastor's dependence on the Holy Spirit for effectiveness (cf. McKee, *Pastoral Piety*, 100, 112ff, 136ff). His customary manner of beginning the prayer following the sermon, "We bow ourselves before the majesty of our good God in recognition of our faults," along with the rest of the prayer that drew from the biblical text, suggest how Calvin's exercise of pastoral duties reflects his understanding of the pastoral office (cf. McKee, *Pastoral Piety*, 100, 126ff, 151ff).

[12] And in keeping with the theme of our colloquium, we should look at Calvin's comments on those passages where a "company of pastors" act together (e.g., Acts 1:12ff, 6:1ff, 11:1ff, 13:1ff, 15:6ff, 15:36ff).

# Pastors in the French and Hungarian Reformed Churches: Two Models of Reform

*Glenn S. Sunshine*

## I. Introduction

As Protestant churches emerged in the middle and late sixteenth century, one of the pressing problems they faced was how to organize themselves in a way that was faithful to Protestant ecclesiology. Systems of local and collective church government had to be developed, clergy had to be recruited and supervised, the Gospel had to be preached and the sacraments rightly administered, moral discipline had to be maintained, children had to be taught the basics of the faith, etc. At the same time, the churches also needed to formulate precise statements of belief, or "Confessions," to define the doctrinal content of the Gospel as they understood it. These two inter-related movements have been incorporated into the broad category of "confessionalization" by recent scholars, though arguably "institutionalization" would be an equally appropriate term.

One significant factor in the creation of church institutions was the local political structure. In most areas where Protestantism took root, it did so with magisterial support. This could lead to tensions between pastors and the government, particularly—though not exclusively—over church discipline: Bucer and Calvin both had struggles with their governments over this issue, and Calvin was even exiled from Geneva for three years as a result. On the whole, however, establishing a Protestant church meant working closely with the state. Generally speaking, the form of government adopted by the church was broadly compatible with that of the civil government: principalities tended toward some form of episcopacy, and republics such as Zurich or Geneva tended toward "representative" forms of church government run by councils or synods.[1] This distinction can be pushed too far, however: continental Protestants insisted that all pastors were fundamentally equal in rank under Christ, and thus churches with an "episcopal" polity generally had much weaker bishops than their Roman Catholic counterparts. At the same time, the "republican" churches often had a single pastor who played a leading role within the church, whether Bucer in Strasbourg, Calvin in Geneva, or Zwingli

---

[1] These correspond to the Aristotelian political categories of monarchies and republics respectively.

and Bullinger as *Antistes* in Zurich. Their role was typically to act as the spokesman for the pastors and as moderator of the pastoral council. This was, in fact, Bucer and Calvin's view of the origin of the office of bishop:[2] they argued that the early church was governed by synods moderated by bishops acting as a *primus inter pares* and overseeing visitations, discipline, etc. Both of them explicitly supported this system of church government, though not the use of the term "bishop" to describe the office. The difference between continental Protestant episcopacy and the conciliar structure of the city-states was thus essentially one of emphasis: the churches in principalities tended to focus on "bishops" or "superintendents," and those in republics on councils and synods.

The situation becomes more complicated in regions which had a strong Protestant movement that was opposed by the civil government. In this paper we will examine two such areas, Hungary and France. In both cases, Protestantism grew out of indigenous reform movements in the Catholic Church, which evolved into various forms of Protestantism before settling on Calvinism. In both cases, the reform was supported by a sizeable percentage of the nobility but opposed by the monarchy. In both cases, the churches struggled with many of the same institutional issues and tried some of the same solutions. Yet the two churches moved in opposite directions with respect to episcopacy, with the Hungarians embracing a far more hierarchical structure and the French opposing any form of primacy within the church. This difference in structure points to a fundamental difference in the patterns of reform in the two kingdoms, a difference that can be illustrated particularly well by contrasting the role of pastors in the two churches.

We will therefore examine the history of the reform in Hungary and France, focusing on the development of institutional structures in the churches, and specifically on the role of pastors in shaping and directing the reform in the two kingdoms. Since the history of the Hungarian Reformed Church is relatively unknown in the English-speaking world, we will begin there with a summary derived from the work of scholars who have specialized in Hungarian and Eastern European Protestantism.[3]

---

[2] See Glenn S. Sunshine, "Reformed Theology and the Origins of Synodical Polity: Calvin, Beza and the Gallican Confession," in *Later Calvinism: International Perspectives*, edited by W. Fred Graham, Sixteenth Century Essays and Studies 22 (Kirksville, Missouri: Sixteenth Century Journal Publishers, 1994), 145-48.

[3] Sources for the history of Hungarian Protestantism are very difficult to come by in English. The most accessible secondary studies (and those on which this paper was based) include David P. Daniel, "Hungary," in *The Early Reformation in Europe*, ed. Andrew Pettegrew (Cambridge: Cambridge University Press, 1992); "Calvinism in Hungary: the Theological and Ecclesiastical Transition to the Reformed Faith," in *Calvinism in Europe: 1540-1620*, ed .Andrew W. Pettegrew, Alastair Duke and Gillian Lewis (Cambridge: Cambridge University Press, 1994); "Hungary" and "Synods: Synods in Eastern Europe," in *The Encyclopedia of the Reformation* (New York and Oxford: Oxford University Press, 1996); and Winfried Eberhard, "East Central Europe," in *Handbook of European History, 1400-1600*, ed. Thomas A. Brady, Jr., Heiko A. Oberman and James D. Tracy, vol. 2, *Visions, Programs, and Outcomes* (Leiden: E. J. Brill, 1995).

## II. The Reform in Hungary: The Essential Role of Pastors

The roots of Hungarian Protestantism extend back to King Matthius Corvinus, who introduced humanism into Hungary in the 1470s and '80s.[4] Under the influence of Ficino, Corvinus saw himself as a Platonic philosopher-king; he promoted arts, education, administrative reform and centralization, and a host of other programs designed to make Buda a new Athens. He promoted people on the basis of education and talent, and appointed humanistically-inspired leaders to key positions within the Church. After Corvinus's death, many of his administrative reforms were dismantled by the jealous Magyar nobility, resulting in a far weaker monarchy. But humanism continued to exert a strong influence within the kingdom, which, together with Franciscan vernacular sermons promoting a simple approach to Christianity and the popularity of the *devotio moderna*, led to an Erasmian-style reform in the Hungarian church in the decades leading up to 1520.

By 1521, Lutheran ideas were introduced into Hungary in a form that integrated well with Christian humanism, and thus Lutheranism developed a following among some of the most influential humanists in Buda, including George of Brandenburg, the military tutor of Louis II, Simon Grynaeus, Viet Winsheim, John Kressling, and Conrad Cordatus, who served for a brief period as Queen Mary of Habsburg's court chaplain.[5] Luther's ideas were also supported by German merchants in the cities and immigrants in the mining towns, and by the cities and towns in Transylvania with extensive trading contacts in Poland and the Empire. On the other hand, Lutheranism was initially opposed by the lesser Magyar nobility, who saw it as another example of "foreign" influence in Hungary, and by the hierarchy of the Catholic Church.[6] The threat posed by the new ideas was so great that the Hungarian Diet decided it needed to take action. It condemned Lutheranism as a heresy in 1523, 1524 and 1525, punishable by confiscation of property and exile or death. Although many reformers were forced to flee Buda, the threat from the Turks prevented the monarchy from taking effective action against the Protestants.

The religious and political situation was further complicated by the disaster of Mohács, (August 29, 1526), which left Louis II, two archbishops, five bishops, twenty-eight magnates, 500 nobles and 16,000 Hungarian troops dead on the battlefield. In the aftermath of the battle, Ferdinand Habsburg claimed the Hungarian throne by right of inheritance and alliance, while the greater part of the Magyar nobility elected John Zapolya king.[7] This resulted in a three-way

---

[4] See Valery Rees, "Pre-Reformation Changes in Hungary at the End of the Fifteenth Century," in *The Reformation in Eastern and Central Europe*, ed. Karin Maag (Aldershot: Scolar Press, 1997), 19-35, for a summary of Corvinus's career as a patron of the Renaissance.

[5] Day, "Calvinism in Hungary," 209.

[6] Ibid., 211.

[7] Day, "Hungary," in *Early Reformation Europe*, 49, 51.

division of the kingdom, with the Turks occupying central Hungary and the Danube basin, the Habsburgs controlling the North and West, and Zapolya in the East and Transylvania. The battle also left the kingdom in disarray ecclesiastically: the deaths of the bishops left appointments to church offices in the hands of the nobility and of the town governments, a growing number of which supported Protestant reforms after "God's judgment" on Hungary at Mohács.[8] Neither Ferdinand nor Zapolya could afford to alienate these groups, so reform movements spread quickly throughout the kingdom.[9] In an ironic twist, over time the Magyars who had initially opposed the spread of Lutheranism out of resentment of German influence in Hungary reversed their position, seeing Protestant ideas as a means of opposing the Habsburgs and thus supporting the cause of nationalism against the Germans.

The 1530s saw the growth of "Evangelical" churches. Frequently led by former Franciscans, these churches were more humanist in orientation than truly Protestant, and even where they were influenced by Luther, they tended to go their own way theologically. Anabaptists made their appearance as early as the late 1520s;[10] as in so many other areas, however, the main point of departure from Luther among Hungarian Protestants was the nature of the presence of Christ in the Lord's Supper. Prominent Hungarian reformers Matthias Biró Dévai (a humanist by training), Michael Sztártai (a former Franciscan), Stephen Szegedi Kis (a graduate of Wittenberg) simultaneously adopted sacramentarian views of the Lord's Supper while paradoxically claiming to be followers of Luther. This would be a long-lasting tendency among Hungarian reformers. One reason for this may be their training. Many Hungarians attended the University of Wittenberg, particularly in the 1540s through 1570s, but they were attracted primarily by its humanism rather than the specifics of its theology. Many of these same students also took advantage of the opportunity to study at Reformed-influenced academies in addition to Wittenberg. They thus felt a kinship with Lutheran ideas—particularly Philippist views—from their connection with Wittenberg, while adopting some Reformed ideas that better suited their theological orientation.

Another important characteristic of the Hungarian reform was that even with Protestant pastors, the churches were still nominally under the umbrella of Catholicism. This fact was particularly important for the subsequent development of Hungarian Protestantism, since as more and more Protestants were appointed as priests, the reformers took increasing control of Catholic pastoral fraternities and synods. In 1538, a pastoral meeting in Sighișoara included rep-

---

[8] Day, "Calvinism in Hungary," 211.

[9] Ferdinand was actually supported by German Lutherans, and Zapolya by the anti-foreign (and especially anti-German) Magyars. As a result, Lutheranism became the dominant form of Protestantism in Habsburg lands, while in the East, a wide range of other forms of Protestantism would take root, with Reformed Protestantism becoming the strongest.

[10] Day, "Hungary," in *Early Reformation Europe*, 60-61; Eberhard, "Hungary," 564.

resentatives of the Catholic church, humanist reformers, and at least one Protestant who was being tried for his views. He was supported by Zapolya's court physician and secretly by the judges appointed to decide his case. Shortly after this meeting, five of the canons who had attended became Protestants, and two of them eventually became bishops in the Hungarian Reformed Church.[11]

By 1545, Evangelicals made up enough of the clerical population that full-scale Evangelical synods were held in Oradea Mare in Rumania and Ardud in Transylvania, both in Eastern (i.e. non-Habsburg) Hungary. These synods affirmed the Augsburg Confession, though with significant disagreements among the delegates about the interpretation of the Lord's Supper. Thus, for example, "[i]n July 1544, a synod at Oradea in Siebenbürgen held that the spiritual body and blood of Christ is present, communicated and dispensed to the believer" while still considering themselves Lutheran. And the next year, a synod at Ardud claimed the Augsburg Confession as its doctrinal standard, though again with some hedging on the interpretation of the Lord's Supper.[12] On the other hand, in Habsburg-controlled upper Hungary, Lutheranism was far more the norm among Protestants, with the five royal free cities of upper Hungary adopting the Augsburg Confession of 1530 (the *invariata*) at a synod at Prešov in 1546, and seven mining cities doing the same shortly thereafter.[13] Doctrinal diversity—frequently coinciding with ethnic divisions—thus entered the Hungarian reform early on.

When the battle of Mühlberg ended the First Schmalkaldic War in 1547, the Hungarian Diet could once again turn its attention to the problem of Protestantism. In 1548, the Diet decreed the expulsion of Zwinglians, sacramentarians and Anabaptists from the kingdom. The Catholic hierarchy, seeking to regain control of the Hungarian church, attempted to apply this to Lutherans as well, citing the earlier decrees against Luther as a precedent, while the Lutherans argued for a narrower interpretation of the decision. In the face of this decree, Hungarian Protestants began the process of confessionalization, as various churches and synods prepared statements of belief to demonstrate their orthodoxy against the charge of innovation.

By this point, the Protestants controlled virtually all of the regional synods and pastoral fraternities in the kingdom, even though these bodies were still nominally part of the Catholic Church. Protestant visitations from 1549-1558 led to the adoption of a series of urban confessions based largely on the Augsburg Confession, though with a growing division between strict Lutherans and those more influenced by Melanchthon and Bullinger. As was generally the case, the process of confessionalization in Hungary hardened the divisions

---

[11] Daniel, "Calvinism in Hungary," 214.

[12] Daniel, "Calvinism in Hungary," 212.

[13] Daniel, "Calvinism in Hungary," 214.

that existed among the Protestants in the kingdom. The division fell in part on cultural, ethnic and socio-economic lines, with Magyar nobility and the smaller market towns adopting Reformed theology, and the Germans, Slovaks, and pro-Habsburg members of the upper nobility adopting Lutheran ideas.[14] The division was also geographic: territories not directly under Habsburg control, or with weak Catholic hierarchies, or that had extensive contact with Italy during the late fifteenth century and that were thus strongly influenced by Corvinus's neo-Platonic humanist ideas, all tended to adopt Reformed ideas.[15] Synods held in Beregszáz (1552), Ovar (1554), and Ardud (1555) all show the growing influence of Melanchthon and Bullinger, and throughout the 1550s Reformed churches were being established in Central and Southern Hungary under the Ottomans and in the East and Transylvania.[16]

Finally, in 1558, the Synod of Czenger adopted the II Helvetic Confession, the first formal acceptance of Reformed theology by a Hungarian synod. This was followed by the synod of Tîrgu Mures's Confession on the Lord's Supper, which took a decidedly Zwinglian-Bullingerian view of the Supper, the synod of Tarcal (1562), which adopted Beza's Confession, and the Synod of Debrecen (1567), which also adopted the II Helvetic Confession, together with confessions in Hungarian and Latin aimed against the growing threat of Anti-Trinitarianism, the third major force in Hungarian Protestantism.

Along with confessions, the Protestant churches also began developing their systems of polity. The Reformed Church adopted a church order designed by Péter Horhi Melius Juhász. Melius had studied with Lutheran teachers and with Stephen Szegedi Kis before attending the University of Wittenberg; upon Melius's return, he was appointed pastor at Debrecen and then in 1558 became "superintendent" (i.e. bishop) of the Reformed Church in the region. His system of government was based on synods operating within a clerical hierarchy of senior pastors (who oversaw the work of the synod and ordained new clergy), archdeacons and superintendents.[17] Although this system is similar to that advocated by Calvin, we can rule out his direct influence on the church order. At this time the Magyars (including Melius [18]) preferred Bullinger's theology to Calvin's; in fact, Calvin's catechism was not even translated into Hungarian until 1562. Calvin did not begin to replace Bullinger as the principal inspira-

---

[14] Day, "Calvinism in Hungary," 216.

[15] Day, "Calvinism in Hungary," 229.

[16] The Lutherans resisted Reformed encroachment in the Habsburg lands of Western and Northern Hungary, however.

[17] The process was completed in 1591-1592 by dividing the church into two large ecclesiastical districts, Transdanubia and Samorín in Upper Hungary.

[18] Day, "Calvinism in Hungary," 221.

tion for the Hungarian Reformed Church until about 1575.[19] Further, the Reformed Church's system of government paralleled those adopted by both the Lutherans and the Anti-Trinitarians.[20] Its roots are thus found in the broader Hungarian Protestant tradition rather than in specifically Reformed or Calvinist ecclesiology.

A more likely source for this system of ecclesiastical government is the institutional matrix in which Hungarian Protestantism arose. The cradle of all forms of Hungarian Protestantism was the Catholic Church's pastoral assemblies and synods. Given that the Protestant church leadership came from these synods, which in turn operated within an episcopal framework, it is only logical that the Protestant churches should adopt (or adapt) this type of church government for their own use. Further, they were operating with at best limited support from the government. The Ottomans did not care which variety of Christianity was in their territories, and the Habsburgs wanted to abolish Protestantism altogether, though they were as yet largely incapable of carrying this out. Only in the East would the government support reform efforts, and even here there was little concern to maintain one form of Protestantism over another.[21] This left the churches in a state of benign near neglect, thereby permitting the system of church government to develop organically out of indigenous church structures—that is, the now-Protestant pastoral synods.[22]

The rest of the story of the Hungarian Reformed Church must be told briefly. During the Fifteen Years War with the Turks (1591-1606), persecution of Protestants and imperial abuses in Transylvania led Istvan Bocskay, prince of Transylvania, to establish an anti-Habsburg alliance with the Turks.[23] This rebel-

---

[19] Ibid., 229. N.b., that at least one pastoral synod adopted his catechism in 1564 (Day, "Hungary," in Early Reformation Europe, 219). Oddly enough, though, Beza began to have a significant influence in Hungary during the 1560s, well before Calvin. For example, he corresponded regularly with individuals in Hungary, whereas only one Magyar (George Belényesi) had direct contact with Calvin, and as indicated above, Beza's Confession had been accepted by the Tarcal synod in 1562 ( Day, "Hungary," in Early Reformation Europe, 217, 219).

[20] Day, "Synods: Synods in Eastern Europe."

[21] A diet held at Thorda in 1550 decreed official religious toleration; in 1557 the diet also affirmed individual consciences and recognized Catholicism, Lutheranism and Calvinism as "approved" religions; in 1571, Unitarianism was also added (Eberhard, "East Central Europe," 564).

[22] Another possible source for this system of church government is Hungarian humanism. Calvin's ecclesiastical system came from a humanisticaly-inspired reading of church history; given the influence of humanism on the Hungarian Protestants, they may have gotten their system from the same source.

[23] The Calvinists supported this effort, but the Lutherans opposed it.

lion combined the themes of religious freedom and liberation of the estates from Habsburg control, common themes in the "political Calvinism" centered on the Palatinate during this period.[24] Bocskay succeeded in driving imperial forces from Transylvania and even seized most of Upper Hungary. The Peace of Vienna (1606) ended the war and guaranteed freedom of religion for Hungary's peoples. The treaty was confirmed by the Diet in 1608, and thus for the first time the Lutheran and Reformed Churches in the kingdom were legally independent of Roman Catholicism.[25]

In the midst of this struggle, however, the churches' work went on. Clerical oversight remained a major concern, as did social discipline.[26] By 1600, especially in the East and Transylvania, superintendents began to order visitations to oversee the clergy in cooperation with magistrates, with each commenting on the others' performance. On the ecclesiastical side, these were typically carried out by archdeacons and the senior clergy with the expectation of support from the synods and local noble assemblies. Fear of the Turks and Catholic repression made such visitations more difficult in Western Hungary, however. The ecclesiastical administration in the West thus became progressively more and more decentralized, with no effective supervision of the clergy.

To fill the gap, lay "presbyteries" patterned after those in Heidelberg were established in Pápa in 1616, illustrating again the influence of the Palatinate on the Hungarian Reformed Church. These worked sufficiently well that in 1630, the superintendent adopted them as the disciplinary model for all Western Hungary. This decision was endorsed by the clergy as more effective than visitations and more consistently Reformed as well, largely because of the precedent set by the national Reformed Churches in Western Europe. A national synod meeting at Szatmar in 1646 decided that the time was not right to introduce presbyteries all over the kingdom, however, since although some nobles supported them, most opposed them: not only did the institution conflict with the traditional role of the nobility in administering justice, but further, the nobles resented being disciplined by their social inferiors. As a result, the presbyteries never spread further within Hungary.

The essential point to be drawn from this history is the central role of pastors in the Hungarian Reformation, from its earliest pre-Protestant days to the

---

[24] See Joachim Balhcke, "Calvinism and Estate Liberation Movements in Bohemia and Hungary (1570-1620)," in *The Reformation in Eastern and Central Europe*, 72-91; Claus-Peter Clasen, *The Palatinate in European History 1559-1569* (Oxford: Oxford University Press, 1963).

[25] There were additional struggles over this issue in the subsequent decades, but the principle articulated in the Treaty of Vienna set a precedent that withstood the later challenges to the Protestants by the Habsburg monarchy.

[26] This summary is derived from Graeme Murdock, "Church Building and Discipline in Early Seventeenth-Century Hungary and Transylvania," in *The Reformation in Eastern and Central Europe*, ed. Karin Maag, St. Andrews Studies in Reformation History (Aldershot, England: Scolar Press; Brookfield, Vt.: Ashgate Publishing Co., 1997), 136-154.

full legalization of Protestantism in the seventeenth century. Pastors led the way in the initial humanist reforms; they adopted Lutheranism early on; after Mohács, priests adopting "Evangelical" ideas took over pastoral synods within the Catholic church, as technically Catholic clergy introduced Lutheran, Reformed and even Anti-Trinitarian ideas into the churches. These synods were the institutional base for all forms of Protestantism in Hungary, whether Lutheran, Reformed or Anti-Trinitarian, as evidenced by the fact that all these churches adopted essentially the same structure of government based on synods operating within the framework of a clerical hierarchy. Pastoral supervision and church discipline were carried out initially via visitations, another holdover from Catholicism. Attempts to introduce lay presbyteries did not get very far: although they were supported by the clergy, who by that point were often trained in the Palatinate and who in any event knew more about and had more contacts with foreign Calvinist churches, the presbyteries were ill-suited to Hungarian culture and thus the national synod recommended against trying to establish them throughout the kingdom.

## III. Reform in France: Pastors and Laity

In France, the situation was much different. Although French Protestantism grew out of some of the same roots as Hungarian Protestantism, the Huguenots rapidly moved in a very different direction. In France as in Hungary, Protestantism started as primarily an urban phenomenon, centered on the educated classes and certain craft and professional groups—though in France it did not attract as many prominent clerics as in Hungary. Instead, early French Protestantism was a largely lay-led movement, with prayer cells and churches developing in private homes around better educated people who could afford to buy Protestant books and pamphlets, or around charismatic individuals who had been exposed to Protestant ideas. Sacramentarian views were common though not universal,[27] and for reasons best explained by Christopher Elwood in *The Body Broken*,[28] this issue became the trigger for royal persecution of Protestants starting in 1534.

The monarchy was a much more significant force in France than in Hungary, and things might have gone very differently for the Protestants were it not for the conversion of large numbers of the nobility in the 1550s. Protestant nobles provided protection and political support to their coreligionists; they also established churches on their rural estates and frequently in their town homes as well, the latter sometimes emerging as independent local

---

[27] See e.g. Denis Crouzet, *La Genèse de la Réforme Française: 1520-1562* (Paris: Sedes, 1996), 207-239, 284-298, etc.

[28] Christopher Elwood, *The Body Broken: The Calvinist Doctrine of the Eucharist and the Symbolization of Power in Sixteenth-Century France*, Oxford Studies in Historical Theology (New York and Oxford: Oxford University Press, 1999).

churches that were patronized by their noble founders without actually being part of their household or retinue. In the hierarchically-minded French world, this large-scale conversion of the nobility changed the center of gravity of French Protestantism: although the majority of Protestants were still in the earlier, largely urban churches, the nobility and their rural power base now became the effective leaders of the movement.

This period also saw a major shift theologically among the Huguenots. Whereas earlier French Protestantism was remarkably diverse in its beliefs—Lucien Febvre referred to it as a period of "magnificent religious anarchy"[29]—in the 1540s and 1550s the Huguenots increasingly moved into the Calvinist camp. There were two primary reasons for this. First, the introduction of Calvin's French theological writings in the 1540s made high-quality theological works available in French for the first time. This had a profound effect on the thinking of the lay leaders of French Protestantism, many of whom were not completely comfortable with Latin. In fact, the threat to French Catholicism posed by works by Calvin and his associates was serious enough that about two-thirds of the books banned by the Sorbonne came from Geneva.[30] Second, Geneva began sending increasing numbers of missionary pastors to France in the 1550s.[31] These missionary pastors had an impact out of all proportion to their numbers on the shape of French Protestantism: as key churches received highly trained Calvinist pastors, they adopted church structures and statements of faith inspired by Geneva, which then influenced the Protestant churches around them. The Protestant nobility also typically supported the movement toward Calvinism, and frequently sponsored Calvinist pastors as their private chaplains.

In the second half of the 1550s, several churches decided it was high time to organize the Protestants of the kingdom into a single ecclesiastical organization with a common statement of faith. After an abortive attempt to produce a church order at a meeting held in Poitiers in 1557,[32] Antoine de la Roche Chandieu and François Morel called a number of churches to meet in Paris in 1559 in what became the first national synod of the French Reformed Churches. As the Hungarian churches had done earlier in this decade, the national synod adopted a vernacular statement of faith known as the Gallican

---

[29] *Au coeur religieux do XVIe siècle*, 2nd ed. (Paris: SEVPEN, 1968), 66.

[30] Francis Higman, *Censorship and the Sorbonne: A Bibliographical Study of Books in French Censured by the Faculty of Theology of the University of Paris, 1520-1551*, Travaux d'Humanisme et Renaissance 172 (Geneva: Librairie Droz, 1979), 62. See also "Index of Authors and Titles of Works in French," 181-189.

[31] This process has been discussed most thoroughly in Robert M. Kingdon, *Geneva and the Coming of the Wars of Religion in France 1555-1563* (Geneva: Librairie E. Droz, 1956).

[32] The meeting produced the *Articles politiques*, a proposed church order that was never implemented. This document exists in one manuscript located in the Bibliothèque Publique de Grenoble. It has been published twice, once in *Documents protestants inédits*, and later in *Bulletin d'information de l'Eglise Réformée de France* 18.3 (October, 1956): 2-4.

Confession. This was based on the earlier Confession of the Paris church and was heavily influenced by Calvin and Bucer.

The synod also adopted a church order, the *Discipline ecclésiastique*, to regulate local and collective church government.[33] The discipline outlined a polity based entirely on representative councils. Local churches were governed by a consistory composed of pastors, elders and deacons; for purposes of pastoral oversight representatives of neighboring churches would get together as needed in a body that would evolve into the colloquy by 1571; the churches of each province would also send a pastor and an elder or deacon to the provincial synod; finally, the national synod would meet as well, initially only on an as-needed basis with delegates from individual churches, and later at regular intervals (in principle, at least) with delegates from the provincial synods.[34] These bodies also acted as a system of courts: local consistories were responsible for administering church discipline, with appeal to the colloquy, then to the provincial synod, and ultimately to the national synod.

Unlike the Hungarian Reformed Church, or for that matter any other church order devised to that point, these synods operated independently of senior pastors, bishops or "principal churches;" instead a moderator would be elected at the start of each synod, and his office would expire at the end of the synod. In fact, the foundational principle of Huguenot polity was the equality of all pastors (and churches) under Christ. The very first article of the *Discipline* insisted that, "No church is to pretend to have any form of primacy or dominion over another." This applied equally to pastors, even within a single church.[35] In short, the Huguenots applied the common Protestant principle of pastoral and congregational equality far more systematically than it had been elsewhere, leading to the creation of an unprecedented, purely synodal form of polity.

If the Hungarian synodal system with its clerical hierarchy grew out of Roman Catholic synods, where did this new synodal system come from? Again, we can be sure it was not from Calvin: though Western European Calvinist

---

[33] The best historical discussion of the Confession remains Pannier, *Les origines*. See Hannelore Jahr, *Studien zur Überlieferungsgeschichte der Confession de foi von 1559*, Beiträge zur Geschichte und Lehre der Reformierten Kirche 16 (Neukirchen-Vluyn: Neukirchener Verlag des Erziehungsvereins, 1964) for a list of the printings of this Confession. The *Discipline ecclesiastique* (hereafter, DE) has been printed a few times, but always in defective texts; further, since the Discipline was modified by every national synod, it is important to establish exactly which edition of the Discipline a particular manuscript contains. This analysis uses accurately dated texts from manuscript sources transcribed either by the author or by Prof. Bernard Roussel. For a more complete discussion of the evolution of Huguenot church government, see Glenn S. Sunshine, *Reforming French Protestantism: The Development of Huguenot Ecclesiastical Institutions, 1557-1572*, Sixteenth Century Essays and Studies 66 (Kirksville, Missouri: Truman State University Press, 2003).

[34] Representation was originally by individual church; this was soon changed to representation by provincial synods.

[35] DE 1563, 1.

churches tended to follow this model, it does not appear anywhere in Calvin's writings. In fact, his ecclesiastical advice to the king of Poland was much closer to the Hungarian system: it did include synods, but it also recommended having bishops and an archbishop over the entire Polish church.[36] Rather, the explanation for the polity of the French Reformed Church is to be found in the conditions in which the *Eglises Réformées* developed. Early French Protestantism was not united doctrinally, much less institutionally, a situation virtually guaranteed by the hostility of the monarchy and the absence of any ecclesiastical support from the Catholic synods. Even with the growth of Calvinism, churches developed more or less independently of each other; in general the churches had few if any direct ties and no common institutional structures.[37] This left the first national synod in a difficult situation: its goal was to unite the churches theologically and organizationally, yet at the same time for practical reasons it was important to respect the autonomy of the individual churches.

The solution was thus a compromise, albeit one that was in line with Protestant ecclesiology: individual churches were left to govern their own affairs for the most part, but in matters of mutual interest they needed to consult with other churches to set common policy, since if any church attempted to act unilaterally it would effectively be assuming primacy over the other churches involved. Thus synods were established to handle matters of mutual interest, but with no on-going offices or bureaucracy in order to avoid alienating the churches they were attempting to attract.

## IV. Pastors and Synods

This difference in synodal structure points to a fundamental difference between the Hungarian and the French Reformed Churches. The Hungarian reform was controlled and directed by the clergy. As the number of Protestant clergy grew, they were able to co-opt existing structures within the ecclesiastical hierarchy and thus absorb the essentially top-down structure of the church. In France, the reform was non-clerical in its origins: unlike their Hungarian counterparts, French Protestant pastors did not typically come from the Catholic clergy. Although not much is known with certainty about early French Protestant leaders, most seem to have been educated laypersons who adopted Protestant ideas from reading Protestant books or pamphlets. Some early French Protestant groups seem to have been led by rogue monks, but once the

---

[36] CO 15: 383. For Calvin's view of the origins of bishops, archbishops and patriarchs, see *Institutes* 4.4.4; note that he labels these offices (though not the titles) as scriptural.

[37] There were some connections between churches. For example, Poitiers seems to have acted as a "mother church" for churches founded by pastors it sent out—e.g. Le Mans, most likely—and as a "metropolitan" church for the Loire valley (*Documents protestants inédits du XVI<sup>e</sup> siècle: synode général de Poitiers 1557, synodes provinciaux de Lyon, Die, Peyraud Montélimar et Nîmes en 1561 et 1562, assemblée des etats du Dauphiné de 1563, etc.*, ed. E. Arnaud [Paris: Grassart, 1872], 83).

national synods began to meet, they made it very clear that former Catholic clergy were to be viewed with extreme suspicion and to be examined closely over a period of time to make sure of their lives and doctrine before they were accepted as leaders in the churches.[38] In fact, the national synods actually warned Protestant nobles not to include Catholic priests in their retinues because of the danger that they would debauch the servants and spread super-stition.[39] Those Catholic clerics that were inclined toward Reform needed the protection of powerful patrons to avoid an unpleasant death at the hands of the *parlements* or the royal courts. There was thus no opportunity to subvert Catholic synods for the cause of Protestantism.

With the arrival of the first missionary pastors from Geneva, things began to change. On a local level, they introduced Calvinist doctrine and discipline and replaced the earlier organization of their churches with a structure patterned on the church of Geneva. We can see this, for example, in the impact Pierre Merlin had on the church in Le Mans. This church's structure was decidedly non-Calvinistic prior to Merlin's arrival; one of the first things Merlin did was to produce what amounts to a local Discipline and completely re-order the church along essentially Genevan lines.[40] The rigorous training these pastors had received increased their stature among a Protestant population that had already been influenced by Calvin's writings; their united theological perspective led them to work together more closely than earlier French Protestants had; and they would be the people who led the movement that resulted in the adoption of the Confession and the Discipline. As time went on, the most prominent leaders within the French Reformed Church were all pastors, including Antoine de la Roche Chandieu, François Morel, Pierre Viret, and Theodore Beza. There is no doubt that these men exerted a strong moral and intellectual influence on French Calvinists.

Further, the synods were inevitably moderated by the pastors; they ran the meetings and helped set the agenda, and thus influenced the action of the synod. For example, the third national synod held at Orléans in 1562 was the first to address the Morély conflict.[41] Unfortunately for Morély, the synod was moderated by Antoine de la Roche Chandieu, who had had a serious falling out with Morély a few years earlier. Chandieu and his supporters worked hard

---

[38] DE 1561, art. 21.

[39] Acts of the fifth national synod (Paris-1565), "Avertissemens generaux aux Eglises," 30.

[40] See "Papier et registre du Consistoire de l'église du Mans réformée selon l'Evangile 1560-61 (1561-1562 *nouveau style*)," in *Recueil de pièces inédites pour servir à l'histoire de la Réforme et de la Ligue dans le Maine* (Le Mans: Imprimerie Ed. Monnoyer, 1867).

[41] The most complete discussion of the Morély controversy is Philippe Denis and Jean Rott, *Jean Morély (ca. 1524-ca. 1594) et l'Utopie d'une démocratie dans l'église*, Travaux d'Humanisme et Renaissance 278 (Geneva: Droz, 1993). See also Sunshine, *Reforming French Protestantism*, 82-90.

to get Morély's book condemned, and only succeeded in doing so with some difficulty. Had someone more sympathetic to Morély's views been the moderator, the result could conceivably have been different.

Can we say, then, that French Protestantism went from being a lay-led movement to being a clerically-led movement? No. This would be a misunderstanding of the nature of the French Reformed Church and the Huguenot movement on a number of levels. First of all, in the context of sixteenth-century France, pastors can only be understood as clerics in a very limited sense. Legally, only people who had taken orders in the Catholic Church were considered members of the clergy, the only recognized legal body (*corps*) that extended across the entire kingdom rather than being limited to one locality. In legal terms, then, pastors were not clergy. Sociologically, the consistory as a whole—pastor(s), elders and deacons—performed the essential elements associated with the clergy: they participated collectively in the celebration of the Lord's Supper and in excommunicating or suspending people from the Supper; they thus functioned as a "*clerc collectif,*" in the words of Bernard Roussel.[42] To Roussel's list, we can add the fact that the consistory as a whole performed some of the non-clerical functions that the Catholic clergy had performed in their communities. For example, despite prohibitions by the national synod, consistories in the Midi were frequently involved as mediators in disputes within their communities, a role traditionally performed by Catholic clergy. Given the fact that these official and unofficial "clerical" functions were performed typically by the consistory as a whole rather than by individuals, Roussel goes so far as to suggest in the title of an essay that the Discipline produced "a kingdom without clergy."[43]

To be sure, pastors did have a unique role in the community: they were given the exclusive right to preach and celebrate the sacraments (with some assistance from the elders and deacons), and were also involved in discipline; they were thus the custodians of the three marks of the church recognized in the Gallican Confession. As a result, it is difficult not to view them as a separate class in some sense from the "lay" leaders of the church, as "clergy" in a non-technical sense. Nonetheless, Roussel makes the very important point that we cannot consider them "clergy" without a great deal of caution, and we cannot use the term for pastors in the same sense that it is used for Catholic priests. It would, in fact, be more accurate to use the term for the consistory as a whole rather than for the pastors alone.

---

[42] "La *Discipline* des Eglises réformées de France en 1559: Un royaume sans clergé?" in *De l'Humanisme aux Lumières, Bayle et le protestantisme,* Mélanges en l'honneur d'Elisabeth Labrousse, textes recueillis par Michelle Magdelaine, Maria-Cristina Pitassi, Ruthe Whelan et Antony McKenna (Paris: Universitas; Oxford: Voltaire Foundation, 1996), 169-191.

[43] Ibid.

Even if we get past technicalities of the definition of the term "clergy," we are still left with the question of the degree to which the pastors directed the Huguenot movement. We can look at this question from several directions. On a local level, there were many Protestant cells that lacked pastors and wrote to Geneva for help; Geneva did its best to fill these requests, but they simply could not train enough people to answer all of them. There was thus a chronic shortage of pastors within the kingdom. The national synods attempted to address this issue by recruiting the leaders of earlier French Protestant communities as pastors in the French Reformed Church, as long as they met the requirements (signing the Gallican Confession and the *Discipline ecclésiastique*, and passing muster with the ministers of neighboring churches, the colloquy, or the provincial synod).[44] In all cases, a mixed body of pastors and elders or deacons made the determination of the suitability of the candidate.

Once a pastor was in place, he undoubtedly had a significant amount of influence within the church, but the structure of the consistory meant that he was always outnumbered by the elders and deacons, and thus could not control the church without winning the agreement of the other leaders. In other words, decision-making power was not in the hands of the pastor, but mostly in the hands of the elders and deacons. Synodical records provide frequent examples of difficulties pastors had with their congregations, notably over such issues as getting paid, reimbursements for synodical expenses, and which church had rights over a pastor that had been "lent" from one congregation to another. One cannot read these cases without getting the impression that the pastors were at the mercy of their congregations, rather than being the driving force within the churches.

In terms of the synods, the role of pastors was quite a bit different from what it was in Hungary. Unlike the early Hungarian synods, French synods were not composed entirely of pastors, but of equal numbers of pastors and elders or deacons; at the national level, the elders and deacons of the host church were sometimes included in the synod as well, making the majority of the voting delegates the lay leaders of the churches. The pastors' advice undoubtedly weighed heavily in the deliberations of the synod, but they could not advance their agenda—assuming they had a unified agenda—without gaining the support of the lay delegates. In Hungary, substantial lay involvement in the government of the church did not begin until the establishment of the "presbyteries" to handle church discipline in the early 1600s. As noted earlier, however, these were limited to only certain areas of Hungary and were never adopted throughout the kingdom due to the opposition of the nobility.

---

[44] DE 1561, art. 9.

## V. Pastors, Church and Nobility

This brings us to the question of the relationship of the pastors, the Reformed Church and the nobility in France. The situation here was complex, somewhat contradictory, and unlike anything else in Europe. As we have seen, Huguenot nobles supported the French Reformed Churches: they helped establish churches in towns they controlled; and they hired Calvinist pastors as chaplains, sharing them with local congregations at least while they were in residence in the area. This seems to have been part of a self-conscious missionary strategy on the part of the Genevan church. By placing some of their best pastors in noble households, Geneva cemented its alliance with the French nobility; this in turn would encourage the noble not to compromise on points that the pastors considered essential, and would enable the spread of Protestant ideas up and down the noble's patronage network.[45] And there was no reason why the noble could not allow a local church to form around his principal residence and share the chaplain with them, so providing the noble with a pastor could actually encourage the development of local churches as well.

In practice, however, this strategy did not always work as planned. First of all, there was no guarantee that the noble would listen to the advice of the pastor. Since the pastor was placed in the noble's household, the noble was in charge almost by definition. Second, if a local church does form around the noble's household, using the chaplain as their pastor, what happens when the noble travels? Is the pastor part of his retinue, or is he assigned to the locality? The nobles frequently (though not always) viewed the pastor as part of their household, and thus when they left, they took "their" chaplain with them, leaving the local church without sermons or sacraments. The national synod was forced to address this problem, and insisted that pastors were assigned to churches, not households, "even if the household is large enough to be a church all by itself."[46] The noble thus had no right to bring the chaplain when the family traveled if this would deprive a church of its pastor. Evidently, the nobles went along with this decision, since the situation is never brought up again in the acts of the national synods.[47]

This decision may have reflected more than simply an attempt to regulate a difficult situation for some local churches; it may also have been an attempt to tie the noble churches more directly into the structure of the French Reformed Church. If this was the case, then there is no sign that the article accomplished

---

[45] On patronage networks, see Janine Garrisson, *Les Protestants du Midi 1559-1598* (Toulouse: Privat, 1980), 22-28.

[46] Acts of the fifth national synod (Paris-1565), "Avertissemens generaux aux Eglises," 30.

[47] The alternative—that the synod simply refused to deal with it further—is unlikely, given the number of charged issues the synod dealt with regularly. The fact that there is no further record of this issue being discussed or the article being reaffirmed suggests it was not a particularly common problem.

this part of its purpose. The nobles founded churches; they sponsored pastors; they supported the French Reformed Church; they even fought for it in the Wars of Religion. Yet paradoxically, they saw no real need for their house churches to participate in the larger church in any meaningful way. Few of the nobles seem to have even established consistories in their house churches, probably because they thought that they were themselves responsible for enforcing moral standards and establishing proper order within their households, and because they did not want to be answerable to their social inferiors (including the pastors).

Further, there is no evidence that any of the house churches participated in any of the synods of the French Reformed Church. This represents a major gap in the representation at the synods, considering that noble house churches constituted up to one half of all Protestant churches in France. The attitude of the nobles seems to have been that synods were nice, but not really necessary for the cause of Protestantism.[48] This impression is reinforced by the interaction between synods and the Huguenot political assemblies. The synods tried to send delegates—typically pastors—to the political assemblies, but the assemblies limited their participation to leading in prayer and pronouncing a benediction at the close of the meetings. Quite simply, the nobles were the leaders of French Protestantism, and they knew it. The pastors were there to pray for them, to preach and administer the sacraments, but that was about it. The noble attitude toward the official organs of the French Reformed Church raises a serious question for the historian of French Protestantism: would it be more accurate to say that there was one French Reformed Church or two: the "official" church centered in the local communities, and the churches of the noble households?

All of this suggests some interesting points of comparison and contrast with the situation in Hungary. There, the conflicts within the parts of the kingdom controlled by Christians centered not on religion as it did in France, but on the pro- and anti-Habsburg parties. In Hungary, neither side could afford to alienate the emerging Protestant communities, so persecution never developed to the degree it did in France. There were political dimensions to Hungarian Protestantism, of course: the Habsburgs more or less tolerated Lutherans, but not the Reformed or Anti-Trinitarians, so the pro-Habsburg Protestants tended to be Lutheran, and anti-Habsburg Protestants tended toward Reformed or Anti-Trinitarian views. Yet when the staunchly Reformed Bocskay fought the Habsburgs, it was not in the name of his theology, but was focused instead on estate liberation and a broad-based tolerance of all faiths, even Anti-Trinitarians. This suggests that as in France, the Hungarian Protestant nobles went their own way without necessarily promoting the interests or agenda of their churches;

---

[48]This consideration may have contributed to noble support for Morély. Morély's "democratic" ideas of church government were hardly compatible with the nobility's sense of their own importance, but his argument that synods could advise churches but not enforce their decisions may have appealed to them.

unlike France, however, with its theoretically united Reformed church, Hungarian nobles did not see religion as inextricably connected to politics. Hungarian nobles undoubtedly sponsored and protected Protestant churches, but the nature of their relationship to Hungarian Protestantism was fundamentally different and more distant than the connections between the Huguenot party and the Huguenot church. And this permitted a fundamentally different type of reform, one that was far more clerically-based than the French.

The Hungarian and French Reformed Churches' approaches to pastoral supervision and church discipline provide another interesting point of comparison between the two systems. As we saw earlier, the Hungarian Reformed Church initially performed these functions through visitations as had been done within Catholicism; when political conditions made this unworkable, they attempted to introduce lay "presbyteries," though with only limited success due to the opposition of most of the nobility. In France, strict moral standards and obedience to established authorities had long been a vital element of Reformed Protestantism, and thus introducing the consistory fit the ethos of the churches and seems to have been accomplished relatively easily—except, again, in the noble house churches where obedience to the magistrate had never been a high priority.

Pastoral supervision had initially been placed in the hands of ad hoc groups of local ministers answerable to the provincial synod. Colloquies evolved out of these meetings relatively quickly—they were clearly in place by 1571, twelve years after the first national synod—and a system of appeals for lay disciplinary decisions was set out, going from the consistory to the colloquy to the provincial synod to the national synod; for church leaders, the chain started at the colloquy. Before this system was established, however, Pierre Viret attempted to introduce visitations in a provincial discipline he prepared for Bas Languedoc.[49] The system he laid out was based on his earlier career in the *Pays de Vaud* where it was uncontroversial. The provincial synod was not sure about some elements of the discipline, notably the visitations, and forwarded it to the national synod for review. The national synod immediately and adamantly rejected the visitations, noting that they could have "dangerous consequences."[50] The reasoning was unexplained, but the problem almost certainly had to do with the implication of a hierarchy within the church: the visitations would have placed pastors and churches under the supervision of an outsider, something not only questionable ecclesiologically, but also problematical in

---

[49] *Documents protestants inédits*, 42. The manuscript is dated February, 1561; the date is 1562 n.s.

[50] Acts of the third national synod (Orléans, 1562), art. 17, cf. John Quick, *Synodicon in Gallia Reformata: or, The Acts, Decisions, Decrees, and Canons of Those Famous National Councils of the Reformed Churches in France*, 2 vols. (London: Printed for T. Parkhurst and J. Robinson, at the Three Bibles and Crown in Cheapside, and the Golden Lion in St. Paul's Churchyard, 1692), third national synod held at Orleans, chapter 2, article 14 (1: 24, second pagination).

practical terms given the history of French Protestantism. The non-clerical origin of the French Reformation and the effective independence of the local churches made this solution unacceptable in France, however well it suited the Hungarians. Ironically enough, by 1594 the French Reformed Church would approve *de facto* visitations to try to end abuses within the church,[51] and a decade or so later, the Hungarians would move toward the colloquy. Neither development changed the fundamental ecclesiology of the churches, however: the French never changed the Discipline to make the practice a permanent, universal part of the church order, and the "presbyteries" likewise never became commonplace across Hungary. These solutions simply did not suit the cultural context of the two kingdoms, though the common problems of pastoral supervision meant considerable overlap in the kinds of solutions the two churches attempted.

# VI. Conclusion

The Hungarian and French Reformed Churches both emerged in the 1550s as part of the Protestant communities' response to pressure from Catholic monarchies. Both sought to prove their orthodoxy through adopting confessions, and both worked to organize their churches as part of this process. Both also survived due to the support of the nobility, though their institutions developed largely without the interference or indeed involvement of the nobility. Yet they adopted radically different forms of government, due in large measure to the differences in the roles of pastors in shaping and directing the reform. In Hungary, Protestant confessionalization began with the takeover of Catholic synods by priests-turned-Protestant; their church institutions thus were built around these synods operating within an essentially hierarchical set of church officers—archdeacons, senior pastors, bishops, etc. This system fit the church's origins and in fact would have been recognized and accepted by all mainstream Protestant leaders—including Calvin—in the 1550s. Visitations fit naturally into this system; lay presbyteries were another matter, however, and were opposed by the Protestant nobility as an infringement on their prerogatives. In other words, the Hungarian Reformed Church, along with the other Protestant churches in the kingdom, was essentially a clerical organization, supported by the nobles but fundamentally independent of them.

In France, the monarchy was able to put much more direct pressure on the Protestants than the Habsburgs could in Hungary, and the Protestant movement was strongly opposed by virtually the entire church hierarchy. Protestant groups developed in people's homes, typically with lay leadership since

---

[51] The thirteenth national synod (Montauban, 1594) called on colloquies or, failing that, provincial synods to appoint two to three ministers to oversee problems in the churches to try to prevent abuses which were occurring; the synod did not change the Discipline, however (Quick, chapter 4, article 6 [161]).

ordained pastors were few and far between. The churches, prayer groups, and cells were largely independent of each other with no common doctrine or organization. The process of confessionalization thus needed to address both of these problems, and specifically had to create a common set of institutions that would preserve the relative autonomy of local churches while uniting them in doctrine and in matters of mutual interest. The solution they devised was the so-called "presbyterian" or synodal system which, like the Hungarian church, was built around synods, but unlike the Hungarian church operated without a hierarchy of pastoral offices or churches. Pastors undoubtedly had a great deal of influence in their churches, but since all decisions in the local church were made by the consistory, they could be outvoted by the "lay" leaders of the church. Synods similarly included as many elders or deacons as pastors. At the same time, there was also a much closer relationship between the nobility and the French Reformed Church than there was in Hungary. The nobles founded, sponsored and protected churches and provided the real leadership for Protestantism in France, and largely ignored the institutional structures developed by the *Eglises Réformées*.

In short, the French Reform was fundamentally non-clerical in contrast to Hungary. Yet in the long run, this non-clerical system, developed in very specific and unusual circumstances, would emerge as the mainstream Calvinist system of polity, even though the Hungarian system of synods and "superintendents" was essentially the one Calvin had advocated. The Dutch Reformed Church and later the Scots kirk would both adopt the French system, albeit in very different conditions and for very different reasons than those for which it was originally developed. But that is a different study. Suffice it to say here that the non-clerical focus of the French Reformation proved to be the more adaptable, given the importance of anticlericalism and lay leadership in the emerging national Reformed churches in Western Europe.

Expl. attitude to war
complex — unambig.